ENCYCLOPEDIA OF
KNOWLEDGE

TREASURE PRESS

Contents

First Published in Great Britain in 1979 by
Macdonald Educational Limited

This revised edition published in 1988 by
Treasure Press
Michelin House,
81 Fulham Road, London SW3 6RB

© Macdonald Educational Limited 1979

ISBN 1 85051 281 7

Printed in Czechoslovakia
50691

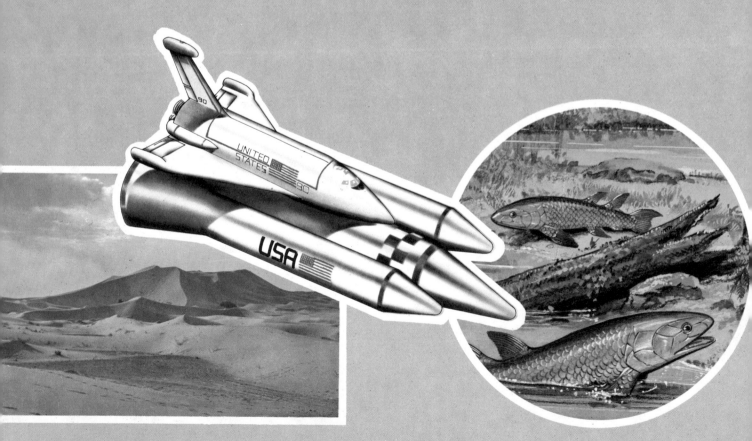

THE LIVING WORLD

Contents

SCIENCE AND TECHNOLOGY

The vastness of space

Take a look at the sky on a clear, moonless, frosty night and try to count the stars. This would be an impossible task but it *would* emphasize the immensity of the universe.

The stars are not scattered evenly throughout the sky but are mainly arranged into groups known as galaxies. Our own galaxy is said to contain some 100,000 million stars and can be seen stretching across the sky in a gaseous cloud we call the Milky Way. If this galaxy was seen from a great distance it would show its spiral structure – a great mass of stars in the centre and streamers of stars reaching out in curves around it, rather like the pattern of cream when stirred into a cup of coffee.

Our Sun lies on one of these curves, about 32,000 light years from the centre of the galaxy. (A light year is the astronomical measure of distance and represents the distance that light travels in one year. When we consider that light travels at a speed of almost 300,000 kilometres per second, we are overwhelmed by the sheer size of astronomical distances.) The Sun is a very ordinary medium-sized star with a diameter of 1,392,000 kilometres and its volume is more than 1,000,000 times that of the earth.

There are nine planets in orbit around the Sun – the smaller ones are rocky and the larger ones are gaseous. Our own earth is the third from the centre of this planetary system and lies in the ecosphere. This is a presumed region around the Sun in which the temperature is neither too high nor too low to support life.

Until recently all that man knew about his planet was what he could study directly on its surface, from the rocks, the soil and the movements of the seas, for example. It is only in the past few hundred years, with the coming of more advanced technology, that he has been able to discover the structure of the earth down to its central core, as well as to appreciate its position and significance, or lack of it, in the universe. Only within the last 20 years has the earth revealed her secrets about the great forces that control the movements of continents and the building of mountains that have given us the earth we know today.

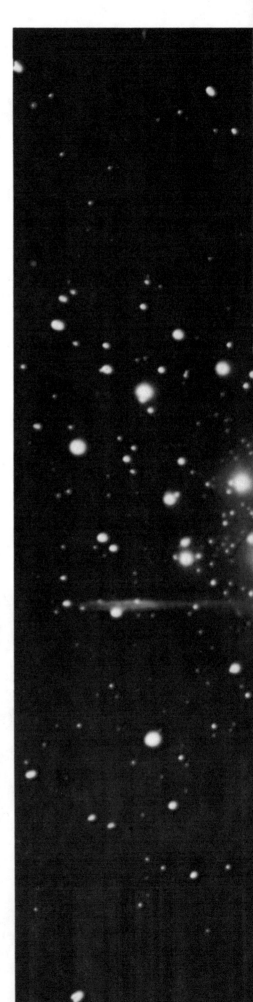

Above: Recent advances in space technology have enabled us to see the earth's surface in a different way. Satellite photography is of great use today.

Right: The size of the universe can be appreciated by looking at the number of stars visible in just one corner of it, as here in the Lagoon Nebula.

How the world began

No one knows for certain how the earth was formed. There are a number of theories. However, before investigating these, we should look at the ideas scientists have had about the origins of the universe and the solar system.

The beginning
Astronomers know that all the galaxies (star clusters) in the universe are moving apart at high speed. Three theories have been put forward to explain this.

In 1927 a Belgian astronomer called Georges Lemaître proposed the Big Bang Theory. He suggested that the universe began as a vast explosion from a central mass of matter. The resulting debris formed the galaxies, which are still moving outwards.

A variation of this theory states that the universe is constantly exploding outwards, drawing back together into a mass and exploding again. This continuous cycle is

Below: Three theories about the creation of the universe. There is strong evidence to support the big bang theory. It maintains that an explosion occurred and the universe is still expanding.

called the Oscillating Universe Theory.

In 1948 Fred Hoyle and two other British astronomers proposed a completely different theory, called the Steady State Theory. According to this, the appearance of the universe remains the same all the time. As the galaxies move apart, new matter is being created to occupy the empty space.

However, recent discoveries show that the universe has changed over the thousands of millions of years since it began. Today, most scientists believe that the universe began with a Big Bang about 18,000 million years ago.

The birth of a star
After the Big Bang there would have been clouds of dust and gas in space. In fact there still are such clouds — astronomers call them nebulae. It is in the nebulae that stars are born.

Every particle or body, whether it is an atom or a planet, is attracted to other bodies by the force of gravity. In a cloud of dust and gas, the atoms and particles are attracted to each other by

gravity and begin to form a solid mass. As the mass contracts, the movement of the particles creates heat and the young star begins to warm up. Among the atoms of gas are atoms of hydrogen. Eventually, the central core of the young star gets hot enough for hydrogen atoms to fuse together to form helium. This reaction is known as thermonuclear fusion.

This thermonuclear fusion gives out a vast amount of energy in the form of heat. Soon the star begins to glow and emit light as well.

Our own star, the Sun, was formed in this way about 5,000 million years ago. Its surface temperature is 5,660° centigrade. But its core, where the thermonuclear reaction occurs, has a temperature of over 15,000,000° centigrade, and a pressure of over 78,000,000 tonnes per cubic centimetre. Although the Sun uses up about 4,000,000 tonnes of hydrogen each second, there is still enough fuel left in its core to last for another 1,500 million years.

The solar system
Several theories have been put forward to explain the formation of

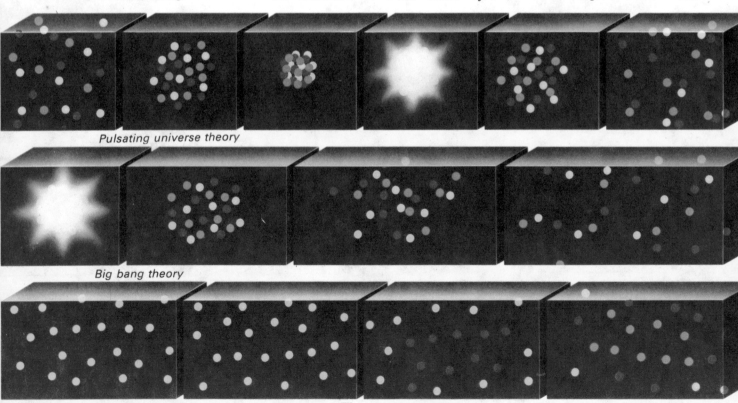

Pulsating universe theory

Big bang theory

Steady state theory

the planets. An early theory suggested that the young spinning Sun threw off rings of matter from its equator. These condensed into separate planets. Another theory suggested that a large star passed near the Sun and drew out a filament of molten material. This broke up into distinct masses that later cooled.

However, the most likely theory is the one known as the Cold Gas Disc Theory. This suggests that the Sun and planets were formed at the same time from a whirling cloud of dust and gas. The Sun formed at the centre of the cloud and the outer parts became a spinning disc of frozen particles. Within the disc, particles began to join up to form lumps. These swept up more particles and, gradually, large bodies were formed round the young Sun.

The earth

As the planets began to form, they, like the young Sun, heated up. However, they were not large enough to generate the very high temperatures needed for thermo-nuclear fusion. Therefore they did not form stars.

At first, the earth was molten and the heavier materials sank towards the centre. These, mainly iron and nickel, formed the solid central core of the earth as it cooled. Around this formed an outer core which remained molten. A thick layer of lighter material called the mantle formed on the outside of the core. The mantle is not completely rigid. Near its top is a semi-molten layer called the asthenosphere. An outer solid layer, the crust, rests on the mantle.

The crust is composed of two layers. Continental crust forms the main continents and their surrounding continental shelves. Oceanic crust forms the bottom of the oceans and lies underneath the continental crust. Scientists now believe that the oceanic crust is divided into plates, like the panels of a football. The plates are moving about on top of the asthenosphere. Where two plates collide, one slides under the other.

As the earth cooled, volcanoes produced gases, which formed the atmosphere. Water in the atmosphere condensed and rained down to form the oceans. And it was in the oceans that the first forms of life appeared, more than 3,500 million years ago.

Meanwhile the surface of the land was changing shape. The movements of the plates caused mountains to appear. At the same time the forces of erosion, such as ice, water and wind, began to wear down the mountains. Soil was formed and sediments were produced that later hardened into new rocks. These processes are still going on today.

Below: The earth formed about 4,600 million years ago. There was no atmosphere and no water. The surface was molten for many millions of years.

The solar system

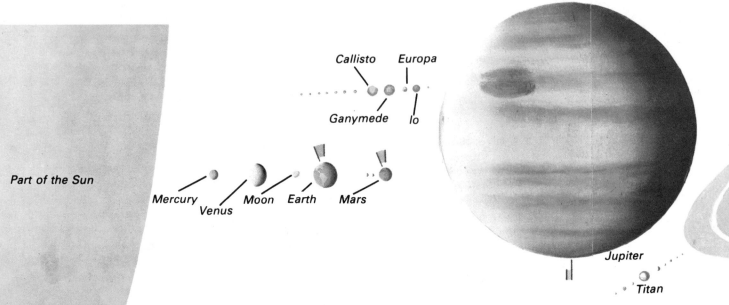

Part of the Sun

Callisto Europa

Ganymede Io

Mercury Moon Earth Mars

Venus

Jupiter

Titan

Our part of the Milky Way galaxy is called the solar system. At its centre is the Sun, a small star described by astronomers as a yellow dwarf. It appears to be so bright because it is quite close to earth – a mere 150 million kilometres away, which is very near in astronomical terms. At one time, the Sun was thought to be burning but calculations showed that this could not be the cause of its enormous output of heat and light. In fact, this energy is produced by a process called nuclear fusion.

At the centre of the Sun, the temperature is about 15,000,000° centigrade, and the pressure is about 400,000 million times that on the earth's surface. Under such conditions, hydrogen atoms com-

bine to form atoms of another light gas called helium. In this process, some of its mass is converted into energy. When even a small mass is destroyed, a large amount of energy is produced, and this accounts for the Sun's high output of heat and light.

The Sun also gives off other forms of energy, such as X-rays, radio waves and ultraviolet waves. It also emits streams of charged particles known as the solar wind.

The Sun's eclipse

Solar prominences are very easy to study during a total eclipse of the

Below: As the earth moves round the Sun, the Sun seems to lie in front of different constellations. The constellations do not lie in the same part of the sky as the signs of the zodiac of the same name.

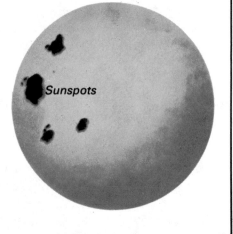

Sunspots

Sunspots are dark patches that can be seen clearly on the Sun's surface. Some last a few days before fading away, others last many weeks. The spots look dark because they are slightly cooler than the rest of the Sun's surface.

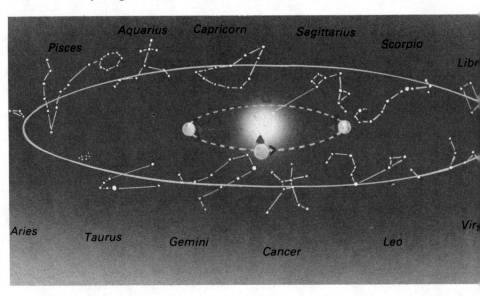

Aquarius Capricorn Sagittarius

Pisces Scorpio

Libr

Aries Vir

Taurus Gemini Leo

Cancer

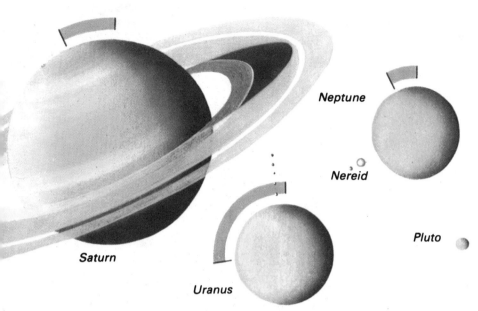

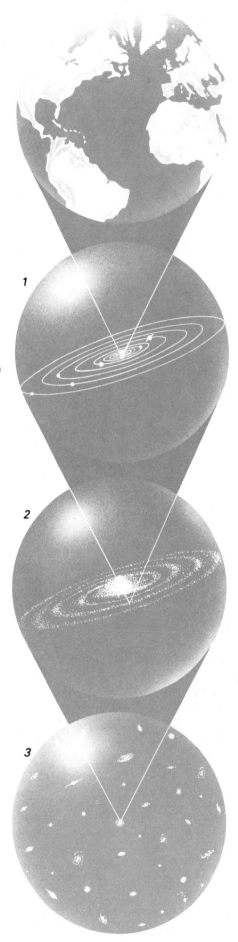

Above: The Sun and the planets that make up our solar system.

Right: The earth is just a tiny speck within the vastness of the universe. Our planet is just one of several planets orbiting the Sun *(1)*, while the Sun is just an ordinary star within the galaxy *(2)*. Our galaxy is one of many galaxies in space *(3)*.

Sun. This occurs when the Moon comes directly between the Sun and the earth. The Moon blocks out the Sun's bright surface, or photosphere, making it easier to see the reddish lower atmosphere, or chromosphere, and the whitish outer region called the corona. During the eclipse, prominences can be seen as red streaks of gas projecting hundreds of thousands of kilometres from its surface.

Another interesting feature of the Sun are the strange patches known as sunspots. Although they are extremely bright, sunspots appear dark in comparison with their even brighter surroundings. Whereas most parts of the photosphere are at a temperature of about 6,000° centigrade, sunspots are relatively cool at around 4,000° centigrade. They appear only in distinct bands on either side of the Sun's equator, and usually occur in small groups.

The planets

The solar system consists of the Sun, nine major planets and many smaller bodies. The planets move in elliptical (oval) orbits around the Sun and are prevented from escaping by the Sun's gravity.

Mercury is the closest planet to the Sun, at an average distance of 58 million kilometres. Then, in order of distance, come Venus, the earth, Mars, Jupiter, Saturn and Uranus. The outermost planets are

Neptune, at an average distance of 4,497 million kilometres from the Sun, and Pluto, at an average of 5,900 million kilometres. The orbit of Pluto, however, is unusually elongated and crosses Neptune's orbit. Therefore, at times, Pluto is temporarily closer to the Sun, and Neptune is the farthest away.

Being so close to the Sun, Mercury and Venus are incredibly hot during the day. Mercury has no atmosphere, while Venus has a dense white cloud cover which holds heat and reduces day-to-night temperature variation. In contrast, Mercury's temperature drops from about 400° centigrade in the day to about –200° centigrade at night. The earth's atmosphere also acts as a temperature regulator and filters out harmful radiation from the Sun. Like the earth, the red planet Mars has icy polar caps, but space probes have failed to find evidence of life on Mars. Jupiter, Saturn, Uranus and Neptune are giant planets, the largest of all being Jupiter. Little is known about the remote world of Pluto except that it may have once been one of Neptune's moons.

The Moon

Apart from the Sun and the major planets, the solar system contains many other orbiting bodies. These include the natural satellites, or moons, in orbit around some of the planets; the asteroids, or minor planets, and the comets and meteoroids (planetary debris). Like the major planets, all these bodies were probably formed from the remains of the gas cloud that formed the Sun some 5,000 million years ago. In addition, the solar system now contains numerous products of the space age. These are mostly orbiting artificial satellites.

Astronomers and space scientists use the word satellite to describe any body in orbit around another. The planets, for example, are satellites of the Sun. The Moon is a satellite of the earth. Other planets also have moons. As far as we know, Mars and Neptune have two, Jupiter has 13, Saturn ten, and Uranus five. In addition, Saturn has a spectacular system of three rings. These consist of orbiting particles of dust, ice or frozen gas.

The Moon

Of all the natural bodies in space, the Moon is closest to the earth. For this reason, it has always attracted a great deal of attention, and it was the obvious target for the Russians and Americans to aim for in the 1960s, when the space race began.

As seen from the earth, the Moon's appearance changes in a regular $29\frac{1}{2}$ day cycle. At any time, the positions of the Sun, Moon and earth determine how the Moon looks to us. When the Sun, Moon and earth form a right angle, for example, we see half of the Moon's face illuminated whereas the other half is in darkness. This occurs during the phases of the Moon known as the first and last quarters. Occasionally the Sun, earth and Moon lie in the same straight line. When this happens, the earth's shadow falls on the Moon, which is then said to be eclipsed.

Right and **below:** Close to, the Moon looks very different from the earth. The terrain that the astronauts found on the Moon was rocky and very dusty. Much of the surface is scarred with shallow pits and much deeper holes called craters. Most of the craters lie in the mountains of the Moon. Through a telescope set up on earth the mountainous areas show up as bright patches, while the darker patches are the Moon's plains. Astronomers call these plains "seas"

From earth we see only one side of the Moon. The far side, or dark side, has been photographed, however, and seems to consist mostly of mountains and craters.

Although it is convenient to talk of the earth's gravitational attraction keeping the Moon in its orbit, in fact the two bodies exert a force on each other. The Moon tries, in effect, to stretch the earth and causes the oceans to bulge on the near and far sides of the globe. As the earth spins, the bulges, or high tides, move around the oceans.

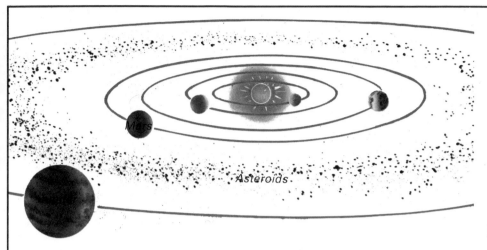

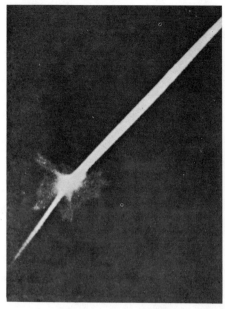

Above: Between Mars and Jupiter lies the asteroid belt. Asteroids are chunks of rock that may measure anything from a few centimetres to several kilometres across. They move in orbit round the Sun.

Right: Fragments from space sometimes plunge through the earth's atmosphere and become white-hot. This is when we see them at night as "shooting stars" or meteors.

Asteroids

We usually think of the solar system as containing nine planets but there are actually thousands. Between the orbits of Mars and Jupiter lies a vast band of orbiting rocks. These are the asteroids, or minor planets. About 2,000 asteroids have been recorded so far, and there are probably about 40,000 more that are large enough to be seen by telescope. The largest asteroid, named Ceres, is only 760 kilometres in diameter, and all but ten measure less than 160 kilometres across. Adonis, the smallest of all the recorded asteroids, measures a mere 150 metres in diameter. There are millions of other asteroids that are thought to exist, some no bigger than grains of sand.

The vast majority of asteroids remain in near circular orbits between those of Mars and Jupiter. A few move in eccentric orbits which sometimes bring them close to the major planets. Eros, for example, moves from the inside of the main asteroid band and crosses the orbit of Mars. The asteroid then approaches the earth's orbit before moving away to rejoin the main asteroid group. Several theories have been put forward to explain the existence of the asteroids. The most likely explanation is that they are materials left over when the major planets were formed.

Comets

Comets, it is thought, are "dirty snowballs" – mixtures of dust, ice and frozen gases. Most of the time they are invisible, for the nucleus of frozen material may be no more than one kilometre across, and comets are usually far from the earth. At regular intervals, though, they approach the Sun and emit a cloud of gas. Some of this forms a glowing tail that may become visible even in the day.

Below: Astronauts have not only walked on the Moon, they have also driven on its surface. Lunar rover vehicles allow the astronauts to roam farther from their landing craft to collect rock samples.

Man in space

In the 19th century almost everyone laughed at the idea of people flying in aeroplanes, and in the first half of the present century they laughed at the idea of travelling into space by rocket. Yet, in the past 20 years, since the beginning of the Space Age, space flight has become accepted as nothing unusual.

Rockets

The first really big rocket was the German A-4 missile, often called the V-2, of the Second World War. In 1945 the Russians captured some of these missiles and developed them further. Then the Russian engineers boldly decided to make a monster rocket with 32 separate engines, far bigger than anything already constructed. The result of this was that in 1957 the first artificial satellite, Sputnik 1, was put into orbit round the earth.

By this time the Russians were thinking about putting a man into space. This needs a large capsule, sealed to make an airtight compartment in which a human can work in comfort for a short time. A

Top left: The launch of the Apollo 15 spacecraft to the Moon in July 1971.

Left: A Soviet Luna unmanned craft, sent around the Moon in 1959.

Below left: The American Space Shuttle is the first space launcher that can be brought back to earth for re-use.

simple idea, but the problems in building such a capsule were enormous.

To be able to live in space, a "life-support system" had to be developed. The life-support system feeds either pure oxygen or a mixture of oxygen and helium to the astronaut so that the atmosphere stays fresh and breathable.

Russian space-explorers are called cosmonauts. The first to be chosen was Major Yuri Gagarin. He was launched into space and completed one orbit of the earth on 12th April 1961 in a capsule called a Vostok. Later, when groups of cosmonauts were shot into space, larger Voskhod-type spacecraft were used.

The American astronauts

America worked hard to catch up with the Russians. It formed a giant organization called NASA (National Aeronautics and Space Administration), and on 5th May 1961 its first astronaut, Alan B. Shepard, was shot 184 kilometres out into space before his rocket returned to earth. NASA's big

Below right: An artist's impression of a future manned space station. Some may be large enough to be called "space towns".

Below: In space the Shuttle has let the tank drift and now opens up to release a large satellite.

goal, however, was to put a man on the Moon.

This took years of effort. In the 1960s bigger and better manned spacecraft spent longer periods of time in space. In 1965 a Russian, Alexei Leonov, opened the door of his Voskhod craft and stepped out into space. This was the first time a man had walked in space, floating alongside the capsule, attached to it by a tether. Leonov wore a special multi-layer spacesuit, and he had a portable life-support system strapped to him.

To the Moon

Astronaut Neil Armstrong stepped out of his Apollo Lunar Module onto the Moon on 21st July 1969. Behind him came "Buzz" Aldrin. They spent over two hours on the Moon, doing various experiments, before lifting off and linking with the main Apollo craft that was orbiting the Moon. The command module and its crew returned to earth three days later, to be picked up by a recovery vessel.

Since then many men have gone to the Moon. In the 1980s the U.S.A. sent astronauts into space in re-usable space shuttles. But in 1986 an explosion on a shuttle shortly after take-off killed the crew and set back the programme. In 1987 the Russian Yuri Romanenko spent a record 326 days in space, while working in the orbiting Mir space station.

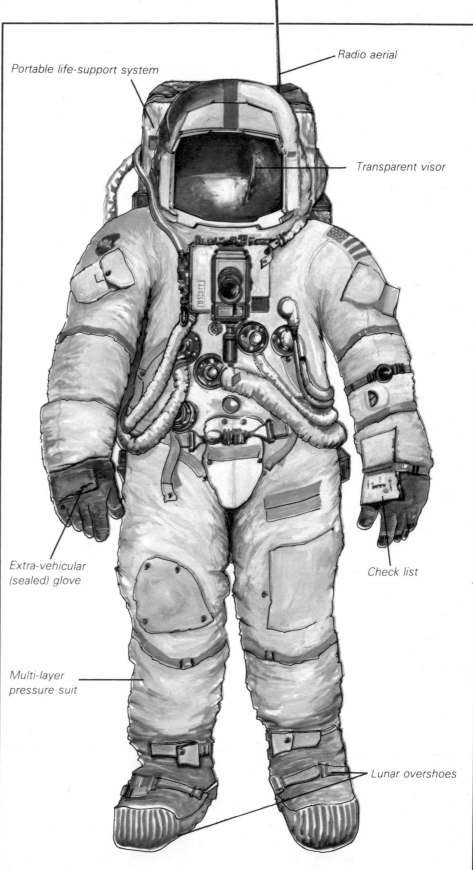

Portable life-support system

Radio aerial

Transparent visor

Extra-vehicular (sealed) glove

Check list

Multi-layer pressure suit

Lunar overshoes

Above: This special space suit was used by American astronauts for working on the surface of the Moon. It is a sealed pressure-suit, fed with a warm breathable atmosphere by a portable life-support system. In theory, anyone could run and jump far better on the Moon than on earth, even while wearing all this!

Galaxies

Stars, like living creatures, are born, live for a certain time, then die. Different kinds of stars have different life histories but the birth of any star takes place in a similar way.

A star forms by the condensation, or coming together, of dust and gas. These are present nearly everywhere in the universe – even "empty" space contains dust and hydrogen gas, although only very thinly. Larger concentrations are visible in the night sky as irregularly shaped clouds called nebulae, which are often rich in young stars.

Our own Sun is a good example of a common type of star. At its birth, as it condensed, it heated up until it began to shine. The energy by which it, and all other stars, shine, is called thermonuclear energy. On earth, we know this kind of energy only as the devastating explosion of an H-bomb.

When youthful, the Sun shone more brightly than it now does in its middle age. As it grows older, it will begin to swell until it becomes the type of star known as a red giant. At this time of its life, it will swallow up its planets, including the earth!

In its old age, the Sun will collapse again into a small, but extremely heavy, form of star called a white dwarf. Compared with the Sun as it is now, this will have very little energy. Gradually, however, it will lose even this energy, to become a black dwarf. The Sun will have died.

In general, smaller types of star than our Sun do not grow to be red giants, but they cool and die in a rather similar way. Stars much larger than the Sun die more spectacularly, by huge explosions called supernovae.

Galaxies

On a clear night, we see the Milky Way shining. This narrow, luminous area of the sky is really our own galaxy, containing a population of many millions of stars, of which the Sun is a fairly ordinary member.

Birth of stars and galaxies

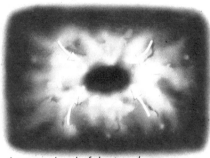

A great cloud of dust and gas

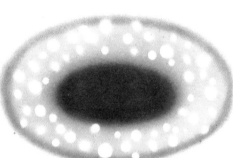

Young stars begin to condense out

The young galaxy contains many stars

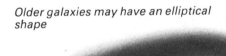

Older galaxies may have an elliptical shape

Stars are born from clouds of dust and gas. Great accumulations of stars, dust and gas are known as galaxies. These have various shapes – irregular, elliptical and spiral.

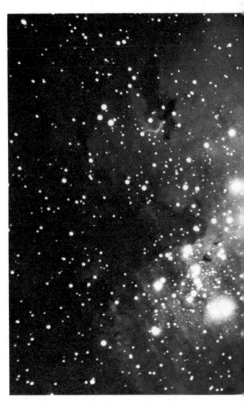

Our galaxy is disc-shaped and the Milky Way appears narrow because we are looking along the disc, the Sun being far out from its centre. If we could view our galaxy from the outside, it would appear as a spiral-shaped disc as in the picture. Astonomers know that it is similar to its nearest neighbour, the Andromeda galaxy, which can be seen to have this spiral shape.

Just as a galaxy contains vast

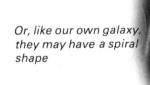

Or, like our own galaxy, they may have a spiral shape

Left: Nebulae are great clouds of dust and gas in space. Astronomers number them by the heavenly constellations in which they occur. This one, for example, is known as M16 in Serpens – it lies in the constellation The Serpent.

Above and **right:** Galaxies are sources of great quantities of radiation, including light, radio waves and X-rays. On earth, radio waves from space are detected with large radiotelescopes.

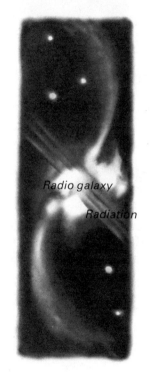

numbers of stars, so the universe contains vast numbers of galaxies. These have various shapes, many being spiral types, sometimes with a bar between their coiling arms, when they are known as barred spiral galaxies. Many others, the elliptical galaxies, are more egg-shaped, without arms. Yet others have irregular shapes.

The irregularly-shaped galaxies contain many young, very hot stars. The elliptical galaxies may contain many old stars. Beyond these observations, it is difficult to

know the age of a galaxy. All galaxies other than our own and its immediate neighbours are so far away that they can be seen only with very powerful telescopes.

For example, certain very remote objects called quasars, although apparently of star-like size, give off more energy than whole galaxies. No-one has yet explained this satisfactorily, although many astronomers think that quasars may be related to radio galaxies, which also emit vast amounts of energy in the form of radio waves.

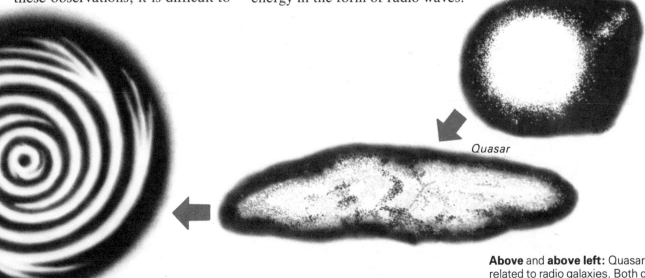

Above and **above left:** Quasars may be related to radio galaxies. Both give out huge amounts of energy.

The atmosphere

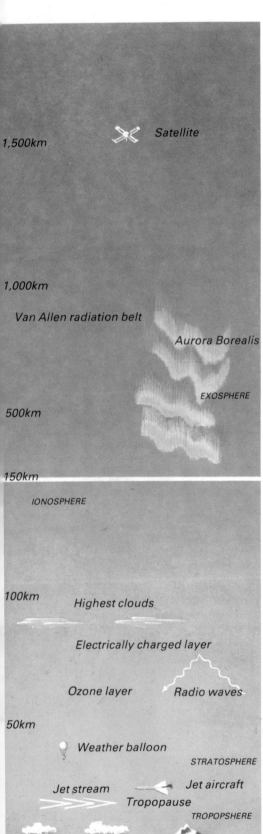

Above: The different levels of the earth's atmosphere do not change abruptly from one level to the next. Instead, the changes are gradual and the different levels merge gently with one another. All life on earth lives in the thinnest layer called the troposphere.

The first atmosphere was probably made up of methane, hydrogen and ammonia gases. As soon as it formed, it began to change. One of the first things to happen was that the hydrogen, being such a light gas, was quickly lost into space.

Water

When a solid crust had formed on the earth's surface, vast quantities of water vapour were released into it from volcanic activity. For a while, the atmosphere was full of this vapour but soon this began to condense and fall as the first rain. But the earth's crust was still very hot, and the water immediately evaporated into vapour once again. This probably continued for millions of years, until the crust had cooled enough for the water to land on it without boiling away.

It probably rained solidly everywhere for the next few million years. The water gathered in the hollows, filling up and spilling over so that the pools united into lakes and then into seas and finally the oceans were formed.

While this was happening, the other gases given out by volcanoes, such as sulphur dioxide and carbon dioxide, collected in the atmosphere.

The first life

About 3,500 million years ago the first known life forms had appeared in the sea. These were simple algae which could use the energy of sunlight to create food out of raw materials. Since the evolution of true oxygen-producing plants, about 1,900 million years ago, the amount of oxygen in the atmosphere has been steadily increasing. The presence of oxygen in the atmosphere has made animal life possible on the surface of the earth – since animals need oxygen to live.

The largest part of the atmosphere – about 80 per cent – has nearly always been composed of the gas nitrogen. This gas does not have much effect on the earth's animal life.

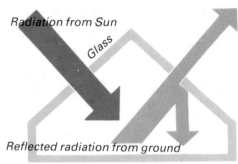

Above: Heat and radio waves are absorbed by different amounts in the various layers of the atmosphere. The glass of a greenhouse *(top)* acts as a barrier stopping the heat waves escaping.

The air

The atmosphere that surrounds this planet is said to be thin, as it only goes up about 700 kilometres. Then it becomes so rarefied that it fades into space. This height, compared with the earth's diameter of over 12,700 kilometres, is very small.

Although we use the expression "as light as air", the air has enough weight to keep the bulk of the atmosphere close to the earth's surface. It also means that the quality of the atmosphere changes the higher one goes above the ground. The lower layers are compressed by the weight of the layers above.

The atmosphere is divided into a number of distinct layers that have different pressures, temperatures and other qualities.

Troposphere

The lowest layer, up to about 18 kilometres above the equator and eight kilometres above the poles, is

Above: Because of the tilt of the earth's axis, it is colder at the poles than at the equator. The Sun's rays pass through more of the atmosphere at the poles, so more heat is lost.

called the troposphere. This is the thinnest layer, but all life forms live within it. The weather in this layer can change from day to day.

Stratosphere

The upper boundary of the troposphere is called the tropopause. Above that, up to about 80 kilometres, lies the second layer of atmosphere. Here the pressure is too low and the air too thin to support life. Aircraft travelling at these heights need to have the atmosphere inside them artificially pressurized, with breathable air supplied by special equipment.

In the stratosphere, there is a very important layer called the ozone layer. This consists of oxygen but its atoms are arranged in groups of three rather than in groups of two as is the case in the atmosphere below. Ozone is able to absorb much of the ultraviolet radiation from the Sun. This radiation could be very harmful to living cells if concentrated.

Ionosphere

Farther up, from the top of the stratosphere to a height of about 500 kilometres, is the third layer, the ionosphere. This is the thickest layer of the atmosphere, but it has in it only one per cent of the atmosphere's mass. Above is the exosphere, which is so rarified that it just fades off into space.

The pressure of the atmosphere decreases regularly with height, but the changes of temperature in the atmosphere are much more complex. The energy radiated from the Sun is absorbed by some of the layers and reflected by others. Only about 45 per cent of the Sun's radiation actually reaches the earth. Some of this is reflected back again, heating the atmosphere from below. In all, the heat radiated from the atmosphere is equal to the heat absorbed from the Sun.

Delicate structure

The structure of the atmosphere is quite a delicate one. This is important if life on earth is to continue. In the late 1980s, scientists found a 'hole' in the ozone layer over Antarctica. They think that the ozone is being damaged by chemicals used in aerosols, refrigerators, plastic insulation and upholstery foam. Further damage to the ozone layer could have disastrous consequences.

An increase in the carbon dioxide in the atmosphere – which happens when fuels are burned – may set up something known as the "greenhouse effect".

In this, the heat balance becomes upset and much of the heat radiated from the earth's surface is trapped in the troposphere. This could cause the temperatures at the earth's surface to rise to dangerously high levels, melting the ice caps at the poles and so raising the levels of the seas and flooding large parts of the populated world.

To prevent these effects, we must keep a close watch on the amount of waste that is allowed to escape into the air.

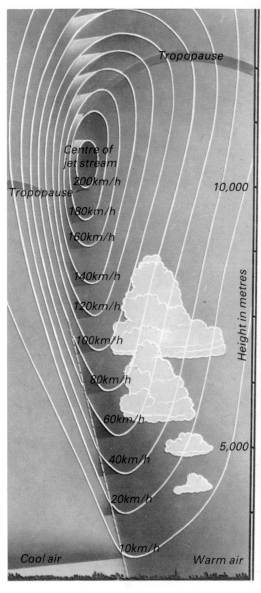

Above: The atmosphere is always circulating. Jet streams are very fast tunnels of wind formed when two air masses meet.

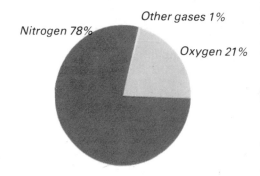

Above: The composition of the atmosphere varies with height, because the heavier gases tend to sink down to the ground. But in all parts of the atmosphere nitrogen and oxygen make up by far the greatest proportion.

Rocks and minerals

Above: Fairly rare minerals are sometimes found in deposits large enough to be mined. An example of this is at the Nebaya copper mine in the copperbelt of Zambia.

Above right: In most places, the solid rock of the earth's crust is covered by a weathered layer of rock, mixed in with plant debris. This very thin layer we know as soil.

The name that geologists give to the substance the earth's crust is made of is "rock". This term covers loose sand, clay and other substances formed naturally by the earth, as well as the hard lumps we usually think of as rocks.

Types of rocks
There are three types of rock – igneous, sedimentary and metamorphic.

Igneous rock forms when magma (molten matter from beneath the earth's surface) cools and solidifies.

This can happen underground, where it forms large masses of coarse-grained rock, such as granite. It can also take place at the surface, where lava flows from volcanoes and hardens into more finely-grained rocks, such as basalt.

Sedimentary rocks form when existing rocks are worn away by

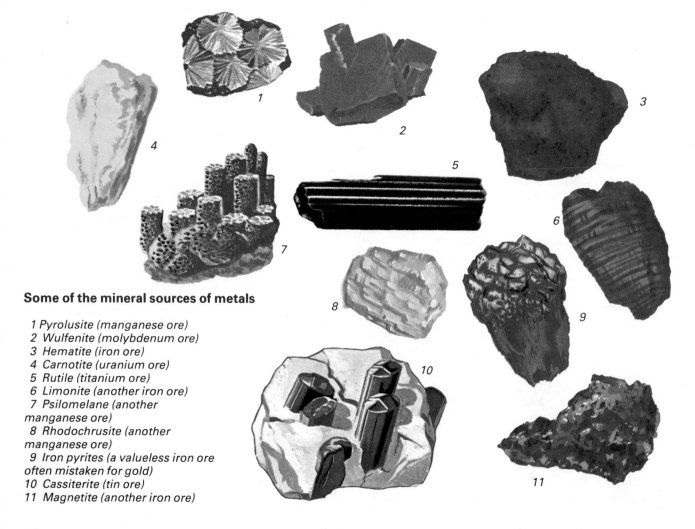

Some of the mineral sources of metals

1 Pyrolusite (manganese ore)
2 Wulfenite (molybdenum ore)
3 Hematite (iron ore)
4 Carnotite (uranium ore)
5 Rutile (titanium ore)
6 Limonite (another iron ore)
7 Psilomelane (another manganese ore)
8 Rhodochrusite (another manganese ore)
9 Iron pyrites (a valueless iron ore often mistaken for gold)
10 Cassiterite (tin ore)
11 Magnetite (another iron ore)

rain and frost. The fragments produced are carried by rivers, glaciers, winds and seas, and when they finally come to rest, they are buried, compressed and cemented together to form rocks. These lie in layers, called beds. Sedimentary rocks include sandstones, formed when sand is compressed and solidified, shales, formed when mud is turned to stone, and conglomerates, made of pebbles cemented together.

The third type – metamorphic rocks – are produced when existing rocks are heated or compressed by great stresses. The chemical structure of the rocks is altered, though the rocks do not actually melt.

Gneiss and schist are both metamorphic rocks. They are often twisted and contorted, which shows the violent way in which they were formed.

The process needed to form metamorphic rocks often takes place when a mountain is being formed.

Minerals

When we look at a rock through a microscope we can see that it is made up of a mass of tiny crystals. A rock usually has crystals of up to five different substances in it. These substances, made up of chemicals, are called minerals.

There are nearly 3,000 different minerals, but each rock has only a few.

Most people use the word "mineral" to refer to the ore-forming kinds from which useful metals can be extracted, but these are only a small proportion of all the minerals that exist. Most are rock-forming minerals such as quartz, calcite and feldspar.

Information from crystals

The types of minerals found can tell us a great deal about how the rock was formed. Granite, for example, is coarse-grained because it is made of mostly very large crystals.

This is because the original molten matter cooled slowly

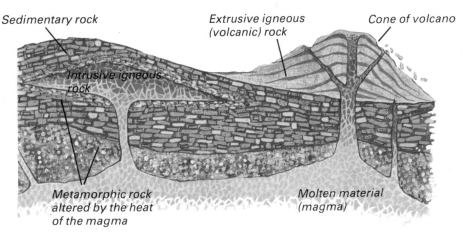

Sedimentary rock — Intrusive igneous rock — Metamorphic rock altered by the heat of the magma — Extrusive igneous (volcanic) rock — Cone of volcano — Molten material (magma)

underground, and as it did so it gave the crystals time to grow large. The crystals formed first are usually the largest, and are best developed. The later ones are much finer.

In sedimentary rocks, the grains may be very small and well rounded. This suggests that the particles from which the rock is made were carried a long way and were worn smooth before they became rock.

Above: The first rocks to form were horizontal beds of sedimentary rock. Later, molten material from the depths of the earth burst through them, and solidified, either underground, or as a heap at the surface called a volcano. The heat of the molten material sometimes changed the nearby sedimentary rock into metamorphic rock.

Below: Wind and weather can erode rocks into strange shapes.

The oceans

When seen from space, our planet looks blue. This is mainly because blue light reflects from the atmosphere, while other colours do not, and also because so much of the earth's surface – over 70 per cent of it – is made up of water, in the form of the ocean.

As we have already seen, the crust of the earth is made up of sial, a lighter material which floats about on top of a heavier material. the sima. The sima is constantly renewing and destroying itself.

Moving panels
If we think of the crust of the earth as a football, then each plate of sima can be thought of as a panel.

Each panel is constantly changing, growing at one side where volcanic material erupts at the seam, while the other side slides under the neighbouring panel.

A look at a contour map of the ocean floor makes the pattern clear. Several ridges can be seen, running up the centre of the Atlantic and Indian Oceans, and up the east side of the Pacific. These ridges are the seams along which the panels are being formed by volcanic activity.

Around the edge of the Pacific Ocean are a series of deep trenches. These are usually next to high mountain ranges, such as the Rockies, or the Andes, or near strings of volcanic islands, such as Japan. The trenches are the points at which one panel is sliding beneath another.

This overall structure and movement has been responsible for the form of the sea bed, and has been responsible for the way in which land and water are distributed over the earth's surface.

Water
The water on the earth's surface and in its atmosphere is always

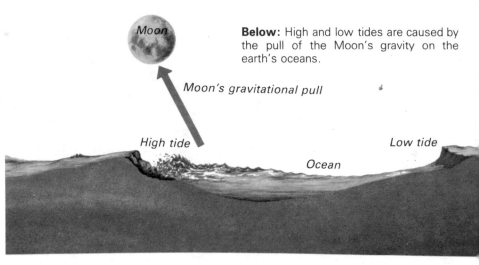

Below: High and low tides are caused by the pull of the Moon's gravity on the earth's oceans.

Moon

Moon's gravitational pull

High tide

Low tide

Ocean

moving. The sun evaporates it from the ocean's surface, the wind blows the resulting vapour over the land, where it falls as rain, collects in rivers and flows back to the sea.

Great quantities of water are locked up as ice on the land and in the seas of the colder parts of the world. But in spite of this, and the amount being evaporated, more than 97 per cent of the earth's water is contained in the ocean at any one time.

Movements
There are movements within the ocean, caused by currents. These form when water heated by the sun rises to the surface and colder water flows in underneath it.

Other movements are caused by the wind, which blows across the surface of the ocean to make waves, and by the tides. Tides are the result of the water being pulled by the gravity of the moon and the sun.

Sea water
Sea water is not pure. It contains large amounts of dissolved salts – as much as 35 grams in one kilo of water. Sodium chloride, or common salt, forms about 80 per

Right: The continental shelf is an area of sea bed less than 200 metres deep which surrounds every continent. From above, the continental shelf looks light blue against the deeper blue of the rest of the ocean.

The ocean depths

Continental shelf	200m
Whale	1000m
Beebe's bathysphere	920m
Barton's bathysphere	1,373m
F.R.N.S. 3	4,051m
Deep-sea camera	
Trieste bathyscaphe	10,915m

1km
2km
3km
4km
5km
6km
7km
8km
9km
10km

Left: Some trenches along the ocean floor can reach depths of over 10,000 metres, but most exploration is confined to the top 500 metres. The deepest dive made so far is 10,915 metres in a submersible (underwater craft) called the *Trieste*.

cent of these salts.

Seventy-five per cent of all the natural chemical elements which exist in the world are found in sea water. Even gold is there, but in such small quantities that it is not worth extracting it. The only products extracted are cooking salt, magnesium and bromine.

Exploration

People have only recently begun exploring the ocean. The technology needed to investigate it is rather like that needed for space exploration. In both cases, robots and remote sensors, rather than people wearing life support systems, actually go to look at the place.

We may have to turn to the ocean in the future to supply many of our needs, as the world's growing population rapidly uses up known natural resources.

Until now, our uses of the sea have been very limited. The fish we take from it forms only a small proportion of our diet. In future we may farm the sea as we farm the land. We already exploit offshore oil, but other minerals are present, and may be extracted one day.

The development of the diving suit

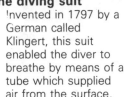

Early divers used skin bladders filled with air. These attempts, though almost unworkable, led to the development of better equipment.

Invented in 1797 by a German called Klingert, this suit enabled the diver to breathe by means of a tube which supplied air from the surface.

Called the "closed" dress, this was the first modern suit. Invented by Augustus Siebe in 1837, its design is almost the same today.

The design of the aqualung allowed the diver to be flexible in underwater movement. Scuba diving has become a popular sport.

For diving to great depths, specially strong suits are needed to protect the diver against pressure. A metal articulated suit is shown here.

Eroded landscapes

As soon as mountains are formed, whatever the cause, the forces of nature immediately begin to wear them down again. The rate at which erosion occurs seems to us to be very slow. But over periods of millions of years the effect is dramatic. Water is the most powerful agent of erosion.

Streams and rivers
Water is constantly being evaporated from the surface of the ocean and falling on the land as rain. There, much of it seeps underground, re-emerging at the surface in springs, forming streams which combine into rivers and flow back to the sea.

Along the way, small pieces of rock are worn off the sides and bottoms of streams. These are rolled and bumped along, knocking off other pieces, wearing away the stream's channel.

This is most obvious in the upper reaches of streams and rivers. Here they flow swiftly down steep slopes, sometimes containing great boulders when the river is in flood. The river beds are worn into deep, V-shaped ravines.

In the lowlands, where the slopes are more gentle and the rivers flow more slowly, the water does not have enough force to go on carrying all the material that has been worn away. Sand, silt and rocks are then deposited on the river bed and at the banks. In times of flood the finer material is spread out over large areas. This can form a flood plain – a vast expanse of flat land, often found stretching away from the foothills of mountain ranges.

Chemical erosion
As well as this physical effect, rainwater also has a chemical effect. As it falls, rain dissolves carbon dioxide from the atmosphere and soil so it becomes a weak acid.

The mineral calcite, which forms limestone, is attacked by this acid, and this erosion can create strange forms in a landscape. The same process in underground streams in limestone areas creates cave systems by dissolving the surrounding rock. The underground water also opens up cracks and joints. Water

Above: Waterfalls and gorges show the great power of falling water. These torrents carry rocks and other debris that scour out the beds and deepen valleys. They carve out the mountain landscape and carry the material to the sea.

Right: Limestone caves illustrate dramatically the effect of rainwater on calcite. Calcite is dissolved by running water and deposited again later, as stalactites and stalagmites.

Main shaft

Side passages

Chimney

Chockstone

Pool

Rimesone

Boulder choke

Roof fall

A cave system showing typical features

Above: A headland is often attacked on each side by waves, making it narrower. Caves are carved out, then worn through to form natural arches. When the arch collapses a sea stack is left.

stalactites and stalagmites, and other related features found in limestone caves.

The sea

The sea itself is a very powerful agent of erosion. The waves batter the coastline, creating headlands and cliffs, cutting caves and carving sea stacks and natural arches.

The sea also has a constructive

Above: A subsiding island in a tropical sea will have a fringing reef of coral. As the island sinks, the coral goes on growing as a barrier reef, and finally forms an atoll when the island has gone.

that seeps through the rock may be exposed on the roofs and walls of the caves. There it evaporates, depositing the dissolved calcite. These deposits build up to form

role to play. The sand and rocky debris produced by all this battering, together with that brought down by the rivers, is shifted and sorted by the currents. Eventually it all accumulates as sand banks or mud flats where the current is slack. These may later be buried and become sedimentary rock.

Coral reefs are a special kind of rock built in the sea. Tiny coral animals (called polyps) build up reefs using the limestone skeletons of previous generations of coral. The surface of the reef is covered by a "skin" of living coral. These animals commonly appear as fossils in some limestones, indicating areas that were once marine.

Once rocks are formed, earth processes may form them into mountains and the whole process of erosion begins again.

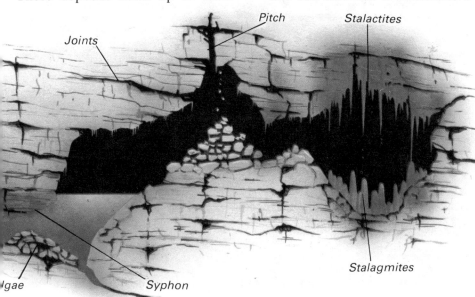

Joints

Pitch

Stalactites

Algae

Syphon

Stalagmites

Mountains and glaciers

Left: The mountains of Antarctica are typical fold mountains – formed where two plates of the earth's crust join. Frost and glaciers are now eroding them.

Folds and faults

Because of the way they are formed, these types are called fold mountains. Another way mountains can form is by a process called block faulting. In this, solid areas of crust are split by vertical cracks called faults.

This forms individual crustal blocks, which move up and down in relation to one another. In doing this, they make either rift valleys, where one block has subsided in relation to those on either side, or horsts where a block has been raised above those around it.

A spectacular rift valley system runs up most of the length of East Africa and continues northwards to form the Red Sea and the Jordan Valley into Syria. The Ruwenzori Mountains which border part of the rift valley in East Africa are an example of a horst.

Once the mountains have been raised they are attacked by a number of processes which wear them back down again.

Mountains are being built all the time. Sometimes this is obvious and spectacular – for example due to earthquakes and volcanic eruptions.

More often it happens so slowly that it cannot be observed in a lifetime. Mountain ranges thousands of metres high and hundreds of kilometres long form gradually over millions of years.

Formation

The most obvious sites for this activity are along the edges of the surface plates of the earth – where a plate is sliding beneath blocks of the continental sial and crumpling it up like the edge of a tablecloth.

The Rockies were formed like this a long time ago, and today the Andes are being formed in the same way.

The worn stumps of similar mountain ranges throughout the world show that the plate boundaries have not always been in the same place. The Urals in the U.S.S.R., the Appalachians of eastern North America and even the Highlands of Scotland are the remains of old mountain systems formed along ancient plate edges which no longer exist.

Right: Although spectacular, volcanoes do not add much to the mountain building processes shaping the world today. They form mountains of loose material, which is easily washed away.

Erosion

This wearing down is called erosion. Rain, running water, frost, ice and the wind all help to erode rocks. Frost and ice tend to produce a particular kind of mountain landscape – either at high altitudes or at high latitudes towards the earth's poles.

Frost makes water freeze in cracks in the rock. The ice forces the crack open and eventually chunks of the rock split away.

The flanks of mountains, where they are not concealed by snow or glaciers, are covered with pieces of rocks broken off by frost action. These form scree slopes which are common in the English Lake District.

When snow piles up in the sheltered hollows of cold mountain areas, it stays there without melting. Eventually it is compressed into ice and flows downhill as a glacier. Although it moves slowly, a glacier is tremendously powerful.

Above: Mount Hood in Oregon is an old volcano amongst the folded Rocky Mountains.
Below: Hot springs and geysers show there has been recent volcanic activity.

It scours out deep U-shaped valleys and carries off vast quantities of the frost-shattered rocks. It deposits them as moraine many kilometres away.

Within the last two million years – during the Ice Age – erosion of this kind was happening all over northern Europe, and formed much of the landscape of the British Isles today.

Wind erosion

The effects of the wind can be seen in arid areas, where there is not enough moisture to hold the fragments of soil together. They are blown about in sandstorms, acting like sandpaper, wearing away exposed rocks and producing yet more fragments. These eventually settle to form the great dunes that are found in the desert areas of the world. These too are constantly being moved by the wind.

Below: The force of mountain building is obvious here. Rocks, still deep underground, were forced apart by molten material which then solidified in the cracks, forming granite dikes.

Left: Erosion by sand and wind in desert areas may carve rocks into fantastic shapes. Sand from this process accumulates as dunes, which spread over huge areas.

Soils

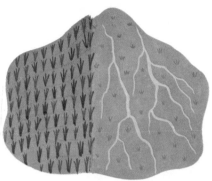

New settlers coming into a fertile forest land cut down trees to clear space so that they can begin farming. The forest is the natural vegetation, established for thousands of years.

Crops are planted, but every year they take more nutrients from the soil. Continuous working compresses the soil so that it cannot absorb much water and therefore rain flows off it.

Much of the soil is eventually washed away with the rain. Its quality gets worse, so that it can no longer be used for crops. Cattle are grazed on it, and soon it will only support sheep.

Most of the rocks of the earth's surface are covered by a layer of material we call soil.

A mixture

Soil is basically a mixture of the fragmented and decomposed bedrock and the rotting debris of the plants that have grown from it.

When it is cut through, the soil's structure can often be clearly seen. At the very bottom is the natural bedrock of the area. Directly above, there is a layer of the same rock, but broken up. The next layer is known as the subsoil and is very rich in minerals leached (dissolved) out of the soil above.

Above this is the topsoil. This contains a large amount of vegetable matter. At the top there is a layer of humus, made up largely of decomposing plant remains.

A soil profile is not always exactly like the example above, as it varies a great deal from place to place and from climate to climate. In desert areas there may be hardly any vegetable matter and the soil covering may be very thin as the wind blows away any rock fragments that are broken off.

In cold marshy areas, on the other hand, the humus layer may be extremely thick, since the plants that die and are buried tend to decompose very slowly, building up layers of peat.

In areas of high temperatures and high rainfall, minerals such as iron ore are dissolved out of the bedrock. These rise to the surface as the water is evaporated, making the upper layers very rich in minerals.

Plants and animals

The animal and plant life in the soil make a big difference to its final appearance. Earthworms, for example, make little tunnels in the soil, allowing air to circulate through it. This speeds up the decomposition of organic matter. Worms also pull down leaves and other rotting vegetation from the

Left: Mountainous areas tend to have very thin soil cover. This is because the rain that falls, runs off very quickly. There is little build-up of rock fragments to give root-holds to plants.

Right: Deserts have very little soil. Although there is a great deal of fine rocky debris, the arid climate means that there is little decomposing plant material to form humus.

Sheep eat everything that is left and, with no plant roots to hold it together, the soil crumbles to dust and is washed away by the rain. Gullied badlands result, useless for agriculture.

surface, which enriches the humus.

Every living thing owes its existence, directly or indirectly, to the soil of its native land.

Different plants need different minerals and different depths in which to stretch their roots. The animal life of the area, which depends on the plant life, is affected in the same way.

People depend on the soil to grow the crops that produce the food they eat and the clothes they wear. A look at a world map shows

the close ties between people and the soil. Populations are sparse where the soil in poor, and large where it is rich and fertile.

It is obviously very important for us to keep the rich soil in good condition so that we can go on benefiting from it for as long as it is farmed.

Balance

People have not always appreciated the delicate balance of the soil. In the early days of settlement in North America, vast areas of rich soils were found. The trees were cleared away and the land was farmed intensively. This led to disaster. Frequent cropping soon took all the nutrients from the soil. The crop yields began to decline. Without a plant cover and a network of roots to hold the soil particles together, the sun dried out the land and the wind blew what was left of the soil away. This caused tracts of deserts, "badlands", where the rich soil had

Right: The prairies of North America are grasslands with humus-rich soil. These areas are now farmed for wheat. They are successful because the wheat is so similar to the natural vegetation.

Left: Climate is the most important factor in soil formation. Here, on the south coast of Turkey, the closeness of both the sea and the mountains influences the climate and thus the formation of soil.

Above: Contour ploughing is often practised to prevent soil erosion. Making the furrows follow the contours helps to stop tilled soil being washed down slopes.

once been.

A similar thing has happened in North Africa. The Sahara was not always as large a desert as it is now. Continuous overfarming and overgrazing at the edges have made it creep southwards in places at a rate of 100 metres a year, bringing with it famine and misery.

Climate and weather

The terms "climate" and "weather" are often confused. Climate is the average or typical temperature, rainfall and so on expected in a particular area. To make sure they know how to describe it fully, people must make a large number of observations over a long time – 50 years or more.

The day-to-day variations that occur within the framework of a climate are known as weather.

Climates

A map of the world shows that climates lie in horizontal bands, partly determined by latitude. These are the result of the way in which the surface of the earth is heated by the sun's rays.

The climate in the band straddling the equator is mostly hot and wet. It is like this because the air heated by the sun here is rising, creating a low pressure air system into which wet winds from the oceans are drawn.

To the north and south of this are belts of hot, dry climates. Here, the air that has risen above the equatorial belt descends once more, creating a high pressure air system, from which winds blow outwards. These are the desert parts of the world, where very little grows. The air here moves at low levels either back towards the tropical zone, as trade winds, or as warm winds blowing north and south towards the temperate zones.

The polar climates are in the far north and south. The sun's rays reach the ground there at an angle so low that they must travel

World climate

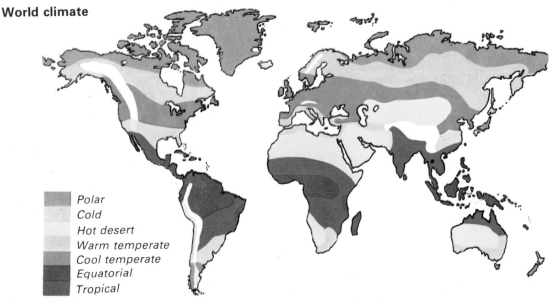

Polar
Cold
Hot desert
Warm temperate
Cool temperate
Equatorial
Tropical

The world's climates are in roughly parallel bands, north and south of the equator. But they do not quite match, as climate is also affected by how near the sea is and where the mountains are. Mountains can cause deserts by intercepting the moisture-laden clouds from the ocean and preventing them from reaching some areas.

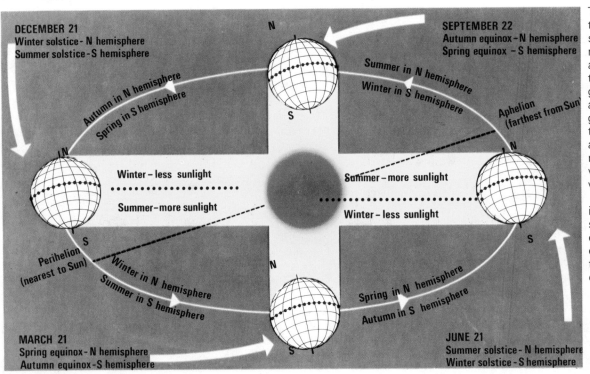

DECEMBER 21
Winter solstice – N hemisphere
Summer solstice – S hemisphere

Autumn in N hemisphere
Spring in S hemisphere

SEPTEMBER 22
Autumn equinox – N hemisphere
Spring equinox – S hemisphere

Summer in N hemisphere
Winter in S hemisphere

Aphelion (farthest from Sun)

Winter – less sunlight
Summer – more sunlight

Summer – more sunlight
Winter – less sunlight

Perihelion (nearest to Sun)

Winter in N hemisphere
Summer in S hemisphere

Spring in N hemisphere
Autumn in S hemisphere

MARCH 21
Spring equinox – N hemisphere
Autumn equinox – S hemisphere

JUNE 21
Summer solstice – N hemisphere
Winter solstice – S hemisphere

The way the earth is tilted gives us the seasons. When the northern part is tilted away from the sun, the rays reach the ground at a shallow angle. They have to go quite a long way through the earth's atmosphere and do not give much warmth. This causes winter.

At the same time, it is summer in the south. When the earth reaches the other side of its orbit, the seasons are the other way round.

through the atmosphere for some distance before they reach the ground. Much heat is lost along the way so these places are never very warm, and are nearly always covered with snow and ice.

Climate varies from area to area within these bands. It is affected by the nearness of the sea and chains of mountains. A high range of mountains can intercept the passage of wet winds from the sea so that the areas behind it receive only dry winds. These areas are called "rain shadow" deserts.

Weather

The greatest variations of day-to-day weather take place in mid-latitude temperate climates. This is because this zone contains a boundary, the polar front, where winds from warmer areas meet the cold winds from the polar regions. The boundary is not fixed and moves from season to season.

Fronts

When warm and cold air masses meet, they slide past each another in different directions. This sets up

eddies like vast whirlpools in the air. Spiral tongues of warm air reach into the cold. The edges of these tongues are known as fronts.

Fronts can be warm or cold, depending on the sort of air they bring with them. Cold air tends to spread along the ground, forcing warm air up over it. When this happens, the moisture in the warm air condenses, forming first clouds and then rain. The variation in the amount of rain which places in temperate zones receive is influenced by the fronts.

Thundercloud

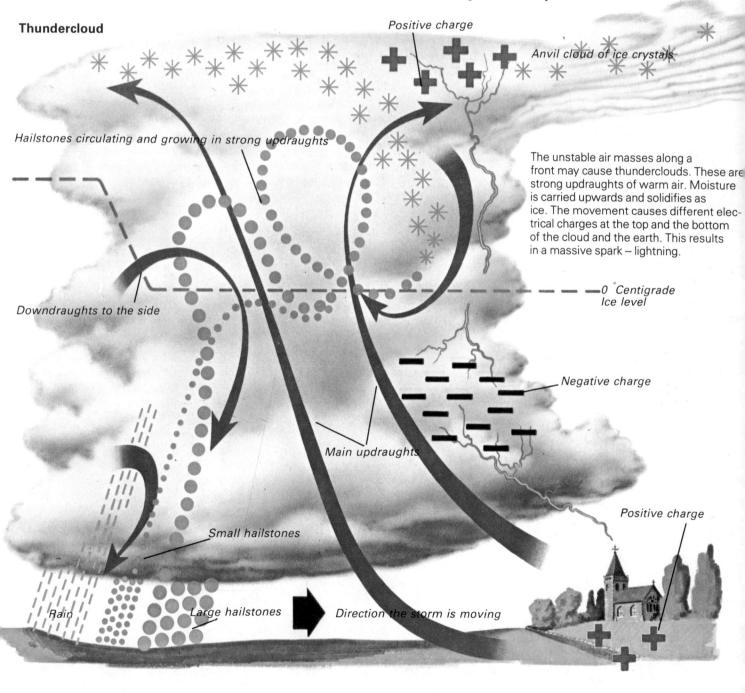

Positive charge

Anvil cloud of ice crystals

Hailstones circulating and growing in strong updraughts

The unstable air masses along a front may cause thunderclouds. These are strong updraughts of warm air. Moisture is carried upwards and solidifies as ice. The movement causes different electrical charges at the top and the bottom of the cloud and the earth. This results in a massive spark – lightning.

Downdraughts to the side

0 °Centigrade
Ice level

Negative charge

Main updraughts

Positive charge

Small hailstones

Rain

Large hailstones

Direction the storm is moving

The food we eat

Early man found his food by hunting down wild animals and eating wild berries, nuts and roots. His first really secure food supply began when he started to farm, cultivating crops and domesticating animals. In time, his tools improved and he learned how to irrigate land and how to breed animals to produce more meat. These early farming endeavours are the basis of farming today.

The food industry
Millions of people work in jobs which produce food. There are farmers and fishermen, manufacturers and suppliers, canners, freezers and packers.

Many major advances in harnessing the world's food resources have been made in the last century. About 100 years ago, hunger was a part of most people's lives: there was a famine every nine years on average in the United Kingdom, for example. Fish was only available to those who lived near the sea. Today, fish farms and sea-going trawlers with refrigeration equipment mean that most of us can eat fish when we want to.

At the same time, scientific advances have meant a greater and more reliable supply of crops. Hardier strains of the cereal crops – rice, wheat maize, oats and barley – have been developed, including some that produce two or even three harvests a year. Leaf and root vegetables are also hardier and some have been developed that produce more in a smaller space. Fertilizers have improved the soil's fertility and chemical pesticides have eliminated or controlled some of the pests and diseases that in the past caused famine. Machinery has also become much more efficient. Since 1900, food production has increased four-fold. Factory farming has also greatly increased the supply of meat.

Top: Pests and diseases that ruin crops can often be controlled by spraying chemical pesticides from a light plane. Because the plane has to fly so low, it is a dangerous job.

Above: Fruit such as raspberries could once only be eaten fresh and for a limited season. Today, quick freezing methods keep them tasty and available all year round.

Right: Large sea-going trawlers operating with refrigerated mother ships have revolutionized fishing. Food from the sea could be one of the ways in which man could find more food for the world population. Every year, the ocean's edible fish supply is estimated to be 120 million tonnes but only about 60 per cent of that is caught. One problem is that people dislike the weird appearance of some edible fish from the deep sea. In some places, like parts of the North Sea, the seas have been overfished and measures have had to be taken to conserve supplies.

Food shortages

As impressive as all these achievements are, their benefits are largely enjoyed by only about 24 per cent of the world's population – those who live in the developed world, comprising Europe, North America, the U.S.S.R., Japan, Australia and New Zealand. The 76 per cent who live in most of Asia, Africa and South America (the developing world), still cannot rely on regular food supplies. This is partly because of a lack of technological development but also not having enough money to finance it. The main problem is that food production cannot keep up with the rate of population growth.

Attempts are already being made slowly to increase the world's food production. The distribution of food is also being improved. More family planning is being encouraged in overpopulated countries.

Right: Plant breeding, fertilizers and pest control have increased the wheat yield per acre threefold in 100 years.

Looking for new land

Only a small part of the earth's land is used for agriculture. People are constantly looking for ways of using the arable land available. Often, however, this is both difficult and costly. Land in the Amazon and Zaire basins, for example, would be suitable for development. But it is presently covered by thick rain forest, expensive to remove and risky because their removal could lead to erosion of the soil.

New sources of food are being looked at and some have already been found. Soya beans can be woven in the same way as textiles to make high protein fibre food which resembles mince, ham and chicken. Different animals are also being exploited for food, for example, the hippopotamus.

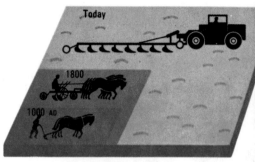

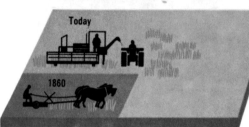

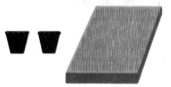

20 Bushels   **Wheat Yield Per Acre**   60 Bushels

Raw materials

The earth is covered with rocks which are themselves often covered with soil or water. These rocks consist of minerals and underneath some of them are seams of coal and pockets of oil and gas. From the ground itself grow great trees. All of these things – the minerals, coal, oil, gas and trees – are called raw materials. They can all be used to make something else.

Energy

Most of the world's energy comes from oil, gas or coal, all of which come from under the ground. Coal was formed over millions of years by layers of dead plant life being compressed and hardened. Today, coal is removed from the earth by cutting deep mines and quarries. The U.S.S.R. has the greatest amount of coal – about 50 per cent of the world's known reserves. It is estimated there is enough coal to last for another 200 years.

Oil, however, could run out quite soon. Even though it has only been taken out of the ground since 1859, it is being used at an unprecedented rate. In the ten years between 1960 and 1970 the world consumed as much crude oil as it had in the 100 years before.

Oil is always found with natural gas and water. It is believed to have been formed from organic matter millions of years old. A great deal of oil is now found under the sea bed – 20 per cent of the world's oil comes from offshore oil wells like those in the North Sea.

Hydro-electricity (power produced from the flow of water) is the next most important form of energy, especially in the mountainous countries which lack coal and oil. Nuclear energy, which uses the mineral uranium, is also becoming increasingly important.

Minerals

Most economic minerals are taken out of the ground in the form of a mixture, called an ore. Although there are valuable minerals in the rocks all around us, they are not often found in sufficient quantities to make it worthwhile starting to mine them.

Iron or plastic
Plastic wood
Nickel copper
Plastics
Ceran
Aluminium

Wood fascia
Galvanized iron
Triplex glass
Nylon seats

Plastics

Aluminium

Nickel/Manganese
Chromium
Lead
Synthetic rubber
Steel

Stainless steel
Pyrex
Steel/silver
Tin
Nickel-chrom
Linoleum

Iron comes from several different ores and is made into steel, one of the most important products in industrialized countries. Some of the rarest metals like gold, silver and platinum, are called precious metals. Like the precious stones – diamonds, sapphires, emeralds, and rubies – these metals are often used to make jewellery. Platinum, the most expensive metal, is also used for electrical resistance wire and laboratory apparatus. Silver is also used for electrical contacts and silver salts in photography.

Some minerals are also taken out of the sea. Sea salt provides about 30 per cent of the world's salt and 65 per cent of the world's magnesium comes from the sea.

Trees are used for timber, paper and also in the chemical industry. About 25 per cent of the land's surface is still covered with forest but these areas are diminishing rapidly, particularly in Europe and North America.

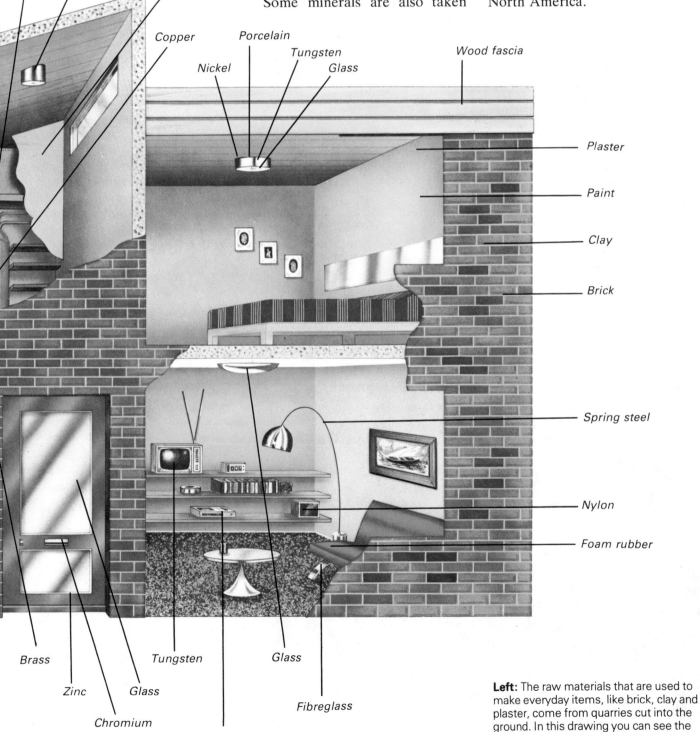

Left: The raw materials that are used to make everyday items, like brick, clay and plaster, come from quarries cut into the ground. In this drawing you can see the vast array of raw materials that go into the building and equipping of a modern house.

Peoples of the world

The different faces of China

The Han account for 94 per cent of the population of China.

Above: These European schoolchildren all belong to the Caucasoid group, which is probably the most varied of all human groups.

Below: Many of the world's largest cities are multi-racial. Here, blacks and whites mix happily at London's yearly People's Carnival.

All human beings belong to the same species, *Homo sapiens*. But within this species there are great physical differences. The people who have certain bodily characteristics form sub-groups of the human species, called races. Racial characteristics include skin colour, type of hair and shape of head.

There are three main races in the world – Caucasoid (so-called white), Mongoloid (yellow) and Negroid (black) – as well as two smaller ones – Australoid and Capoid.

The individual members of each race do not always look similar. This is because each race is really a mixture of other races. The Caucasoid people, numerically the largest group, include people as diverse as the blond northern Europeans and the darker-skinned Arabs, while the Mongoloid people include Japanese and other Asians as well as the American Indian and the Eskimo.

The reason why the races are mixed can be traced through history. The earliest records show that people have always been on the move. The different racial groups intermarried and the distinctive features of each group began to blend into one another.

It is believed that all the races developed from a common ancestor and as he migrated to other areas, he developed different characteristics which often allowed him to adapt to a new environment. Negroid people, for example, have a layer of melanin (a black pigment), under their skin to protect them from the hot sun in Africa where they originated. In

The Uighur number 4 million, and form the second largest group in China.

The Tibetans number 3.5 million. Tibet has been part of China since 1250.

The Yi people are scattered throughout China. There are 3.5 million of them.

colder lands, such as northern Europe, this protection is not necessary so skins are white. During the Ice Age the sea level was probably lower than today and "land bridges" linked many land masses that are now separate. This meant that people could move around more easily. Some Mongoloid peoples from Asia spread to America at this time where they became the Eskimos and the Indians, and to Europe where they became the Lapps. In the Pacific they migrated by boat to new lands, where today they are called the Polynesians. Mongoloids are either yellow- or brown-skinned with round heads and straight black hair. Their noses are usually flat and their eyes almond-shaped.

Caucasoids spread throughout Europe and the Middle East and much later to North and South America and to Oceania. Caucasoids are a mixture of types. The Nordic types are found in north and west Europe and have fair colouring, blue eyes and are quite tall. Alpine types are darker with round heads, blue or brown eyes, and are found from central Europe to Persia. Mediterranean types are

Right: The Aborigines are Australoids. They are believed to have arrived in the north of Australia some 30,000 years ago, probably across a "land bridge" from southern Asia.

dark-haired, smaller and are found around the Mediterranean Sea. All three groups have mixed so much that there are few "pure" types.

The Negroid people, the smallest in number of the three main groups, originated in Africa and spread to North and South America and to Europe. They have black skin, black eyes, short woolly hair and flat noses.

The two smaller groups are only tiny in number. The Australoids are found in Australia and similar types are also found in India. They

have black skin and wavy hair. The Capoids have yellow-brown skin and include the Bushmen of South Africa.

Other groups

The Congo Pygmies appear to be a different group again and there are many people in South-East Asia who cannot be easily classified. In Papua New Guinea and some of the Pacific Islands, some people appear to be Negroid in type although their noses are long and they may have long hair.

Europe

Surtsey

Europe is the western part of the land mass that comprises Russia, Asia and Europe. Unlike the eastern part, it is not a solid land mass but a peninsula or a series of peninsulas with sea inlets. It is bounded on the west by the Atlantic Ocean, and by the almost tideless Mediterranean Sea to the south. Western Europe is separated from Scandinavia by the Baltic Sea. No part of the continent lies more than 1,600 kilometres from the sea.

The closeness of the sea and its position on the globe – half-way between the equator and the North Pole – give it a mainly temperate climate with three main climatic zones: maritime (cool summers, mild winters) in Western Europe; continental (hot summers, cold winters) in Central and Eastern Europe; and Mediterranean (hot summers, mild winters) in the south. Iceland and the northern parts of Sweden, Finland and Norway lie within the Arctic Circle, but the moderating influence of the ocean current called the North Atlantic Drift means the Atlantic Ocean is ice-free for most of the year. The Baltic Sea, however, freezes over in winter.

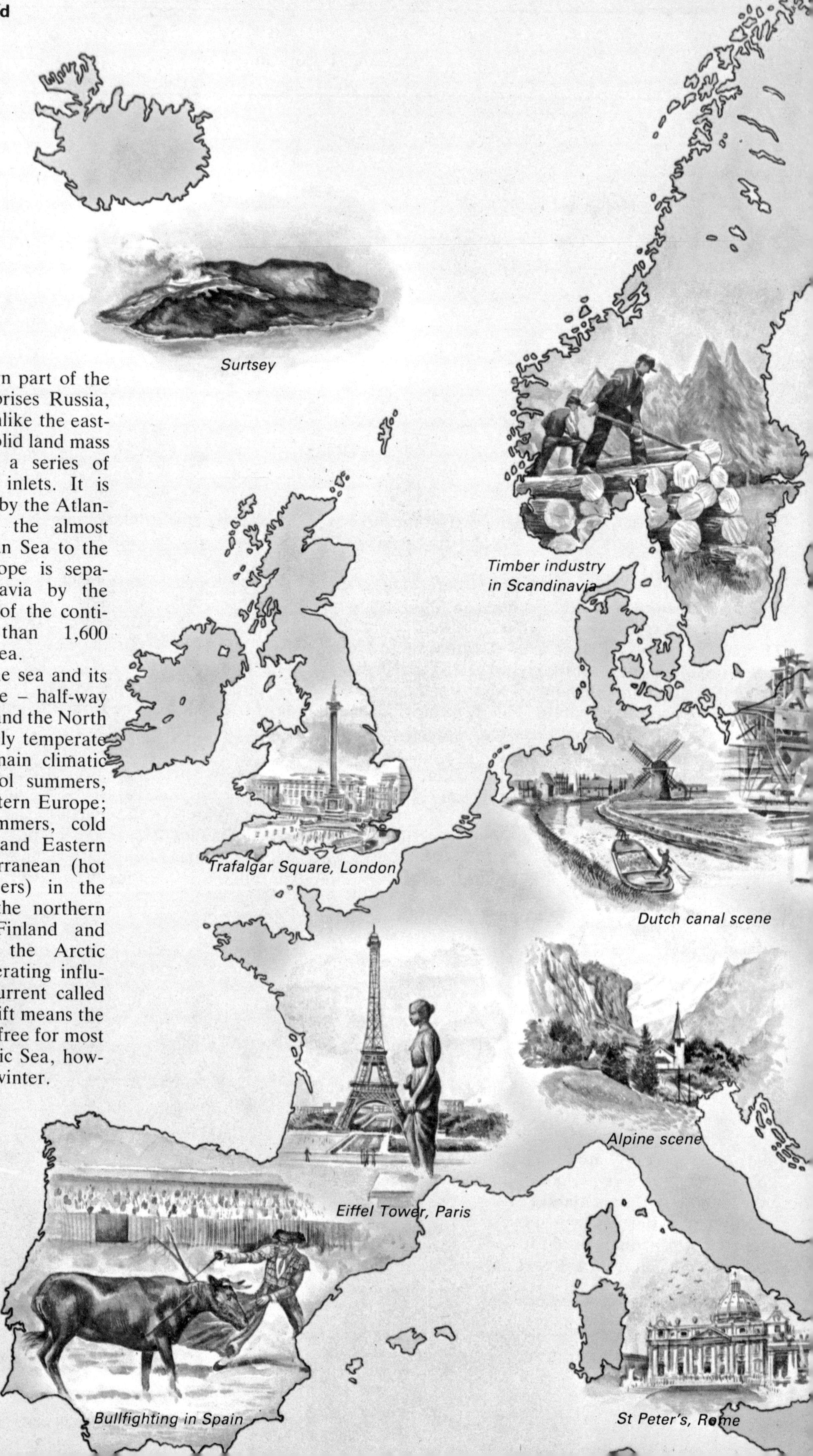

Timber industry
in Scandinavia

Trafalgar Square, London

Dutch canal scene

Alpine scene

Eiffel Tower, Paris

Bullfighting in Spain

St Peter's, Rome

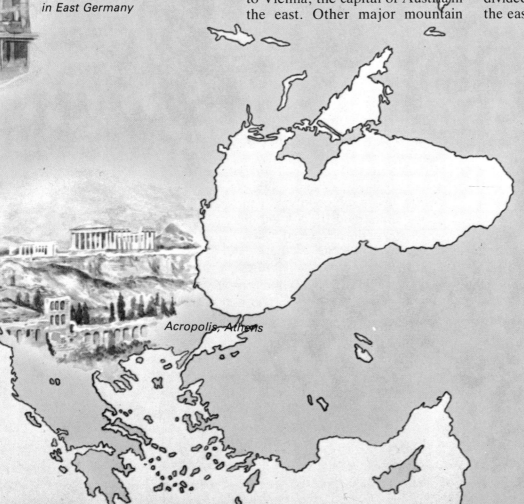

Excluding European U.S.S.R., Europe occupies only 3.3 per cent of the world's land surface area though its population of over 490 million makes it the most densely populated. Its nations vary considerably from modern industrial countries like Britain and West Germany to large agricultural countries in Eastern Europe such as Romania, and small principalities such as Monaco and Liechtenstein. Twelve countries – Belgium, Britain, Denmark, West Germany, Greece, France, Ireland, Italy, Luxembourg, Netherlands, Portugal and Spain – belong to an economic union, the European Economic Community, or the EEC. Others, such as Hungary, Poland, East Germany, Czechoslovakia, Bulgaria and Romania belong to the Communist economic union which is called Comecon.

Europe is not a very mountainous continent, the average height being only 300 metres above sea level. There are two great plains, the Great Plain of Hungary and the North European Plain. Its largest mountain system is the Alps which stretch for 1,200 kilometres from Nice in southern France in the west to Vienna, the capital of Austria in the east. Other major mountain systems are the Pyrenees between France and Spain and the Apennines in Italy.

Europe has an extensive river system. Many of its great rivers are linked by canals so that they form a huge inland waterway system that is used for transport and communication. The largest river is in fact the Danube, 2,700 kilometres long. The Rhine, 1,370 kilometres long, carries more traffic than any other river in the world. It passes through some of Europe's most productive areas.

Europe's cities vary greatly. London has a population of about 6.8 million, while Greater Paris is a huge urban area with over 10 million inhabitants. Rotterdam in Holland is the largest port in Europe and the second largest in the world. Paris is traditionally the centre of culture while Rome and Athens both have many superb historic remains.

World War Two divided Europe into two opposing political camps. Germany was divided into two halves and a fortress-like frontier was erected from the Baltic coast in the north to the Adriatic Sea in the south. Berlin was left as a divided city, with half of it lying in the eastern zone.

Chemical industry in East Germany

Acropolis, Athens

Asia

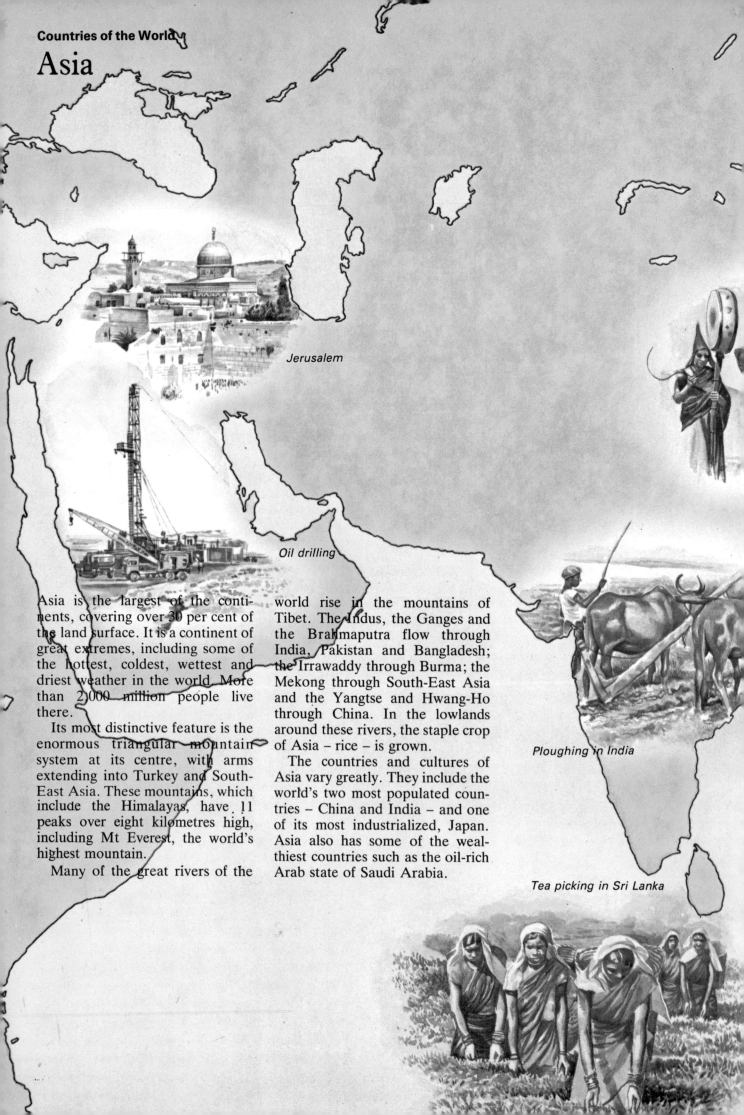

Jerusalem

Oil drilling

Ploughing in India

Tea picking in Sri Lanka

Asia is the largest of the continents, covering over 30 per cent of the land surface. It is a continent of great extremes, including some of the hottest, coldest, wettest and driest weather in the world. More than 2,000 million people live there.

Its most distinctive feature is the enormous triangular mountain system at its centre, with arms extending into Turkey and South-East Asia. These mountains, which include the Himalayas, have 11 peaks over eight kilometres high, including Mt Everest, the world's highest mountain.

Many of the great rivers of the world rise in the mountains of Tibet. The Indus, the Ganges and the Brahmaputra flow through India, Pakistan and Bangladesh; the Irrawaddy through Burma; the Mekong through South-East Asia and the Yangtse and Hwang-Ho through China. In the lowlands around these rivers, the staple crop of Asia – rice – is grown.

The countries and cultures of Asia vary greatly. They include the world's two most populated countries – China and India – and one of its most industrialized, Japan. Asia also has some of the wealthiest countries such as the oil-rich Arab state of Saudi Arabia.

Mongol encampment

Himalayan musicians

Chinese commune team

Japanese industry

Sampans and junks

Luzon, Philippines

Rubber tapping in Malaya

U.S.S.R.

Moscow

Grain harvest in the Ukraine

Rural scene

Russia, the commonly-used name for the U.S.S.R. (the Union of Soviet Socialist Republics) is the world's largest nation, covering 16 per cent of the total land surface. It is not a continent by itself but its massive size has led it to be considered separately. Twenty-five per cent of it lies in Europe, while the rest is in Asia.

Despite its great size and resources, it mostly lacks easy access to the open ocean. The parts of its coast on the Arctic and Pacific oceans are ice-bound for much of the year and the Black Sea to the south and Baltic to the west are both enclosed seas. Only at the extreme north at the Arctic towns of Murmansk and Pechenga does this huge country have year-round access to open seas.

The country is for the most part low-lying, and much of it is taken up by the European Russian plain. Nearly 65 per cent of this plain is the basin of the Volga River. To the south lies the Caucasus Mountains, rising to Mt Elbruz (5,633 metres), and forming a barrier between the Black and Caspian Seas. The mineral-rich Ural Mountains divide European Russia from Siberia.

The U.S.S.R has a great deal of land that cannot be put to productive use, such as the vast northern tundra whose soil is frozen for much of the year. Almost 50 per cent of the country is occupied by forest, the steppes of central Asia providing grazing land. The Uk-

raine, north of the Black Sea, is the major agricultural area, often called the granary of Russia. Its mineral resources are immense. The U.S.S.R. leads the world in output of petroleum, natural gas, iron ore, lead and manganese and is in the top three for diamonds, chrome ore and gold. Her coal resources are estimated at about 25 per cent of world reserves.

Although the U.S.S.R. is just one nation, it is in fact made up of some 100 different nationalities, many with their own language and culture. Russia was for centuries ruled by a Tzarist regime but has had a communist form of government since its revolution in 1917. The U.S.S.R. is made up of 15 republics.

Siberian seasons

Trans-Siberian Express

Africa

Left: The River Zambezi downstream from the Victoria Falls. The Zambezi forms one of Africa's main river systems. It rises in Angola and travels 3,540 kilometres eastwards to the Indian Ocean.

Vegetation closely follows climatic conditions with equatorial forests close to the equator merging into savanna – great grasslands with shrubs and scattered trees – as the rainfall decreases. This is where much of Africa's famous wildlife (lions, elephants, giraffe, zebras and antelope) is to be found. To the north and south-west are deserts: the Kalahari and Namib in the south and the world's largest desert, the Sahara, in the north. The Sahara stretches for about 5,150 kilometres from west to east and 2,250 from north to south.

Most of Africa's rivers rise on the surface of the plateau and drop to the coastal plain via great waterfalls or rapids. A spectacular example is the Victoria Falls on the Zambezi River. Four other main rivers drain the continent: the Nile which, at 6,680 kilometres is the world's longest river, the Zaire (formerly Congo), the Niger and the Orange rivers.

About 555 million people live in the 55 separate countries of Africa, including the islands. Politically, the continent has completely changed over the last 50 years. In the 1920s, for example, only four African states – Egypt, Liberia, South Africa and Ethiopia – were independent. Today most of the continent is self-governing.

In South Africa, and in Zimbabwe until it became independent in 1980, white minorities rule black majorities. Much of Africa's known mineral wealth is to be found in South Africa, particularly diamonds and gold. Zaire and Zambia are rich in copper, cobalt and uranium and several countries, such as Sierra Leone, Liberia, and Morocco have iron ore deposits. Huge deposits of oil have been found in Libya, Nigeria and Algeria.

Africa, bounded by the Atlantic and Indian Oceans, is the world's second largest continent. It is joined to Asia, the world's largest, by a short neck of land, through which runs the Suez Canal. At its nearest point it is just 15 kilometres from Europe. It is believed that prehistoric man first evolved in Africa, where some of the world's oldest cities still exist. These include Alexandria and Thebes, established by the Ancient Egyptians, and Timbuktu and Kano, whose 1,000-year-old walls still stand in modern-day Nigeria.

Africa is cut almost in half by the equator and the seasons are reversed on either side. For example, when it is winter in northern Africa it is summer in the south. Around the equator, the climate is hot and wet all year round and 65 per cent of the continent lies in this tropical zone. Parts of the south-west (the Namib and Kalahari) and the huge Sahara region in the north have desert climates. The northern coast of Africa and the very tip of South Africa have a Mediterranean climate.

The majority of Africa is occupied by a huge plateau surrounded by a narrow coastal plain. The plateau is higher in the south than in the north. In the north-west, the Atlas Mountain system belongs to the European alpine system. From the north-east down through East Africa lies an enormous rift valley. In it lie several large lakes, such as Lake Victoria. The highest mountains in Africa – Mt Kilimanjaro at 5,895 metres and Mt Kenya at 5,199 metres are found here. Despite their proximity to the equator, they are perpetually covered with snow.

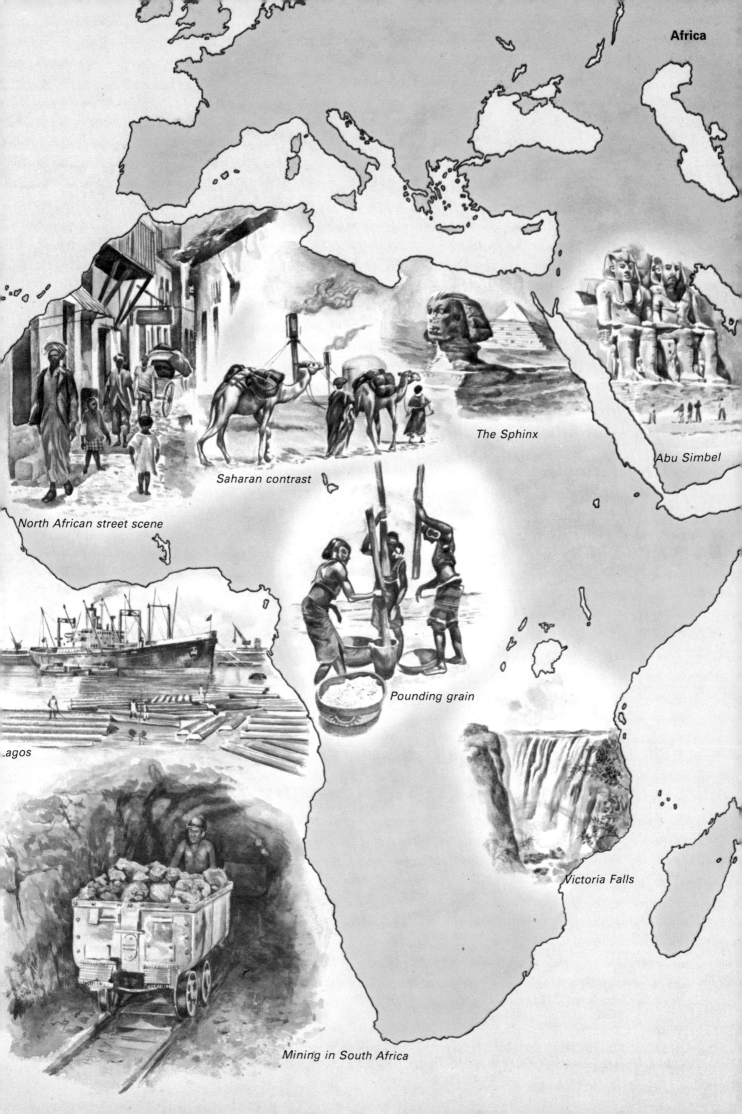

The Sphinx

Abu Simbel

Saharan contrast

North African street scene

Pounding grain

agos

Victoria Falls

Mining in South Africa

Oceania

The Australian outback

Sheep farming

Oceania comprises land masses as varied as the continent of Australia, Papua New Guinea (the eastern half of the world's second largest island), New Zealand, and literally thousands of smaller islands scattered around the South Pacific Ocean. More islands are found here than in all the rest of the earth's oceans. The larger islands are often volcanic and the low-lying islands are coral atolls such as the Kiribati Republic and Tokelau. Some islands – Canton and Johnson islands for example – are completely treeless while others have dense forests.

Even in one country like Australia, the climate can produce huge barren deserts in the west, plains in the centre and the Australian Alps in the south-east. New Zealand enjoys a mild, temperate climate while islands like those in the Solomons and Papua New Guinea groups are tropical. Generally, the range of temperatures in the Pacific Islands is moderated by the influence of the sea around them.

Australia is able to support large-scale agriculture, notably wheat. Yet some of the islands can support only a subsistence agriculture, the main crops being coconuts, bananas, yams and taro.

By far the richest countries are Australia and New Zealand, where high standards of living are in stark contrast to those of their poorer neighbours. Much of the mineral wealth of the area is to be found in the ancient land of Australia, particularly iron ore, nickel, uranium, bauxite, lead, copper and zinc. New Caledonia has the world's largest-known nickel deposits, Papua New Guinea has considerable copper, and Fiji mines gold.

Europeans began to colonize the area in the late 18th century and Oceania is still dominated by European customs and culture.

Native trimaran canoe

New Guinea islanders

Coconut harvesting

South Pacific scene

Volcanic activity in New Zealand

North America

North America, the third largest continent in the world, stretches for 9,700 kilometres from the Arctic Circle in the north to just short of the Tropic of Cancer in the south. It is bounded by three oceans – the Pacific on the west, the Atlantic on the east and the Arctic to the north. The continent tapers down in a triangular shape to the Mexican peninsula, the link between the two American continents. Just two nations – the United States of America, the world's richest and most powerful country, and Canada – dominate this vast continent. While Canada occupies a slightly greater area than the U.S.A., its population of 25 million is only just over 10 per cent of that of the United States.

Geographically, the continent contains three main divisions – the Rocky Mountain system in the west, the eastern highlands and in-between the vast central plains. The Rockies consist of several ranges running parallel to the coast, stretching from Alaska in

Above: The deserts of the U.S.A. contain rocks carved into fantastic shapes by the effects of sand and wind.
Below: Vermilion Lake in Banff National Park, Canadian Rockies. Spectacular scenery like this makes the Rockies a popular holiday area.

the north where Mt McKinley (6,194 metres), the highest peak, is found, to Mexico in the south. In-between the parallel ranges are many plateaus and river valleys. The north-east consists of part of a very old rock formation called the Canadian Shield in Canada. The Appalachian Mountains in the east extend from Canada to Alabama. Rich in coal, they are low mountains and to their east lies the coastal plain.

The agricultural and grazing lands of the central plains contribute much to the wealth of the two countries. In the U.S.A., the plain is drained by the Mississippi and its tributaries. In Canada, the Saskatchewan and Red rivers flow into Lake Winnipeg and then into Hudson Bay via the Nelson River. On the border between the two countries are the Great Lakes – Superior, Michigan, Huron, Erie and Ontario. These are connected by the St Lawrence Seaway to the Atlantic. A canal bypasses the massive Niagara Falls. The St Lawrence Seaway enables large vessels to reach Chicago on Lake Michigan.

Climate varies from the extreme cold in the north of Canada, much of it being uninhabitable, to the healthy, sun-drenched beaches of Florida. The centre of the continent has very cold winters because it lies so far from the sea and Arctic winds sweep down from the north. The west coast enjoys the most temperate climate.

The U.S.A. and Canada are among the four biggest countries in the world (China and the U.S.S.R. are the others) and two of the wealthiest. They were settled by Europeans only 300 years ago and have small indigenous Indian populations. The U.S.A. also has a large black population of 26 million originally brought into the country as slaves. The United States, with its vast agricultural and mineral resources, particularly coal, oil and iron, has become the greatest industrialized country in the world.

North America

Alaskan oil

Wheat farming on the Prairies

California

Grand Canyon

New York

Washington

Texas

Temple of the Sun

Mississippi River

Cape Canaveral

Panama Canal

Sugar harvest

South and Central America

South America is almost completely surrounded by the Pacific and Atlantic oceans. Only the narrow isthmus of Panama joins it to North America. This narrow bridge of land called Central America was cut through in 1914 to form the Panama Canal. On the Atlantic side of this bridge are the West Indies, a great arc of islands spanning 5,000 kilometres from just south of Florida in North America and nearly reaching the coast of Venezuela in South America. The Caribbean Sea lies between the islands and the mainland.

Central America has a backbone formed by a southern extension of the Rocky Mountains. Mexico is frequently thought of as part of this area, although geographically it has strong links with North America.

In the southern continent lies the great Andes mountain system, the longest chain of mountains in the world and the highest after the Himalayas. The Andes stretch for 7,100 kilometres along the west coast, leaving only a narrow coastal strip between them and the Pacific. They are at their broadest in Bolivia – 640 kilometres wide. The highest peak is Mt. Aconcagua (6,960 metres) in Argentina. In the north-east of the continent, the Guiana Highlands are separated from the Brazilian Highlands by the massive Amazon River. This river is the second longest in the world and, with its tributaries, drains at least half the continent. The other rivers draining the central plain of South America are the Orinoco in the north-east and the Paraná-Paraguay system in the south.

The equator passes through the mouth of the Amazon, the Tropic of Cancer through Mexico and the Tropic of Capricorn near Rio de Janeiro in Brazil. This means the vast majority of the land lies within the tropics. The Amazon Basin has a hot, wet climate, but the west coast, south of the equator, is largely desert. Patagonia in the far south, lies in the rain shadow zone of the high Andes, and is also arid.

The sub-tropical and warm temperate areas are the most productive agricultural areas, where coffee, wheat, maize, cotton and sugar cane are grown. Sheep and cattle are reared, particularly in Argentina. The continent is also rich in minerals including oil, tin, copper and iron. Mexico and Venezuela are among the world's leading producers of crude oil.

Apart from Mexico which is eight times the size of the United Kingdom, the other countries of Central America are fairly small in area with El Salvador, the smallest, being the most densely populated. In contrast, some of South America's 15 countries are enormous, notably Brazil, which is almost as big as the United States, and also Argentina. Their larger populations – 135 million in Brazil and 30 million in Argentina – reflect this and the two countries are among the most developed in a generally underdeveloped continent.

Much of South and Central America was colonized by the Spanish and Portuguese during the 16th and 17th centuries. In the process, the civilization of the Incas was wiped out. Most of the population today are of mixed descent. The continent has a very high rate of population growth and overpopulation is becoming a burden on the continent's economy. Much is being done by means of education to try and limit this growth rate.

Left: In the Peruvian Andes, ores such as copper, lead, zinc and silver are mined, but not on a very large scale.

South and Central America

Oil platforms on Lake Maracaibo

Amazon forest Indians

Reed boats on Lake Titicaca

Machu Picchu

Cape Horn

Gauchos on the Pampas

Life on earth

Almost every part of our world is inhabited by some kind of life. Even inhospitable regions of perpetual cold, like the Arctic and the Antarctic, support a little vegetation and a few animals. In sharp contrast to this scanty population, the polar oceans are as rich in life as any seas in the world.

In all, there are about a million different types of animals and more than 300,000 kinds of plants. In addition, there are some kinds of life forms that are neither wholly plant nor wholly animal; they include primitive organisms such as bacteria and yeast.

Below: In the scorching heat of the grasslands of Africa, water is scarce, especially in the dry season.

The teeming array of plants and animals that exist on earth today has evolved over millions of years. Yet despite their great differences, all forms of life have one thing in common. All depend on another living thing and none could survive in isolation for long. The leaf of an oak provides food for all sorts of animals like caterpillars, beetles and worms. In turn, the uneaten leaves and the dead bodies of animals decay in the soil, making it fertile for other plants to grow in. Most important of all, plants provide the oxygen animals breathe.

Delicate balance
The earth contains a wide variety of habitats, each of which builds up its own pattern of plant and animal communities. The species within each community contain just the right number to keep the balance of nature – neither too many nor too few. Remove just a single species from that community, and the whole community might suffer, or even die.

The balance of nature is a delicate one. In the past, man's activities have radically altered that balance and damaged the environment. It would be a tragedy if our tampering with the environment meant that many wild species could not adapt quickly enough to survive.

Right: Alligators belong to the reptile family which evolved millions of years ago and once dominated the earth.

Michael Lyster/Zoological Society of London

Dawn of life

How did life begin? Nobody really knows the answer to that question but scientists have put forward a few theories to try to explain it. It seems likely that the first form of life must have been simply a molecule that could absorb atoms and build up another molecule of exactly the same type. The way it did this must have been very similar to the way a modern virus reproduces itself. A virus is little more than a very complex molecule.

Amino acids

The very first molecule must have been some kind of protein. Experiments carried out in laboratories show that when hydrogen, ammonia and methane gases are mixed with water vapour and an electrical spark passed through them, amino acids are generated. Amino acids are the substances that form proteins in living organisms. Scientists know that large quantities of hydrogen, ammonia and methane, as well as water vapour, were present in the earth's atmosphere millions of years ago when the earth first solidified. Bolts of lightning may very well have brought about the same chemical reaction in this atmosphere and amino acids would have formed. They collected in warm pools of water where they underwent further chemical changes that built them into proteins. One of these proteins was a molecule that could reproduce itself. Life had begun.

Evolution

Each new generation of molecules could change and adapt, or evolve, in some small way. As time went on, the original molecule became more and more complex. A change in the make-up of the molecule that made it easier to reproduce itself was passed on to the offspring. A change that made the

Below: It was probably a bolt of lightning that caused the chemicals in the earth's waters to react in such a way that the first living substance was formed.

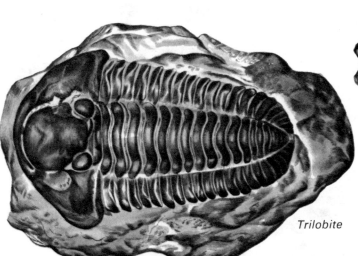

Trilobite

Sea urchin

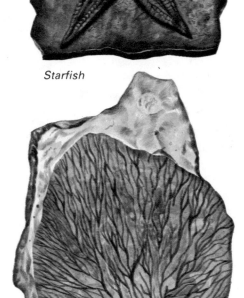

Starfish

Coral

We cannot say precisely when the earliest life forms first appeared, because there are no fossil traces of them. However, the oldest fossils have been found in rocks about 3,500 million years old. Fossils of sea animals are common only in rocks less than 600 million years old. Fossils show that coral was once a solitary organism that slowly evolved into the creature we know today that lives in colonies. Sea urchins and starfish have survived almost unchanged in 500 million years. Trilobites and graptolites, although common once, have both become extinct.

Graptolite

process more difficult died out.

Gradually, the molecule developed into a compact little unit called a cell. This consisted of a nucleus, containing the machinery for reproduction, surrounded by a blob of jelly called cytoplasm. On the outside was a protective covering. Individual cells began to join together, forming more and more complex organisms. Each cell evolved its own particular function within the organism, keeping it alive and helping it to reproduce.

Primitive plants were the first complex organisms to develop. Their cells were able to absorb sunlight and use its energy to transform mineral substances in the waters round them into food. Animals could only develop after plant life had been established

because they had no method of manufacturing their own food. They ate the food generated by the plants. This meant that animals had to be able to move around to find enough to eat.

What we have said so far is largely guesswork. The organisms so far described had no hard parts, so they left few remains to fossilize in the rocks that formed at the time. It was only 570 million years ago, at the beginning of the Cambrian Period, that animals developed shells and hard parts that were easily fossilized. All the animals and plants at this time lived in the sea. There were arthropods which resembled crabs and shrimps, bivalves and brachiopods with recognizable seashells, corals and starfish, along with most of the other major groups of organisms found in the sea today.

Oxygen

This spectacular development in life forms continued through the succeeding Ordovician and Silu

rian Periods. By that time the atmosphere above the oceans was changing too. As we have read, the water-dwelling plants were able to use the energy of sunlight to make food from mineral substances. As they did this, the plants released oxygen into the hostile atmosphere of hydrogen, ammonia and methane gases. The oxygen gradually built up and conditions became right for life to move out of the seas and on to the land. The plants were the first to live on land. Initially they were probably left high and dry at low tide and those that lived, flourished. In the Silurian Period the teeming seas were fringed with the greenery of the first land life.

Prehistoric fish and amphibians

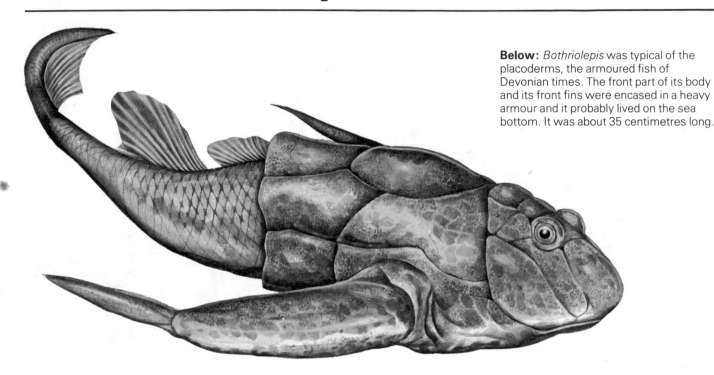

Below: *Bothriolepis* was typical of the placoderms, the armoured fish of Devonian times. The front part of its body and its front fins were encased in a heavy armour and it probably lived on the sea bottom. It was about 35 centimetres long.

During the Silurian Period, some 430 million years ago, a development took place in the animal kingdom that was very important from our point of view. The nervous system of certain worm-like animals became supported by a bony beam that ran the length of the body. This was the beginning of the vertebrate, or backboned, skeleton. Eventually, the first men evolved with such a backbone.

The first vertebrates were fish-like creatures. They were not true fishes because they did not have jaws. However, they did have a backbone and a series of ribs that suggested they were descended from segmented worms. Over millions of years the ribs at the front modified to carry gills, and other ribs developed as jawbones. The first true fish had arrived.

Devonian fish

The Devonian Period lasted from about 395 to 355 million years ago. It is often called the Age of Fishes because of the great number and variety of fish fossils found in rocks dating from that time. Three main groups developed from the first jawless fish. The placoderms had a heavy, bony armour covering their heads and sometimes their fins. One, called *Dinichthys*, was nine metres long.

The second group, the chondrichthyes, comprised sharks and rays, and the third group, the osteichthyes, were the bony ray-finned fish. Both groups exist

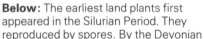

Below: The earliest land plants first appeared in the Silurian Period. They reproduced by spores. By the Devonian Period there were many new types of land plants. Some were the distant ancestors of today's little horsetails.

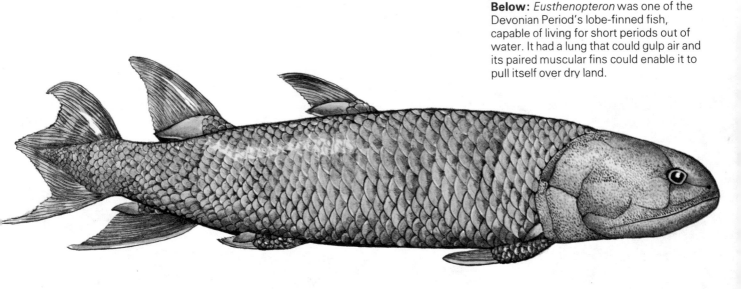

Below: *Eusthenopteron* was one of the Devonian Period's lobe-finned fish, capable of living for short periods out of water. It had a lung that could gulp air and its paired muscular fins could enable it to pull itself over dry land.

today in our oceans.

While the Devonian seas were teeming with fish, some of the osteichthyes developed two important features. A lung formed from the swim-bladder and paired muscular fins began to develop. For the first time, a creature had evolved that could clamber over dry land to seek a new home, if its pool of water dried up in hot weather. And, most importantly, a lung meant it could breathe air. Before long, the amphibians had evolved.

Amphibians

The first known amphibian dates from the end of the Devonian Period. This amphibian was much better adapted to land life than its fish predecessors. It had well developed lungs and toes on its limbs, but it still retained a fish-like skull and a fin on its tail. It also had to return to the water to breed.

During the following Period, the Carboniferous, the amphibians flourished in all sorts of shapes and sizes. They had adapted to life in many environments, except hot and dry ones. Some were the size and shape of alligators, some looked like snakes; the range was far greater than today's frogs and toads, salamanders and newts.

Left: In the Upper Devonian the land plants were quite luxuriant. *Ichthyostega*, the first known amphibian, lived amongst them feeding on the abundant insects. Much later some amphibians like *Seymouria* (*below*) became very reptile-like. It represents a transitional stage between amphibians and reptiles.

Prehistoric reptiles

Below: All these animals date back to the end of the Cretaceous Period, when the dinosaurs ruled the earth. *Tyrannosaurus* was an armoured carnivorous dinosaur, over five metres tall. *Triceratops* was an armoured herbivorous dinosaur. In the foreground are small, early mammals eating dinosaur eggs.

The reptiles were the first vertebrates to be able to live a full life on land. They evolved from the amphibians in the Carboniferous Period that ended some 280 million years ago. During the Permian Period that followed they spread over all the continents. The reptiles' success was due to their leathery or scaly waterproof skins,

Pterosaur

Tyrannosaurus

Triceratops

and the fact that their eggs had shells. They laid their eggs on land and there was no tadpole stage.

The Triassic, Jurassic and Cretaceous Periods are together called the Age of Reptiles. It lasted from 225 to 65 million years ago and the reptiles were the dominant life forms throughout that time. Pterosaurs took to the skies and flew like birds, ichthyosaurs, plesiosaurs and mosasaurs returned to live in the sea, and the land was ruled by the most spectacular animals that ever lived – the dinosaurs. All these varied reptile groups unaccountably died out suddenly about 65 million years ago. Today, there are only four groups of reptile left.

Ornithomimus

Anatosaurus

Triconodon

Prehistoric mammals

With the lack of reptile competitors the mammals suddenly came to the fore, changing and adapting to suit a great variety of life-styles. In the early part of the Tertiary Period there were many strange mammals wandering the tropical forests that covered most of the world. Many of them soon became extinct but some of them were the ancestors of the wildlife we know today. Horses, rhinoceroses, cats and monkeys were around at this time, but only in primitive, unrecognizable forms.

It was not only the land that had suddenly become populated by the mammals. Some developed wings and took to the air. These flying mammals are still with us in the form of bats. Other mammals returned to the sea and developed fish-like bodies. These were the ancestors of the whales.

Many of the early mammalian forms became extinct. Some of them would look as strange to us today as would any of the great dinosaurs. Some might look a little familiar, for example, the

rhinoceros-like *Arsinoitherium*, but they were in fact quite different from any of today's living species.

Alongside the mammals, the birds were undergoing great developments. Birds had evolved from the reptiles during the Jurassic Period, about 150 million years ago.

By half way through the Tertiary Period, about 30 million years ago, the climate had become more temperate. The animals of the temperate woodlands had become more like those of today. Most of

the horses, elephants and rhinoceroses would not have looked strange to us, but they were often gigantic. One rhinoceros grew to the remarkable height of seven metres and browsed for food on the tops of trees like a giraffe.

The apes had developed into forms that were similar to today's chimpanzees. They were destined to make great advances. As the Tertiary Period finished about two million years ago and became the Quaternary, a group of apes left the trees to become ground dwellers on the plains. The Quaternary opened with the great Ice Age when vast areas of the earth's surface were covered with thick ice sheets. The apes learned to come to terms with this harsh environment. They killed other animals and they learned to make tools. In this way they were able to survive, not by adapting to suit their environment, but by adapting their environment to suit themselves. Man had arrived.

Below: The left-hand part of this painting shows mammals from the Eocene Period, about 65 million years ago. The right-hand part shows mammals from 30 million years ago.

Nesodon

Baluchitherium

Dinohyus

Deinotherium

Proconsul

Merychippus

Evolution and extinction

In the last few pages we have been looking at the changes that have taken place in the animal and plant life throughout the history of our planet. Let us now examine how these changes have come about.

Better chances of survival

The most basic form of all life was the molecule of protein that had the power to reproduce itself from surrounding raw materials. Any change that enabled this reproduction to take place more easily meant that the molecule that made the change had a better chance of surviving. Gradually, the molecule

became an organism that had different structures for carrying out different functions. It evolved a digestive system that enabled raw materials to be taken in and used, not just to produce new organisms, but to repair damaged or worn parts of itself.

Animal organisms quickly developed vital senses, such as sight, hearing and touch. These helped them to find their raw materials – or food – more easily. A nervous system developed and a breathing system formed that supplied the energy-giving oxygen to the tissues.

Adapting to new conditions

So gradually, over millions of years, a simple organism developed into something much more complex. The vast array of animals and plants we know today are the result of a whole series of developments. Whenever conditions on the surface of the earth changed, a change took place in the life there. This constant adaptation of life forms is called evolution.

Below: The woolly mammoth evolved its woolly coat to protect it from cold during the Ice Age. Its tusks helped it to scrape for food. It is now extinct.

Beneficial changes

Evolution is based on two concepts – adaptive radiation and natural selection. Adaptive radiation takes place when an organism changes its form in one or a number of ways so that the offspring are slightly different from the parent. Natural selection is the process by which changes that are beneficial to the organism are passed on to successive generations while those that are not are allowed to die out. An organism cannot bring about change consciously; any changes that take place are quite random. It is the environment that determines whether or not a change is beneficial.

Room to expand

The rise of the mammals at the beginning of the Tertiary Period demonstrates this well. The mammals had existed for about 100 million years before and, presumably, during this time were constantly undergoing changes that might lead them to adopt different forms. Such new forms, however, would lead them into direct competition with the great reptiles that had adapted quite successfully to life in all kinds of environments. As long as the reptiles could continue exploiting the environment, the mammals' ability to adapt was kept in check.

When all the great reptiles died out, the mammals found themselves with enough room to expand and adapt. It took only a few million years for a dog-like creature to develop into an animal the shape and size of a modern whale. Yet, over the last 60 million years the whale has changed little, because it has adapted so successfully to its life in the ocean.

Convergent evolution

The term "convergent evolution" is used to describe the fact that creatures living in a particular environment often adopt a standard shape.

When the first sharks appeared in the seas about 400 million years

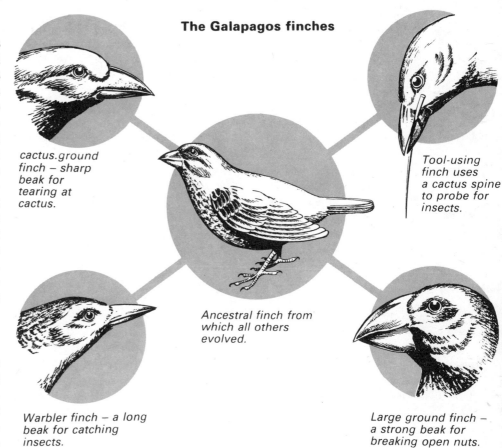

The Galapagos finches

cactus.ground finch – sharp beak for tearing at cactus.

Tool-using finch uses a cactus spine to probe for insects.

Ancestral finch from which all others evolved.

Warbler finch – a long beak for catching insects.

Large ground finch – a strong beak for breaking open nuts.

Above: Charles Darwin realized that the many forms of Galapagos finches have a common ancestor. The beaks of the finches are adapted to their diets.

ago, they developed a streamlined shape with fins and a powerful tail. During the Age of Reptiles a lizard-like creature evolved into a very similar shape with paddle-like limbs and became *Ichthyosaurus*. Later, after *Ichthyosaurus* had become extinct along with many other reptiles, dolphins evolved. They are mammals with almost precisely the same bodily shape as *Ichthyosaurus*.

It was the observation of just such a situation that first led Charles Darwin to make a study of the science of evolution. Between 1831 and 1836 Darwin was the naturalist on board HMS *Beagle*, a British survey ship. The Galapagos Islands in the Pacific Ocean appeared to him to be a relatively new environment that had been colonized by the descendants of relatively few species. Giant tortoises varied from island to island according to environments found there, but all had obviously de-

scended from a common ancestor.

On his return home Darwin continued to study the question of evolution for many years, and in 1859 he published his conclusions in his book *On the Origin of Species*. This book shocked society with its idea that man could be descended from ape-like ancestors.

Evolution is still taking place today. During the Industrial Revolution of the 18th century the pale peppered moth turned black. It could then blend in with the soot-covered trunks of the trees on which it lived. Today, with the advent of clean air laws, the moth is returning to its original mottled pattern, resembling clean bark.

It is tempting to speculate about what will happen in the future. Man has brought about such far-reaching changes to the environment so swiftly that the world's wildlife is under constant threat. But, whatever happens, life will evolve to cope with it.

How plants live

Without plants, man could not live. In fact, without plants there would be no life at all on earth. They provide the oxygen that we breathe and the food that we eat.

Nobody knows how many different kinds of plants there are, but scientists have recorded more than 350,000.

Every living thing is either a plant or an animal. Almost all plants stay anchored to one spot, whereas almost all animals move about. Most plants make their own food from sunlight, air, and water. Animals cannot make their own food. Most plant cells (the basic units of life) contain a carbohydrate called cellulose. Animal cells lack this substance.

Kinds of plants

The plant kingdom can be divided into two main groups: the thallophytes and the embryophytes. Thallophytes are simple plants such as fungi and algae that do not have true roots, stems, and leaves.

Embryophytes are all the other kinds of plants: mosses, liverworts, horsetails, ferns, conifers and flowering plants. They all grow from an embryo, which is a baby version of the plant.

Fungi cannot make their own food. They attach themselves to living plants and animals and draw nourishment from them, or they live on rotting organic matter. Algae are simple plants that live in water or damp places. Mosses and liverworts are tiny plants that often crowd together to form cushion-like clumps. They grow in damp places. Conifers are trees and shrubs, usually with needle-like leaves, and include pines, cypresses and cedars. Broad-leaved trees include the majority of the world's trees and in most cases their broad, flat leaves are shed each autumn. Flowering plants, including grasses, are the dominant land plants, with about 250,000 known species. They are very varied in appearance.

The parts of a plant

Most flowering plants have four main parts: roots, stems, leaves and flowers.

Most plant roots grow underground in soil. There they take in minerals and water which help to feed the plant. Some plants such as radishes, beets and carrots, store food in their roots. All roots help to anchor the plant in the soil.

The stem of a plant grows upwards from the roots and helps to support the leaves, flowers and fruits. Cells inside the stem carry water and minerals up from the roots to other parts of the plant and they also carry the food manufactured in the leaves to the rest of the plant.

Stems may be woody, as in trees and shrubs, or non-woody, as in

3

1 The trees of the tropical rain forest grow tall and thin. They often grow large buttresses at their bases for extra support. Most of the trees have broad leaves and are evergreen. Little sunshine is able to filter through the thick tangle of branches.

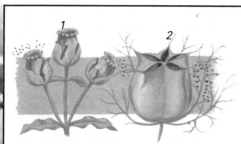

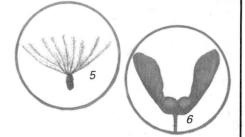

Seed dispersal The campion (*1*) and the nigella (*2*) each have seed boxes from which the seeds are shaken out.

The violet (*3*) and balsam (*4*) both have seed pods which when ripe burst open and scatter the seeds.

The seeds of the thistle (*5*) and the sycamore (*6*) are wind-borne.

tulips. Woody stems are made up of three layers of materials, one inside the other: bark, vascular tissue and pith.

Bark is the hard, corky outer material that protects the stem. The vascular tissue consists of water-conducting (xylem) cells and food-conducting (phloem) cells. In between is a ring of cells called the cambium which grows to form new xylem and phloem cells. Each new layer of cells it makes leaves annual growth rings in the wood. Pith is the soft, light green heart of the stem. It disappears as the tree gets older.

Non-woody plants are also called herbaceous plants. Their stems are green and soft and have no bark. The cells that carry food are arranged differently from those of woody plants; they are in bundles or groups and are scattered throughout the pith.

Leaves are usually the greenest

parts of a seed plant. Their most important job is to manufacture food for the plant. But they also have several other functions. Some store food; others store water. Some attract insects; others protect the plant from grazing animals.

The flowers of a flowering plant are the parts that produce seeds and thus enable new plants to grow. Some flowers are highly coloured, sweetly scented, or hold a sweet liquid called nectar. These are all aids to attract insects to them to help in reproduction.

←————— 4

2 On land at higher levels, the temperature gets cooler. Small evergreens and deciduous trees grow there. It is damp and there are many mosses and ferns.

3 Above 1,500 metres the trees give way to warm, temperate grasslands. At that level grow beautiful flowers like rhododendrons.

4 Above 2,600 metres alpine gentians are found. These are like the gentians that grow in northern Europe. Some of the mountains in New Guinea reach as high as 4,900 metres. At that height there will sometimes be snow.

5 Back in the hot, wet, tropical rain forest, some of the trees act as supports for other plants such as orchids and ferns. Plants that use others for support are called epiphytes. They absorb water from the damp air through their leaves, or through roots that hang in the air.

Fungi, mosses and ferns

Fungi are non-flowering plants without a green pigment and thus they cannot make their own food. They are classified into two main groups: saprophytes and parasites.

Saprophytes feed only on dead matter. Parasites feed on living matter, that is, on another plant or animal. Some saprophytes, such as edible mushrooms, are good to eat. Other kinds, popularly called toadstools, are deadly poisonous. Parasitic fungi cause many crop diseases. These include various rusts, mildews, and potato blight.

Scientists believe that there are at least 100,000 different kinds of fungi. They grow in all parts of the world. They vary in size from those that can only be seen with the aid of a microscope to some that are about 70 centimetres across. Some fungi, such as yeasts, are used in the manufacture of food and drink; others are important in medicine, being the basis of antibiotics such as penicillin.

Growth and reproduction

The main body of a fungus is made up of a mass of tiny hair-like stems called hyphae. If you look at a piece of mouldy food through a

Below: The bladder wrack is a common seaweed. You can recognize it by the nodules or bladders that grow in pairs, and the midrib along each frond.

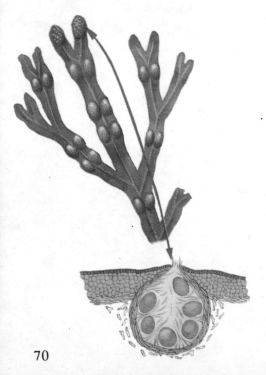

magnifying glass you will see these clearly. The hyphae are woven into a network which is called a mycelium.

Some fungi produce tiny erect stems with boxes or knobs on top of them. Such a knob is called a sporangium and it is full of minute, single-celled bodies called spores. Spores do the same job as seeds do for flowering plants. When the spores are ripe they burst out of the sporangium and float away on the breeze. If they land where conditions are favourable they grow into new fungi. Other fungi reproduce merely when pieces of a fungus body break off, fall into a suitable place and develop into new plants.

Mosses and liverworts are primitive plants that scientists believe may have been the world's first plants. There are about 14,000 kinds of mosses in the world.

Mosses help to make soil by breaking up rock with their root systems. They also tend to hold the rain and keep the ground damp. They usually grow in damp or wet places and form cushions or carpets of tiny green plants growing close together. Their tiny rootlets, called rhizoids, grow from the bottom of the stems and look like hairs. Some types of moss, such as sphagnum, are extremely spongy and make very useful packing material.

Sexual reproduction and budding

Each moss plant has male and female sex cells in organs that grow at the top of the stem. When, in wet weather, a male cell is washed into contact with a female cell, the two cells join and develop into a new plant.

This new plant is a long, thin, brown stalk with a knob on top. The knob contains spores and it opens when the spores are ripe, allowing them to scatter on the wind.

Some mosses have a simpler way of reproducing. They merely grow tiny buds which eventually break off and fall to the ground, where

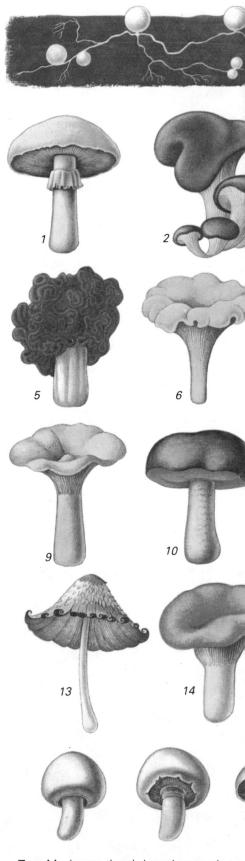

Top: Mushroom theads branch out and join up with other threads.

Above: Examples of different fungi.
1 Horse mushroom *(Agaricus arvensis)*;
2 Oyster mushroom *(Pleurotus ostreatus)*;
3 Parasol mushroom *(Lepiota procera)*;

they grow into new plants.

Ferns are non-flowering plants with feathery fronds. Most of the 10,000 different kinds favour moist, shady regions. Some are as small as mosses; others grow as large as trees. Bracken is a well-known fern.

Life-cycle of a fern

On the back of each frond (fern leaf) are a number of dark brown patches. These are containers in which the spores ripen. When the spores are ripe the patches open and the spores are blown away on the wind. Those that land in moist, shady soil will begin to grow. But the first stage is a very small heart-shaped plant known as a prothallus. The male and female cells that grow on the prothallus eventually unite to form a new fern.

Seaweeds

Seaweeds belong to a group of simple plants called algae. They contain the green colouring matter called chlorophyll which can make use of the energy from sunlight to manufacture sugars. (This process is described in more detail on pages 76-77).

Seaweeds may be either green, brown or red. The green seaweeds are found at the top of the shore, the brown seaweeds grow just beneath the surface of the water, and the red seaweeds can grow at depths of up to 100 metres. The giant kelps of the Pacific Ocean are brown seaweeds. Some grow to a length of 70 metres. Fertilizers and explosives are made from dried kelp, and the chemical called iodine is extracted from it.

Most seaweeds reproduce by the joining of male and female cells through spores, although some merely split in half, with each half developing into a completely new plant.

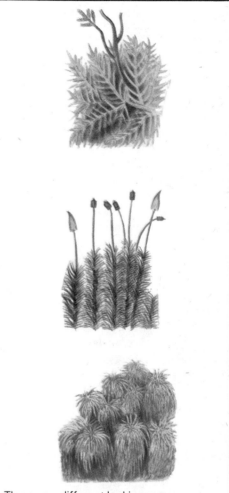

Three very different looking mosses are the heathland moss *(top)*, the hair moss *(middle)*, and the bog moss *(bottom)*. The hair moss shows the capsules with spores, and their straight stalks.

4 St. George's mushroom *(Tricholoma gambosum)*; **5** Turban fungus *(Gyromitra esculenta)*; **6** Chanterelle *(Cantharellus cibarius)* **7** *Amanita caesarea*; **8** Morel *(Morchella vulgaris)*; **9** *Clitocybe geotropa*; **10** *Boletus luridus*; **11** Grisette *(Amanita vaginata)*; **12** *Lactarius zonarius*; **13** Shaggy cap *(Coprinus comatus)*; **14** *Lactarius volemus*; **15** Cage fungus *(Clathrus cancellatus)*; **16** *Clavaria flavia*. **Bottom left:** The cap breaks away from the stalk, exposing the gills.

Above: The undersides of fern fronds have small, brown cases which contain the spores.

Coniferous trees

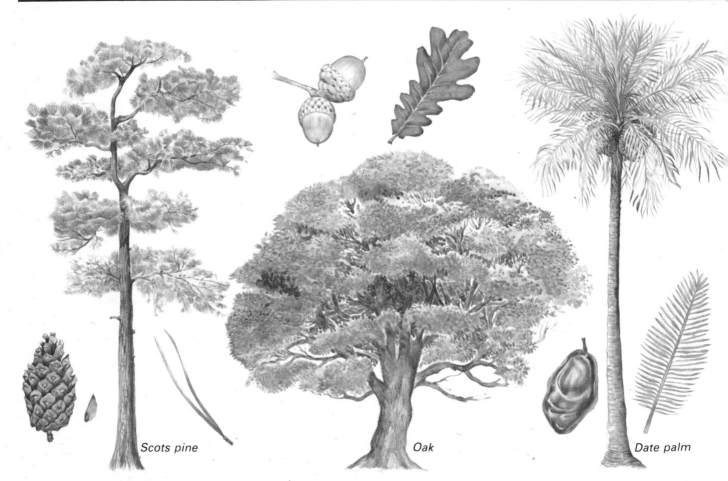

Scots pine

Oak

Date palm

Trees are the biggest plants in the world. Scientists define a tree as a plant with a single trunk that is topped by a branching crown and is at least three metres high when fully grown. There are many thousands of different kinds of trees throughout the world and they are divided into two main groups: needle-leaved trees and broad-leaved trees.

Needle-leaved trees

Needle-leaved trees are almost all evergreens. This means that they appear to stay green all the year round. The secret of their evergreen appearance is that they shed their leaves one by one throughout the year and replace them regularly. The two exceptions are the larch and the swamp cypress. These two trees shed their leaves in the autumn.

Needle-leaved trees are also called conifers because they bear cones. They include pines, firs, cedars and spruces. Their leaves are called needles because they look much more like narrow, sharp, green spikes than ordinary leaves. Because the leaves are so narrow, they present very little surface area to the wind and prevailing climate and, as a result, they are not much affected by changes in temperature.

In some needle-leaved trees, the leaves are less than 2.5 centimetres long. They may grow singly at intervals out of the twigs or they may grow in clusters from knobs on the branches. Other kinds of trees have long needles that grow from the branches in groups of two, three, or five. Yet other kinds have flat, scale-like needles that grow close to the twigs and tend to overlap.

Cones

Cone-bearing trees belong to a large class of seed plants called gymnosperms. The term comes from two Greek words meaning "naked" and "seed". This is because the seeds are naked – they are not enclosed by pods or fruits. There are two kinds of cones: male cones called pollen cones, and

Above: The outlines, leaves and fruits of three very different kinds of trees are compared: the Scots pine with its needle leaves and cone; the oak with its broad leaves and acorns; and the date palm with its feathery leaves and fleshy fruit.

female cones called seed cones. Both kinds are usually found on one tree.

The pollen cones are much smaller than the seed cones. They release their powdery pollen to be carried on the wind to the ovules (structures that contain the female sex cells) of the seed cones. The combining of the male and female cells is called pollination.

The pollinated ovules eventually develop into seeds. The fully ripe seeds fall from the trees to the ground and, if conditions are right, they may grow into new trees. If conditions are not suitable, the seeds may lie in the earth for years before showing signs of growth.

Individual species

The Scots pine is the only conifer native to Britain. It grows up to 30

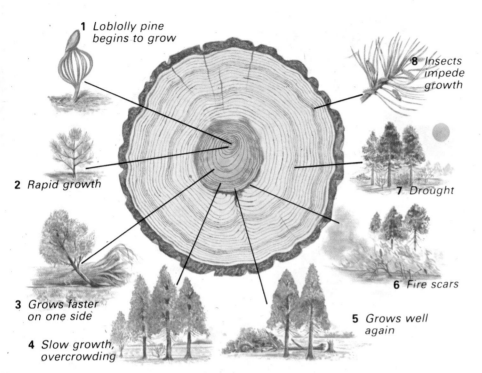

1 *Loblolly pine begins to grow*

2 *Rapid growth*

3 *Grows faster on one side*

4 *Slow growth, overcrowding*

8 *Insects impede growth*

7 *Drought*

6 *Fire scars*

5 *Grows well again*

Above: The sweet chestnut has a distinctively furrowed bark which is a good means of identification.

Above: The bark of the cherry or sweet birch covers a dark, hard, close-grained wood that is used for furniture. The thin bark peels off in horizontal layers.

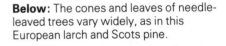

Below: The cones and leaves of needle-leaved trees vary widely, as in this European larch and Scots pine.

metres high with a trunk 1.5 metres across. Because it grows in poor soil and often lacks protection from the fierce winds, its roots have to go deep down into the earth to provide a firm anchorage. The needles are straight, about nine centimetres long, and grow in pairs. The cones have stout stalks and are about five centimetres long. The timber is yellowish, rather soft, and with a coarse grain. It yields quantities of resin, pitch, tar and turpentine.

The Douglas fir is a giant among trees. A native of North America, it has also been introduced into Europe. It may grow up to about 90 metres tall and 3.6 metres thick. Its large, feathery branches grow in downward-pointing spirals. The needles have blunt ends and give off a strong fragrance. In Europe, this tree is grown for its fine timber.

The cedar of Lebanon, originally a native of Asia and Africa, has now been introduced into many other parts of the world. King Solomon is reputed to have built his great temple at Jerusalem from cedars of Lebanon supplied from Tyre. The tree has a massive trunk that sends out spreading branches in flat layers. It grows up to 40 metres in height.

Above: The life history of a tree can be read by an expert from examining a cross-section of its trunk. Rapid and slow growth rates leave their imprint in the timber.

As the tree grows older, it changes its shape. It starts off as a pyramid with a pointed top and the lower branches turning upwards. Later, the top flattens out and the branches poke out horizontally. The short, dark green needles grow from the twigs in small rosettes. The cedar produces a large upright cone with a blunt end.

The Norway or common spruce is perhaps better known as the Christmas tree. A native of Europe, it can reach a height of 60 metres and have a trunk 2.5 metres across. It has four-sided prickly needles that grow in spirals round the branches. The cones hang straight down. Timber from the Norway spruce is known as white wood, or deal, and is used for building.

European larch

Scots pine

Broad-leaved trees

Broad-leaved trees are also called deciduous trees. Deciduous trees, unlike evergreens, shed their leaves in winter. The reason for this shedding is linked to the availability of water. Water is absorbed from the earth by a tree's roots, from where it travels up to the leaves and then out into the air in the form of water vapour. But in the winter the frozen ground yields very little water. So rather than have its leaves go short of water, and run the risk of killing the whole tree, the tree merely sheds the leaves. It does not grow new ones until the spring, when enough water is freely available again for the whole plant.

When the time comes for the leaves to drop off, they do not break off as a broken branch might do. This could cause wounds that might become infected. Instead, the place where the leaf detaches itself from the twig is protected beforehand by the formation of a double layer of cells at the base of the leaf stem. This occurs in the summer, and only when the process is complete do the leaves begin to turn brown and golden before dropping off. The old leaves are actually pushed off by the power of new growth waiting to take its place behind them.

Before the leaves fall off, some of the food they contain is drawn back into the twigs and branches.

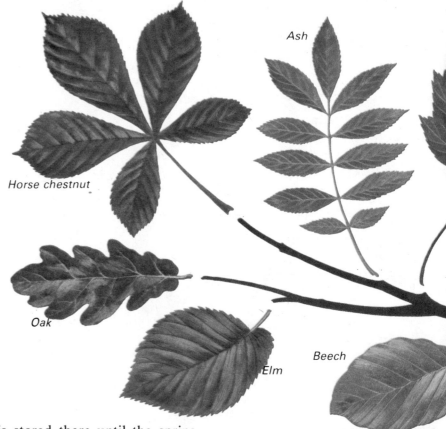

It is stored there until the spring and used by the developing leaf buds.

Oaks

Possibly the most famous of all broad-leaved trees is the oak. There are more than 300 kinds of oaks scattered around the world, and they have a reputation for sturdiness and strength. The two oaks native to Britain differ in their trunks, leaves, and acorns (fruits). The English oak has a shorter

Below: Broad-leaved trees assume various shapes according to their size and foliage. They range from the drooping, graceful weeping willow to the squat, straggly hawthorn and the tall, straight poplar.

trunk with many branches, and its crown is broader than that of the sessile oak. The leaves of both oaks have a wavy outline but the English oak's leaves have short stalks, whereas the ones on the sessile tree have long stalks. In contrast, the acorns of the English oak grow on long stalks (peduncles), and those of the sessile oak are stalkless (sessile).

The flowers of the oak grow in clusters called catkins. Some catkins have male flowers only, while some have female flowers only. But both types of catkins grow on

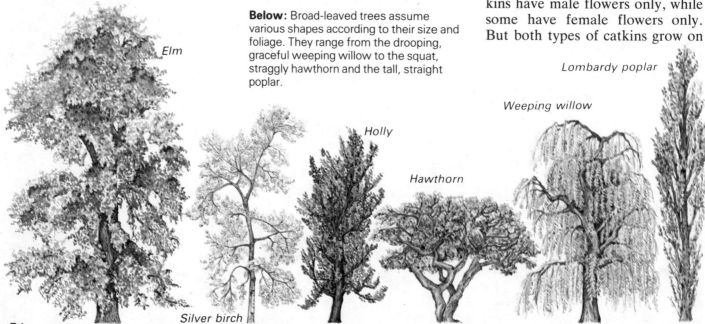

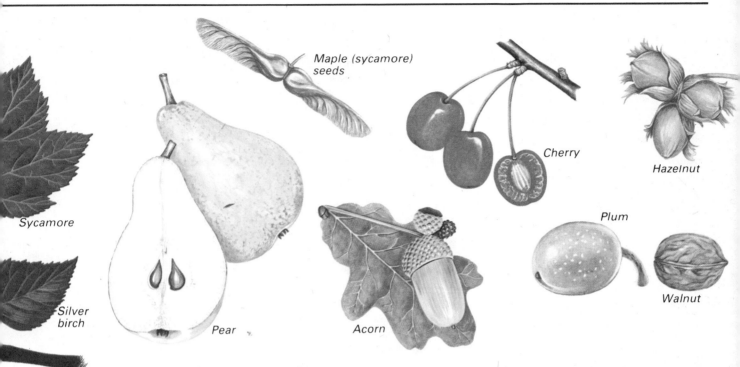

Maple (sycamore) seeds

Cherry

Hazelnut

Sycamore

Silver birch

Pear

Acorn

Plum

Walnut

the same tree. The females, after pollination by the wind, ripen into acorns.

Oak timber lasts almost forever. That is why it was used for building ships in the old days. Today it is still highly valued for furniture, buildings, and fencing.

Elms

The elm is a large, beautiful tree, often planted to provide shade. About the size of an oak, it usually lives for a long time, often for about 200 years. Sadly, in Europe particularly, elm trees have been struck in great numbers by a disease called Dutch elm disease, which is carried by insects. A stricken tree will die in four weeks. Elm fruits have a little wing which enables them to be carried easily on the wind.

Maples

The maple is found in northern temperate regions. The maple leaf is the national symbol of Canada. There are more than 100 kinds of maples, one of which, the great maple or sycamore, grows 33 metres high. The whitish or yellowish green flowers ripen into two-seeded fruits called keys. Each fruit has a pair of thin brown wings giving it the appearance of a propeller.

Above left: Leaf shapes vary as much as tree shapes.

Above: Winged seeds, like those of the maple, are scattered by the wind. Seeds within fleshy fruits are eaten by birds and animals to help dispersal.

Below: Roots serve the dual purpose of providing nutrients for the plant and anchoring it in the soil. Some roots are light and fibrous. Other plants have a single taproot that goes down deep. Some trees, like the beech in the picture develop gnarled and twisted root systems that cover a lot of ground.

Flowers and grasses

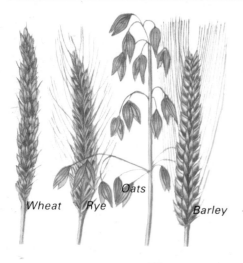

Wheat

Rye

Oats

Barley

Rice

Meadow foxtail

Common quaking grass

Common cat's tail

Left (top and **centre):** The cereal grasses are among the most important food plants grown by man. They include wheat, rye, oats, barley, rice, maize, sorghum and millet.

Flowering plants are the ones we usually visualize when we think of plants. They are made up of roots, stems, leaves, and flowers. There are about 200,000 different kinds of flowering plants and they grow all over the world except at the North and South Poles.

Flowering plants are classified in two main groups – monocotyledons and dicotyledons.

Monocotyledons grow from a seed with a single seed leaf. There are about 40,000 kinds of monocotyledons. Most of them have narrow leaves with parallel veins, and their flower parts usually occur in threes or sixes. Well-known examples of monocotyledons are daffodils, reeds, grasses, pineapples and bananas.

Dicotyledons grow from a seed with two seed leaves. Their leaves are usually broad and have a network of veins. Their flower parts usually occur in fours or fives. Well-known examples of dicotyledons are daisies, dandelions, privets and oaks.

Gardeners, who are concerned with plants that do not grow wild,

Below: Various flowering plants are commonly found in meadows and hedgerows. These include the cuckoo-pint and the foxglove.

Cuckoo-pint

prefer to classify flowering plants according to their life-cycles. They divide them into three main groups: annuals, biennials, and perennials.

Annuals usually complete their life-cycle within a year. Biennials complete theirs in two years, and perennials are those that live for several years and, in some cases, indefinitely.

Photosynthesis

The functions of roots, stems, and leaves have been described to some extent on pages 68-69. But there is one aspect of all green plants (and that includes flowering plants) that has not been touched on. This is their ability to manufacture their own food.

Green plants make their own food by a process called photosynthesis. The term comes from two Greek words which together mean "putting together with light". Water is absorbed from the soil through the roots, and carbon dioxide is taken from the air through the leaves. The water and the carbon dioxide, activated by energy from sunlight, combine to make sugar. Oxygen is given off and sent back into the air through the leaves.

Green plants are able to use the sun's energy in this way by means of tiny organs called chloroplasts which hold a green pigment called

Foxglove

Bindweed

Above: The common cat's-tail or timothy is a valuable grass crop used by farmers for making hay. Quaking grass has slender stalks that sway easily in the wind.

chlorophyll. The energy from the sunlight splits the water into hydrogen and oxygen, and it is the hydrogen that combines with the carbon dioxide. The sugar that is produced is called glucose, and from this, the plants can make starches and fats. They can also make proteins by using the nitrogen, phosphorus, and sulphur which they obtain through their roots from the soil.

What flowers are for

Flowers are the sexual parts of flowering plants and their job is to produce seeds. Some plants, such as the coltsfoot and apple tree, flower before the leaves appear.

Most flowers grow on an enlarged part of the flower-stalk called a receptacle. Most flowers also have four sets of parts: calyx, corolla, stamens, and carpels.

The calyx is made up of sepals. These are small, green, leaf-like parts whose job it is to protect the delicate inner flower bud.

The corolla lies within the calyx. This is usually made up of a group of brightly coloured petals, often the most obvious part of the flower. Their bright colours attract insects and birds to pollinate the flower.

The stamens are the male reproductive parts of the flower. Most stamens have a long, thread-like stalk, on top of which is a bulbous structure called an anther. Each anther has two bag-like sacs called anther sacs in which the powdery yellow pollen is produced.

The innermost set of parts are the female parts called carpels.

Each carpel has a stigma, style, and ovary. The stigma is on top and when it is ripe, its sticky upper surface catches the pollen grains. Underneath the stigma is a long, slender stalk called a style. This leads directly downwards to a chamber called the ovary. The ovary holds the ovules (egg cells) that develop into seeds.

The pollen grain on the stigma sends down a narrow tube through the style and into the ovule. Cells from the pollen grain use the tube to enter an egg cell. Once fertilized, the egg cell grows into an embryo (tiny plant) and the carpel surrounding it ripens into a fruit.

Above: The glacier crowfoot is a member of the buttercup family. The name crowfoot comes from its leaves, which are deeply divided into three parts and look remarkably like the feet of a bird.

Below: Climbing plants cling to supports in various ways. The bindweed puts out stems that twine counter-clockwise. The honeysuckle prefers to go in the opposite direction and twines clockwise. Peas have tendrils that grasp wire or other supports firmly. Roses, both wild and cultivated, hang on by means of their sharp thorns. Ivy clings to its support with tiny roots growing from its stems.

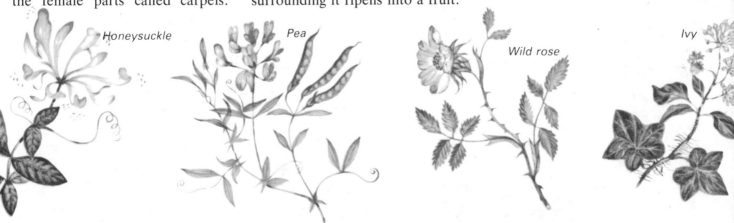

Honeysuckle　　　*Pea*　　　*Wild rose*　　　*Ivy*

Animal groups

There are two basic groups in the animal kingdom – the vertebrates and the invertebrates.

There are more than a million different kinds of animals, and scientists need a way to put them in groups and give them names. It is not enough just to say that they are vertebrates or invertebrates.

The vertebrates have backbones and are the more advanced animals. But they make up only a small percentage of all the different kinds of animals known to exist on earth.

Below: The constant high temperatures and humidity in the moist tropical forests provide an ideal environment and ample food for a wide variety of animal life.

The invertebrates – animals without backbones – make up 95 per cent of all known species. They include some of the most primitive animals, such as the tiny one-celled amoeba and others which, like the sea anemone, look more like plants than animals.

Scientists group together animals which can interbreed with one another and call each group a species. A number of species that have a lot of features in common are called a genus. Several genuses make up a family. Families are grouped into orders and orders into classes. Several classes make up a large group called a phylum, and there are about 20 of these.

The simplest animals
The simplest phylum comprises the Protozoa, or single-celled animals. There are about 30,000 species of Protozoa, some of them too small to see with the naked eye. They live in soil and in water.

The most primitive animals with more than one cell belong to the phylum Porifera. They are the sponges that live in colonies in water, always attached to a rock or the sea bottom.

The next phylum, the Coelenterata, contains about 9,000 species. Each one looks like a bag, with a single opening surrounded by tentacles. Some, like the sea anemone, are attached to a rock or

Bush baby

Gibbon

Jaguar

Orang-utan

Sloth

Macaw

Emerald tree boa

Okapi

Toucan

Hummingbird

Tapir

Goliath frog

the sea bed while others, like the jellyfish and the Portuguese man o' war, float on the currents.

Two other small phyla found in water are the Echinodermata (starfish, sea urchins and sea cucumbers), and the Ctenophora (sea walnuts and comb jellies).

There are three phyla that contain the worms. One phylum consists of flatworms, another of round worms, and the third phylum are segmented worms, like the earthworm. This last phylum is called Annelida.

Molluscs

The phylum Mollusca is the second largest of the invertebrate groups and includes 80,000 species. They have a shell and include the snail, the oyster and the clam. The octopus is also a mollusc. It once had a shell but this disappeared

during the course of evolution.

Arthropoda and Chordata

The arthropods are the largest of the invertebrate groups and make up 75 per cent of all the known species of animals. They are divided into three classes: the Crustacea (lobsters, shrimps and crabs), the Arachnida (spiders and scorpions), and Insecta (insects). Arthropods are found on land, in the sea and in the air. They have an external skeleton and a complex nervous system. Arthropods already existed 500 million years ago.

The most varied of all phyla is Chordata. This includes all the vertebrates and a few invertebrates. They all have a hollow nerve cord along their backs, with a supporting rod. In the vertebrates, this forms the backbone.

The vertebrates

Life began in the sea, millions of years ago. The bony fishes, the largest group of vertebrates, are the oldest in terms of evolutionary history, and still live in the water. The amphibians – the frogs, toads, newts and salamanders – live both on the land and in the water and are the descendants of the first animals to come out of the sea. But they cannot live for long away from water. The reptiles were the first animals able to live on land all the time. A number of them, like crocodiles, alligators and turtles, still live in the water, but most, like the snakes and lizards, are land animals.

Below: Fish of varying shapes, sizes and colours are found in the ocean's shallow waters. Some, such as the starfish, are not really fish, but a more primitive form of animal.

Portuguese man o' war · Flying fish · Low tide line · Herring · Mackerel · Kelp · Shark · Tuna · Ocean sunfish · Red mullet · Sea perch · Parrot fish · Puffer fish · Surgeon fish · Butterfly fish · John Dory · Sea anemone · Frogfish · Gunard · Skate · Plaice · Sea urchin · Starfish

Senses and adaptation

Above: The red clown fish and the sea anemone live in harmony. The fish has a covering of slime which enables it to swim safely among the anemone's tentacles.

Above: The chameleon is a master of disguise. If it is put on green leaves, it will change colour to match them in 15 minutes.

Birds probably developed from reptiles. Their feathers, it is believed, evolved from scales and they still have scales on their legs. Unlike the reptiles, however, they are warm-blooded. In this respect they are similar to the mammals, the most advanced class in the whole of the animal kingdom.

Basic needs
Mammals care for their young, the mothers nourishing them with their own milk. All of them, except for the monotremes, such as the Australian platypus and spiny anteater, give birth to live young. Mammals include a large variety of groups, including rodents, whales, marsupials and bats. The primates, the group to which man belongs along with monkeys and apes, are also mammals.

Every species of the animal kingdom has two basic needs – the need for food and the need to escape being another animal's food. Different animals have adapted in various ways to meet these needs.

Birds have developed different shaped beaks to suit the food they eat and owls and bats have developed excellent eyesight for hunting in the dark. All animals have also developed ways of escaping their enemies. Some, like bees

Below: The water buffalo allows birds such as the oxpecker and the cattle egret to pick flies, lice and ticks from its body. The birds also warn of danger.

Cattle egret

Oxpecker

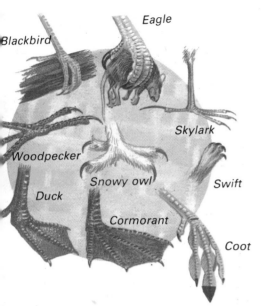

Above: The different types of birds' feet reveal their ways of life. The bird of prey has sharp claws, and the duck has webbed feet for swimming.

and wasps, can sting, while others, such as the antelope can run away swiftly.

Camouflage

Many animals that are not fleet-footed or cannot defend themselves, escape attack another way – by camouflage. They are usually able to hide from their enemies because their shape or colouring makes them blend in with their surroundings. Stripes and other types of marking are commonly found because they break up the outline of the animal, so that enemies cannot easily detect it against it's natural background.

Colour change

Prawns, chameleons and some flatfish can actually change colour to blend in with their surroundings. A flatfish can adopt a whole range of colours according to its background while a brown chameleon put among green leaves can change to green in just 15 minutes.

Adaptations

These features developed because they helped the species survive. They are adaptations that happened over vast stretches of time, as conditions changed. Species that did not adapt became extinct.

Senses

An animal's senses help it to obtain information from its surroundings about possible sources of food and danger. Sometimes one or two

Above: The nocturnal tarsier has developed owl-like eyes to see in the dark. By day the irises are narrow slits but at night they open very wide.

senses may be very well developed and others hardly at all.

In some animals the sense of sight is very simple and can only distinguish light from dark. Many mammals have quite good sight, but probably only primates can see in colour. Fish and most reptiles and birds can see in colour.

Hearing also tells an animal a lot about its surroundings. Birds have excellent hearing, and some animals, such as dogs, can hear noises that the human ear cannot pick up.

Below: Scallops have sensory cells in their tentacles for touch and smell. They have many small eyes but these can only distinguish light from dark.

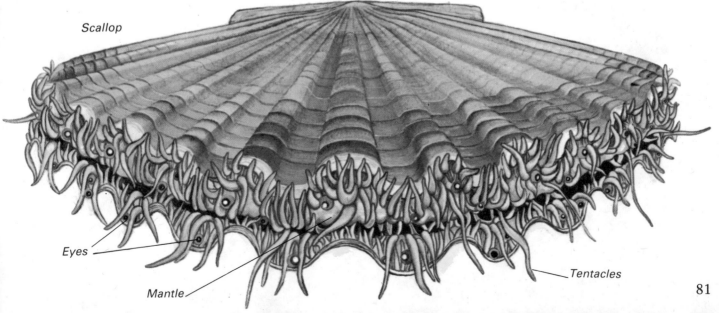

Migration and hibernation

Above: The cheetah lives on the plains and does not stalk its victims through the long grass. Instead it runs very fast over open ground, though only in short bursts. It tires after the first 400 metres.

Sense of smell

Most animals have a much stronger sense of smell than human beings. It is important for them to smell out their own food and to smell danger from approaching enemies. Dogs, for example, have a highly developed sense of smell, whereas in birds it is weak. Being able to see and hear well is much more important to birds.

Below: The dormouse hibernates in winter, curling itself up into a tight ball and becoming cold and stiff.

Smell is also important to some animals at breeding time, when the male is attracted to the female by the scent she produces.

Touch

Some animals are covered in tiny hairs that are connected to touch-sensitive areas all over the body. Many insects have poor eyesight, but highly developed touch areas. Scallops and some other molluscs have sensory cells around their shells to communicate both touch and smell.

Temperature

A few animals are very sensitive to temperature. The female mosquito, for example, uses her antennae to hunt out warm-blooded victims some distance away. Mammals and birds are warm-blooded and keep their bodies at a constant temperature through extremes of heat and cold.

Hibernation

Animals such as reptiles, which cannot adjust their body temperatures, rely on the sun for warmth. In cold regions, along with some warm-blooded animals such as bats, mice and hedgehogs, cold-blooded animals go into a long sleep during winter, when they can-

Below: The type of beak shows the foods a bird eats. The bullfinch cracks seeds, the shoveller duck strains mud, the rook eats anything, the falcon kills with his beak, and the curlew probes in mud.

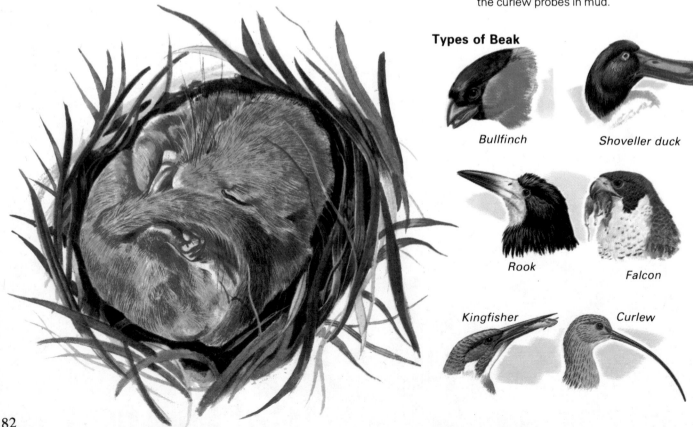

Types of Beak

Bullfinch

Shoveller duck

Rook

Falcon

Kingfisher

Curlew

not count on the sun for warmth.

This long sleep, called hibernation, brings about a drastic change so that the animal may appear almost dead. Breathing and heartbeats are much slower than normal and the body temperature drops. In some cases the body becomes quite stiff. Very little energy is used up in this state. Hibernation may last for several months until the warmth of spring wakes the animal. If bats, for example, did not hibernate, they would starve in winter, when there are few insects to eat.

Migration

Many birds solve the problem of finding winter food by migrating from cold regions to warmer ones. Insect-eating birds such as the swallow and cuckoo make long treks from Europe to Africa and from North America to South America. Land animals also often migrate for food though their journeys are not as spectacular as those of birds. The Alaskan caribou, for example, spends spring in the Arctic tundra and winters in the mountains farther south.

Migrations are not always for food. Often, animals migrate to established breeding grounds at a particular time of year. Salmon and eel are the most spectacular travellers. Eels travel from freshwater rivers and ponds in northern Europe and America to south of the Sargasso Sea in the mid-Atlantic – a journey of thousands of kilometres. There they spawn and die. Salmon swim from the sea to fresh water to breed. Rapids and waterfalls do not stop them – some salmon can leap almost five metres to clear a waterfall.

Right: Male emperor penguins incubate the eggs during the Antarctic winter. They adapt to the cold by huddling together in groups for warmth.

Primitive animals

The most primitive members of the animal kingdom are those without backbones – the invertebrates. Some are so simple they are made of just a single cell while others, like insects and spiders, have quite complex nervous and circulatory systems. Many of the simplest animals are found in the sea where life began millions of years ago.

Protozoa
The simplest forms of life are the single-celled animals which belong to the phylum Protozoa. There are about 30,000 different kinds and they live in water and on land.

The *amoeba,* one of the most primitive of all animals, belongs to this group. The size of a pin-point, it looks like a shapeless blob of jelly. The *amoeba* changes its shape constantly as it flows along in the water. Small finger-like projections push out and move the body forwards. As it flows, it takes in tiny particles of food and absorbs oxygen from the water. It reproduces itself by simply dividing into two.

Other protozoans, such as *Euglena,* move by using a whip-like cord, which they twirl in the water to pull themselves along. A third group, the ciliates, are covered in tiny hairs, and move by beating these in the water.

Sponges
Porifera, or sponges, are also simple and look like a collection of protozoa. They are in fact multi-cellular and are always attached to the sea bed or a rock. They have a

Above: A sea anemone looks like a harmless plant, swaying gently in the shallow water. Yet, its tentacles can paralyze unsuspecting prey.

Below: A yellow sponge growing on red coral. There are about 5,000 different species of sponge. Most types live in the sea but some inhabit fresh water. Both types are found in warm seas like the Mediterranean and the Caribbean. It is their dead skeleton that forms the familiar bathroom sponge.

supporting skeleton and come in a variety of shapes and colours. They may be fan-shaped or they may look like a branching tree. Their colours range from scarlet to green, yellow, brown and white.

Coelenterates
There are about 9,000 species of coelenterates. They all have in common their bag-like shape and the fact that they all have one cavity which is ringed by tentacles. The tentacles have stinging cells along them which are used to stun prey before drawing in the paralyzed food. Coelenterates have no circulation system and no brain.

Sea anemones are in this group. They are always attached to something – usually a rock – though they are able to glide slowly along. Their tentacles are shaped like petals and are very colourful.

Some coelenterates belong to a sub-division called Medusa. These include the jellyfish, which are some of the largest animals without backbones.

Another sub-division called the polyps include the tiny *Hydra* which live in the bottom of fresh-water ponds and lakes. *Hydras* are only 12 millimetres long and look like frayed bits of string.

If one is cut into pieces, almost every piece becomes a new *Hydra*. Because of this, it is named after a mythical Greek monster, Hydra, which had nine heads and could grow a new one if one was cut off.

The *Hydra* can also reproduce by budding. A bud-like lump forms on the side and breaks off to grow tentacles and a mouth. It may also produce male and female cells which unite to form a new *Hydra*.

Another coelenterate is coral, which is related to both the anemones and jellyfish. Corals are made of a collection of polyps – soft, tube-like creatures – which form a colony. They take lime from the sea water and build it up to form a hard skeleton which, over hundreds of years, may form a coral reef.

Echinoderms
Another primitive group found in the sea are the echinoderms, of which there are 400 different kinds. They are built on a radial plan. This means that all the parts of their body meet at a central point, rather like the spokes of a wheel. They all have skeletons of lime.

The group includes the starfish, sea urchins and sea cucumbers. The starfish has five arms covered with hundreds of small suckers, which it uses to grip and prize open mussels and oysters.

Sea urchins are globe-shaped and burrow into sand, while sea cucumbers live on the sea bed and have spiny skins.

Annelids
Annelids are worms whose bodies are divided into segments. From the outside these look like rings. The earthworms are the best-known annelids. They burrow their way into the earth by eating through the soil.

The marine version is the bristleworm, which has small feet on each segment of its body. It uses these for crawling and burrowing in sand.

Below: All these animals live near the water surface. Ianthina makes a raft of bubbles to stay afloat. The Portuguese man-o'-war trails its stinging tentacles in the water to catch and paralyze its prey.

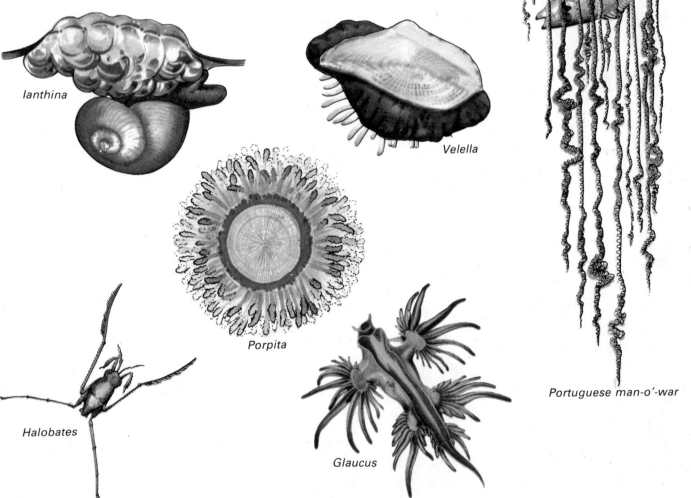

Ianthina

Velella

Porpita

Halobates

Glaucus

Portuguese man-o'-war

Molluscs

Molluscs are a large group of animals which usually live in the sea though some of them, such as snails and slugs, live on land.

The great majority of them have shells, although the octopus and the slug have none, and some other molluscs have only a small one.

The name mollusc comes from the latin word *mollis* meaning "soft" and refers to the soft body usually found under the shell.

Shells
The shell of a mollusc has a double duty. It houses the animal and protects it. Between the shell and the body is a layer of tissue called the mantle. As the animal grows, the outer rim of the mantle becomes part of the shell. This growth sometimes causes lines or ridges to form on the shell. The mantle is made from a tough, horny substance. Most molluscs have two or three layers which form the bulk of the shell and are made of lime. Some molluscs have another inner layer made of mother-of-pearl. This lining material covers any irritants that get into the animal's shell. In an oyster, the material can sometimes form a pearl.

Molluscs can be divided into five types – univalves, bivalves, cephalopods, chitons and tusk shells.

Univalves and bivalves
The first group, the univalves, are also sometimes called gastropods. They have their shell in a single piece. Limpets, winkles, whelks and land and freshwater snails are all univalves, as are slugs. Slugs either have no shell or one so reduced that the slug cannot draw back into it, unlike the snail. The shapes and colours of the sea slugs are among the most varied of the marine world. One member of the group has flaps attached to each side of its feet which act like wings, and so it is called a sea butterfly.

Univalve shells are all coiled in a spiral at some time in the animal's life. Young limpets, for example, have coiled shells, while parent limpets have cone-shaped shells.

The bivalves have shells composed of two parts, joined by a hinge. This group includes mussels, scallops, cockles, oysters and clams. They are all water animals and usually bury themselves in sand or mud. They move very slowly and cautiously, using a single foot. Only the scallop is a good swimmer. It moves backwards in great leaps, clapping its shells together to expel water and propel it along. Some, like the mussel, attach themselves to hard surfaces using threads.

Other kinds of mollusc
The third group, the Cephalopoda, has no visible shell. The cuttlefish and the squid both have bone-like structures inside, covered by a skin. These animals evolved from snail-like ancestors and have lost their outer shell. The octopus also once had a shell but has now lost it completely.

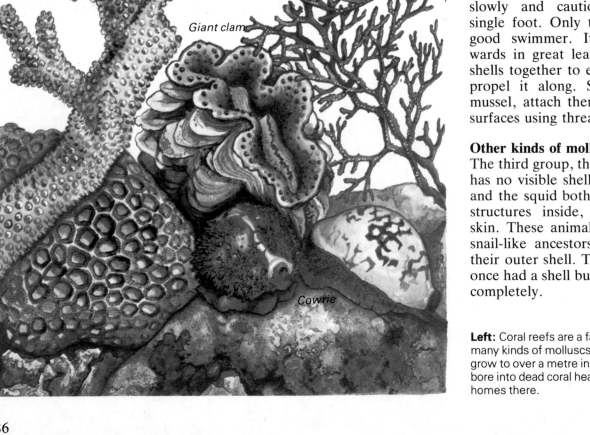

Coral

Giant clam

Cowrie

Left: Coral reefs are a favourite haunt of many kinds of molluscs. Giant clams can grow to over a metre in length. Bivalves bore into dead coral heads and make their homes there.

Both the octopus and the cuttle-fish can change colour to protect themselves and all members of this group can shoot out an inky substance to hide their movements.

Squids, like scallops, move by a sort of jet propulsion and can reach high speeds in bursts. They vary in size from just a few centimetres to the giant squids which can be up to 20 metres long.

Chitons, the fourth group, are also called coat-of-mail shells and are commonly found clinging to rocks on seashores. The shell is made up of eight plates surrounded by a scaly girdle. The chiton can curl itself up to protect its soft inner surface. It is the most primitive of all the molluscs.

The smallest group consists of the tusk shells, which are single-valve shells shaped like an elephant's tusk. They live in sand far below the low-water mark but their shells are sometimes found washed up on the seashore.

Feeding

Molluscs feed on a variety of foods. Snails eat plants, while bivalves draw in microscopic particles from the seawater. Some sea snails eat seaweed while others, together with the whelks, eat other molluscs. Octopuses eat crabs and

Above right: Most sea hares have a flap-like extension to the foot which is folded over their back.

Right and **below:** Dorids are sea slugs with feather-like gills on their backs.

cuttlefish and small squid eat shrimps. Larger squid eat fish.

Development

All molluscs begin life as eggs. Some species lay many thousands of eggs, shedding them into the sea where they drift away to hatch and survive by themselves. Oysters lay up to two million eggs at a time. Some marine snails protect their young by laying their eggs in a kind of jelly or on the backs of their neighbours. The whelks lay many hundreds of eggs in a tough egg case up to 12 millimetres wide. After a couple of months, only

about 12 have hatched. They then eat all the others.

An unusual and risky way of caring for its developing young is used by the swan mussel. This mollusc lays its eggs in summer and keeps them tucked away in its gills until the following spring. Each larva then drifts out of its mother's shell and hitches a lift on a passing fish, sheltering there until its own shell has begun to form. It then detaches itself and falls to the river bed. The swan mussel has to produce about half a million eggs to ensure the survival of only one of its young.

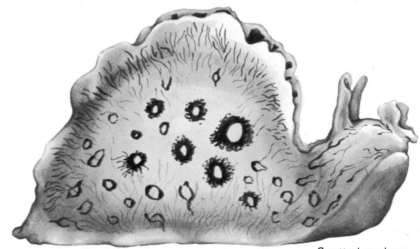

Spotted sea hare

Chromodoris

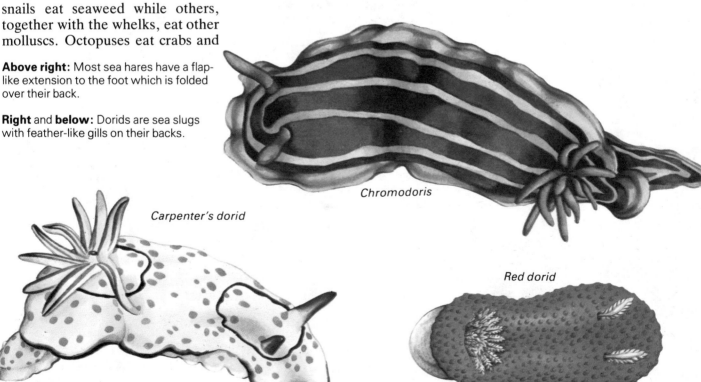

Carpenter's dorid

Red dorid

What is an arthropod?

The term arthropod comes from a combination of Greek words meaning "having jointed feet". Arthropods are more accurately animals with jointed legs. They make up more than 75 per cent of all the known kinds of animals. They include five major groups: arachnids (spiders, scorpions, mites and ticks); crustaceans (crabs, lobsters, shrimps, and barnacles); millipedes; centipedes; and insects (bees, ants, butterflies, cockroaches, beetles, and others).

The bodies of arthropods, as well as their legs, are jointed. Some species have wings. They may have either simple or compound eyes, or a mixture of both.

All have an outside skeleton which protects the softer, inner parts of their bodies. This skeleton may be thick and horny, like that of a crustacean, or thin and weak, like that of a fly.

The arachnids

Arachnids are small land animals that look like insects. But they differ by having four pairs of legs and no feelers, and their bodies are divided into two main parts. Arachnids often have poisonous stings or fangs, and some are dangerous to man.

Spiders are useful because of the large numbers of insects they eat, although many people are horrified by them. A great many spiders spin webs to catch their insect prey. Scorpions have elongated, spider-like bodies with powerful claws in front and a slender, curved tail tipped with a poisonous sting. The sting is used for defence as well as for paralyzing prey.

Mites and ticks are tiny arachnids that have piercing and sucking mouth-parts. They live on plant juices or animal blood. Many types of mites and ticks are a great nuisance to farmers, as they can damage crops and animals.

The crustaceans

Crustaceans are arthropods that are covered with a hard shell. They

Below: A few of the many types of insects are shown below. The rhinoceros beetle can fly, but its wings are small compared with its heavy body. The gaily coloured ladybird helps man by eating harmful insects. The well-known swallowtail butterfly has a 70-millimetre wingspan. The frail, wingless booklouse lives on paper, glue and starch. Ants live in large colonies.

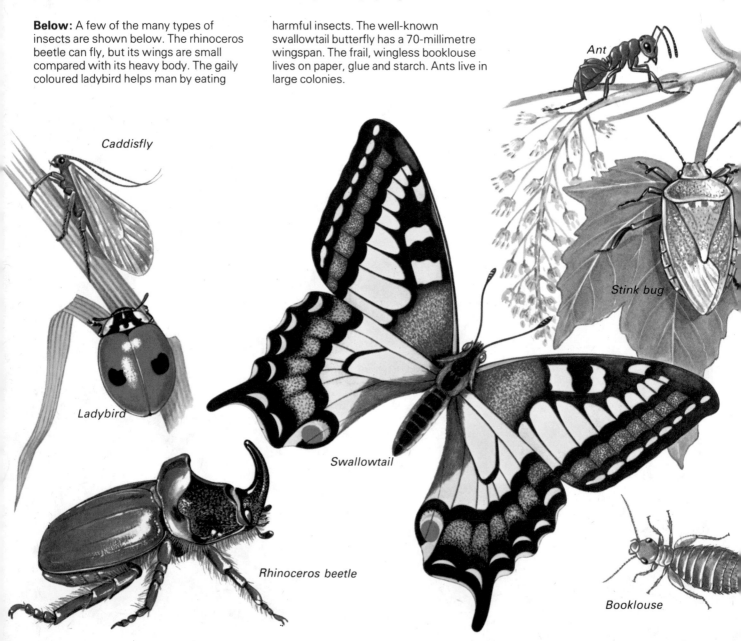

Caddisfly

Ant

Stink bug

Ladybird

Swallowtail

Rhinoceros beetle

Booklouse

have two pairs of feelers. There are about 25,000 different kinds, and most of them live in or near water. A crustacean's shell does not change in size, so when the animal's soft body grows with age the shell has to be cast off or moulted, and then replaced.

The best known crustaceans are crabs, lobsters, shrimps, and barnacles. There are about 1,000 different kinds of crabs, many of which are good to eat. They help to clean up the beaches by eating dead animals there.

Lobsters are also a popular food. They are blue or green when alive, and only turn red when cooked. Crayfish are small freshwater lobsters about 15 centimetres long. Shrimps and prawns are small, fast swimming crustaceans. Prawns look like big shrimps. Barnacles are salt-water crustaceans. They are covered with a tough shell and usually cement themselves permanently to some support such as a ship, the foundations of a pier, or even an animal such as a whale.

Centipedes and millipedes

Centipedes and millipedes are fairly similar-looking arthropods with many legs. Centipedes are flesh-eating, fast-moving creatures that look like caterpillars. They have a pair of poison claws and may have any number from 15 to 170 pairs of legs. Millipedes are slow-moving vegetarians and are completely harmless. They look more like worms and may have up to 115 pairs of legs.

The insects

There are about three times as many insects in the world as all the other animals put together. New kinds are being discovered every day. Insects can survive under almost any conditions and they are found all over the world. They live in burning deserts and icy wastes; on the tops of mountains and far out to sea; in hot springs and even in vinegar. Their small size has helped them to become the most successful animals on earth.

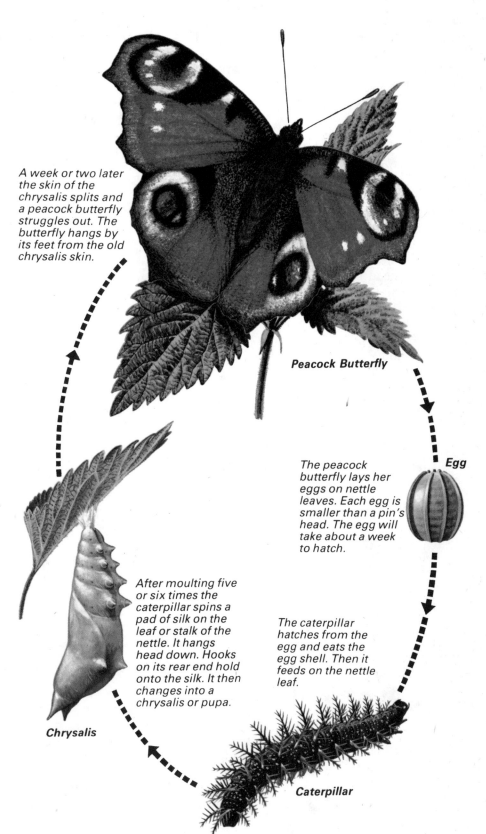

A week or two later the skin of the chrysalis splits and a peacock butterfly struggles out. The butterfly hangs by its feet from the old chrysalis skin.

Peacock Butterfly

The peacock butterfly lays her eggs on nettle leaves. Each egg is smaller than a pin's head. The egg will take about a week to hatch.

Egg

After moulting five or six times the caterpillar spins a pad of silk on the leaf or stalk of the nettle. It hangs head down. Hooks on its rear end hold onto the silk. It then changes into a chrysalis or pupa.

The caterpillar hatches from the egg and eats the egg shell. Then it feeds on the nettle leaf.

Chrysalis

Caterpillar

Above: The diagram shows the stages in the complete metamorphosis of the peacock butterfly. The caterpillar or larva thrives on nettle leaves, which it chews continuously. (The adult butterfly always manages to lay its eggs on the right plant.)

After the adult butterfly has crawled out of the old skin of the chrysalis, it lingers for an hour or two while its moist wings dry in the sun. When its wings are dry, it takes off for its first flight and a new life. The cycle begins again.

Insects

Insect bodies

Adult insects differ from all other arthropods in having three pairs of legs and three main parts to their bodies. They have two feelers at the front of their heads and most of them have one or two pairs of wings.

The three main parts of the body are the head, a middle part called the thorax, and the hind part called the abdomen. All insect bodies are protected by a hard outer skeleton, which is also waterproof. An insect smells, feels, and tastes either with its feelers which it waves about in front of its head, or with its feet. Insects also have compound eyes, made up of a number of smaller eyes. A dragonfly, for example, has 28,000 of these smaller eyes in one compound eye.

Insects may have been the first animals to fly, long before birds or bats. This ability has also helped them to survive. Most insect wings are thin and papery, and heavily veined. Some, such as those of butterflies and moths, are covered with scales, and may be beautifully coloured. Flies and mosquitoes have only one pair of wings, the stumpy hind wings being used only as balancing aids. The front wings of beetles are toughened into shell-like cases that protect the folded hind wings.

What insects eat

Some insects such as cockroaches will eat almost anything. Others will eat only one kind of food, such as the silkworm which lives on mulberry leaves. Butterflies and moths, which have very long sucking tubes, feed on plant nectar. Others, such as the mosquito, have long, sharp, needle-like tubes and suck blood. But other insects may eat wood, wool, fur, paper, cork, rotting vegetables, meat, flour or leaves. That is why most insects are regarded as pests. Some insects, such as the ladybird and the dragonfly, eat other insects and small animals.

Changing their shapes

Most insects pass through various stages in their lives from the egg to the adult (as shown in the diagram on page 89). This kind of growth is called metamorphosis, a Greek word meaning "change in shape". The grubs or larvae that hatch out of the eggs look like baby worms. Caterpillars, for example, are the larvae of moths and butterflies.

The newly-hatched larva eats

greedily and continuously until it grows too big for its skin. Then it moults (sheds its skin). This may happen several times. When the larva can grow no more, it stops eating, attaches itself to some support such as a tree, and turns into a pupa. This is a resting stage in which the larva protects itself with some sort of covering. The butterfly larva grows a shiny, transparent case called a chrysalis. The moth larva spins a silky covering called a cocoon.

During the pupal or resting stage the insect's body changes drastically. After anything from a few weeks to a few months, the case splits and the new insect crawls out.

Insects that go through all four stages – egg, larva, pupa and adult – are said to go through a complete metamorphosis. These include beetles, ants, wasps, butterflies and moths. But other insects, such as grasshoppers, crickets and dragonflies miss out one or more of these stages and undergo incomplete metamorphosis.

How insects live
Most adult insects live by themselves in cracks, in holes in the ground, or under stones and trees. But some, the so-called social insects, live in colonies. These include most bees, ants, termites, and some wasps. The colonies are very well organized, with soldiers to guard them, workers, "nurses", and queens who lay eggs and regulate the colony's activity.

Below: A composite picture showing some of the varied ways of life adopted by ants (1-7) and a typical early life story (8-13).
1 Wood ants build nests of soil and leaves
2 Ants clearing away a caterpillar carcass
3 Harvester ants collect a store of seeds for winter food
4 Honeypot ants hang from the roof of the nest as living food stores
5 Leafcutter ants cut off pieces of leaves
6 In the nest, the leafcutters grow a mould on the leaf compost for food
7 Ants herding aphids on plant roots
8 A queen ant lays her eggs (enlarged so you can see them)
9 Workers tend the eggs until they hatch into larvae
10 In the larval chamber, larvae are fed by nursemaid workers. In return, the larvae secrete juices which are eagerly licked up by the adults
11 Larvae are taken to a pupal chamber where they spin the cocoons in which they pupate
12 In the hatching chamber, the workers help the young ants out of the cocoons
13 Waste material is stored in a refuse chamber

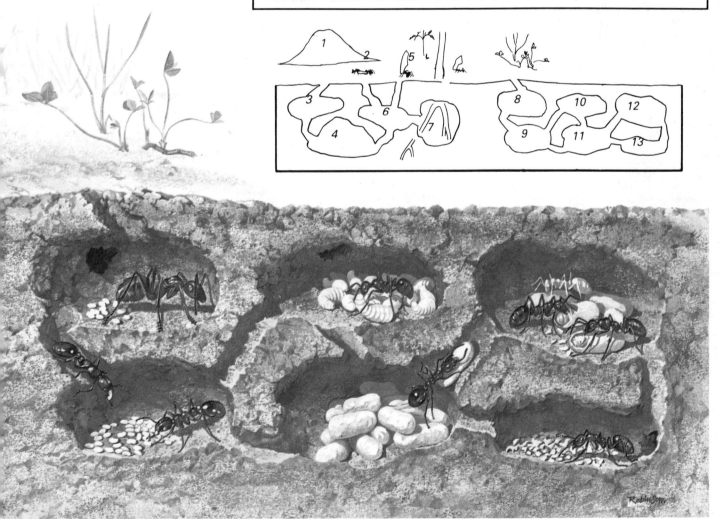

Fish

Rudd

Bleak

Barbel

Crucian carp

Pike

Bream

Perch

Tench

Gudgeon

Roach

Above: All the fish shown here live only in fresh water.

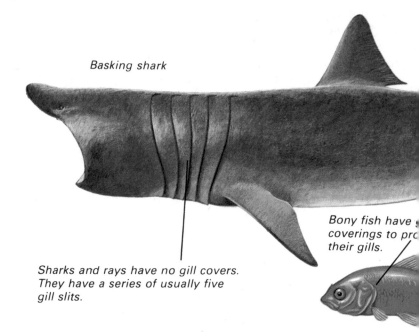

Basking shark

Sharks and rays have no gill covers. They have a series of usually five gill slits.

Bony fish have coverings to pro their gills.

Fish are cold-blooded animals, found in both fresh and salt water all over the world. Because of the variety of environments offered by the open sea, most of the 25,000 types of fish are found there.

Scientists divide fish into three categories – bony, cartilaginous and jawless.

The great majority of fishes are bony, or true fish, with skeletons made of bone. Cartilaginous fishes, such as sharks, rays and skates, have skeletons made of a gristly substance called cartilage.

Lampreys and hagfish are jawless fish. They also have skeletons of cartilage but are distinguished by the fact that they have no proper jaws and no scales.

Movement

The body of a fish is adapted to make movement through water easy. The head is smooth and bullet-like and the body cigarshaped and streamlined so that it offers little resistance to water. Fish swim by wriggling their bodies from side to side while their tails propel them forwards.

The dorsal fin, along the top of the body, and the anal fin, on the underside, help the fish to keep its balance. Two more pairs of fins – the pelvic in the middle of the underside and the pectoral behind the head – help control movement.

Above: The shark is an example of a cartilaginous fish, the goldfish is a bony fish. Only bony fish have gill coverings.

Scales

The bodies of most fish (except jawless ones) are covered with scales. These are mainly protective. In the case of the sea-horse and the pogge, this protective covering is actually bony armour, while the stickleback and the sturgeon have bony plates on parts of their bodies. Sharks have toothlike scales that make their skin feel like sandpaper, and the porcupine fish has long spines that stand out.

Most bony fish, however, have scales that overlap one another. Scientists can identify the fish's species by the number of scales on its body.

Breathing

Fish need oxygen just like land animals. They breathe through gills which are slits at either side of the head. In bony fish, the gills are covered by a plate. Sharks have no such covering. Water is taken in through the mouth and forced out through the gills after oxygen has been extracted from it.

The lungfish has a lung and can use it to breathe in oxygen from the air. It also has gills.

All fish have backbones and a well-developed blood system,

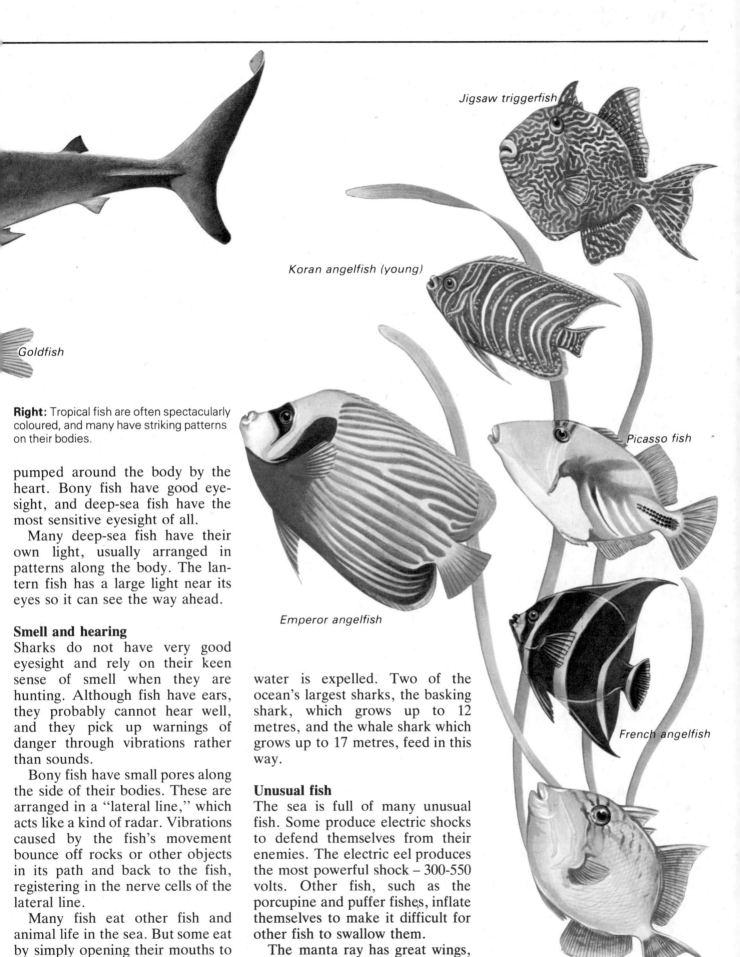

Jigsaw triggerfish

Koran angelfish (young)

Goldfish

Picasso fish

Right: Tropical fish are often spectacularly coloured, and many have striking patterns on their bodies.

pumped around the body by the heart. Bony fish have good eyesight, and deep-sea fish have the most sensitive eyesight of all.

Many deep-sea fish have their own light, usually arranged in patterns along the body. The lantern fish has a large light near its eyes so it can see the way ahead.

Emperor angelfish

French angelfish

Smell and hearing
Sharks do not have very good eyesight and rely on their keen sense of smell when they are hunting. Although fish have ears, they probably cannot hear well, and they pick up warnings of danger through vibrations rather than sounds.

Bony fish have small pores along the side of their bodies. These are arranged in a "lateral line," which acts like a kind of radar. Vibrations caused by the fish's movement bounce off rocks or other objects in its path and back to the fish, registering in the nerve cells of the lateral line.

Many fish eat other fish and animal life in the sea. But some eat by simply opening their mouths to take in water containing tiny plankton and plant life. These are filtered through the gills as the

water is expelled. Two of the ocean's largest sharks, the basking shark, which grows up to 12 metres, and the whale shark which grows up to 17 metres, feed in this way.

Unusual fish
The sea is full of many unusual fish. Some produce electric shocks to defend themselves from their enemies. The electric eel produces the most powerful shock – 300-550 volts. Other fish, such as the porcupine and puffer fishes, inflate themselves to make it difficult for other fish to swallow them.

The manta ray has great wings, which make its body up to six metres wide. It can also leap out of the water.

Queen triggerfish

How fish breed

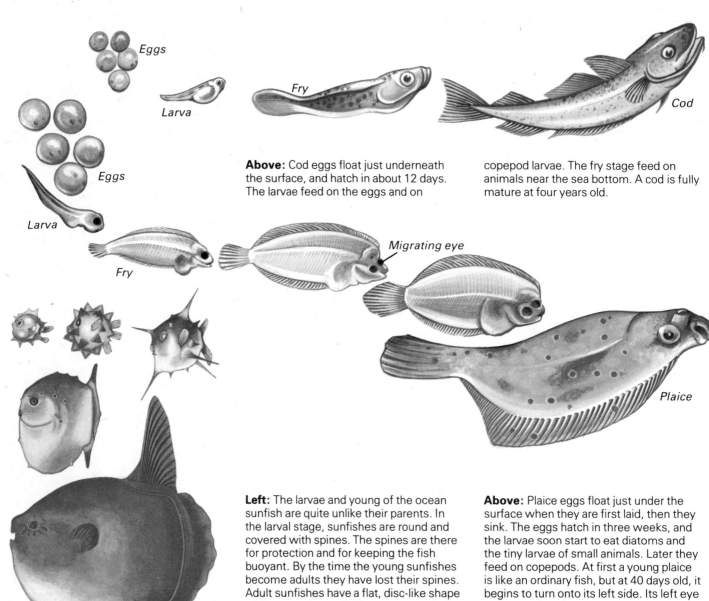

Eggs

Larva

Fry

Cod

Above: Cod eggs float just underneath the surface, and hatch in about 12 days. The larvae feed on the eggs and on copepod larvae. The fry stage feed on animals near the sea bottom. A cod is fully mature at four years old.

Eggs

Larva

Fry

Migrating eye

Plaice

Ocean sunfish

Left: The larvae and young of the ocean sunfish are quite unlike their parents. In the larval stage, sunfishes are round and covered with spines. The spines are there for protection and for keeping the fish buoyant. By the time the young sunfishes become adults they have lost their spines. Adult sunfishes have a flat, disc-like shape with a very short tail. They use their dorsal and anal fins to swim.

Above: Plaice eggs float just under the surface when they are first laid, then they sink. The eggs hatch in three weeks, and the larvae soon start to eat diatoms and the tiny larvae of small animals. Later they feed on copepods. At first a young plaice is like an ordinary fish, but at 40 days old, it begins to turn onto its left side. Its left eye migrates through the skull to lie near the right eye.

Almost all fish are born from eggs, but the ways in which these are laid and looked after varies enormously. Some fish simply lay their eggs and then leave them to hatch and fend for themselves. In these cases, since the chances of survival are slight, a huge number of eggs are laid, usually in hundreds of thousands, or even millions. A single cod may lay up to five million eggs and a turbot eight million. A ling holds the world record. One was found with over 28 million eggs in her ovaries. Fish that live in fresh water tend to lay fewer eggs than sea fish because they face fewer natural hazards than in the ocean.

The cichlid scoops out sand from the river bed to provide a place for the eggs. The stickleback and some wrasse build a proper nest which the male guards until the young are safely born. The male sea-horse carries the eggs in a pouch until they hatch. The male Siamese fighting fish catches the females' eggs in his mouth, then he blows bubbles made of a sticky substance, with the eggs enclosed inside. The female tilapia takes the eggs into her mouth and keeps them there until the young hatch.

Shoaling fish all shed their eggs and sperm at the same time, so that the eggs shed by the females are fertilized at random.

Migration
Some fish will migrate thousands of kilometres to return to their breeding grounds to spawn. Eels are an outstanding example of this. Every autumn, eels from north America and European rivers swim all the way to their breeding grounds south of the Sargasso Sea in the mid-Atlantic. There they spawn and then die. Salmon are so determined to reach their breeding grounds that they will try to leap up rapids and even waterfalls in an effort to get there.

Courtship

Some fish carry out elaborate courtships before they breed. Their colours brighten and some swim around one another in an almost ritualistic dance. The stickleback is an interesting example of fish courtship. The throat and breast of the male turn bright red in the breeding season. He swims towards the female in a zig-zag pattern. When he has caught her attention, he leads her back to the nest he has already prepared. First the female enters the nest to lay her eggs, then the male goes into the nest to fertilize them.

Colour

Apart from courtship colours, a great number of fish are brightly coloured all the time. This is particularly true in the tropics. Deep-sea fishes are often quite different in colour from those that live in shallower seas. Deep-sea fish are usually darkly coloured – red, black, brown and violet – while fish that live close to the surface in tropical waters are generally sky blue or silvery in colour. No-one knows exactly why the colours of fish vary so greatly though it may depend on the amount of light that reaches them.

Colour is almost always a form of camouflage so that the fish cannot be seen by its enemies. The dark, vertical stripes of an angel fish, for example, make it very difficult to pick out the fish among weeds on the sea bed. Some fish have the power to change colour to fit in with their backgrounds. This is particularly true of flatfishes such as sole, turbot, plaice and flounders. They live on the sea bottom and are therefore open to attack from above. The upper side of their bodies are mottled grey and brown but they can quickly take on the colour of a sandy, muddy or gravel background. Most fishes are darker on the top than the bottom so that seen from above, they merge with the darker water, and from below, they merge with the light surface.

Above: Flatfishes, such as plaice, can change colour to imitate any background. This one has turned a mottled colour to match gravel stones.

Above: This flatfish has been put to an extreme test. It has been put on a chessboard to see if it can change colour to match the black-and-white squares.

Above: The upper surface of this flounder will darken so much that it will almost disappear into the mud it is lying on.

Above: Flounders can also become pale. On sand, they lighten in colour and become very difficult to detect.

Above: Fish that live in the sea or in rivers have a dark back and a silvery underside. A sea fish's body is also sometimes iridescent, or mirror-like. The silver of the belly is caused by crystals in the skin reflecting light, like a mirror.

Amphibians

The tongue of a frog or toad is flat and broad. When a frog or toad sees an insect, it opens its mouth and throws out its

tongue. The tongue moves so quickly that it whips the insect into the mouth. The whole movement takes less than 0.1 of a

second. When it is fully stretched, the tongue is about 30 per cent of the length of the frog or toad.

There are about 4,000 different kinds of amphibians. These are animals that live both on land and in fresh water. They were the first form of life to move out of the sea onto the land, evolving from fish about 400 million years ago.

Double life
The name amphibian comes from a Greek word meaning "living a double life". Different amphibians spend varying amounts of time on land. Salamanders, for example, spend most of their lives on land. Frogs and toads, the best-known amphibians, divide their time equally between land and water, while newts spend most of their time in water. Nearly all amphibians breed in water and when they do live on land, it is almost always close to a pond or river.

All amphibians are cold-blooded animals with backbones. Most of them have four limbs. They usually have lungs, though some have both lungs and gills and most of them can take in oxygen from the air through their skins. Amphibians absorb water through their skin rather than drinking it.

Eggs
Most amphibians hatch from soft eggs laid in water by the female and fertilized there by the male. The development of their young is very like the evolutionary steps taken by the amphibian's fish ancestors millions of years ago.

The tadpole of a frog begins life with gills, and swims by using its tail. As it becomes an adult, it loses its fish-like characteristics. Gills are replaced by lungs and its tail disappears as its limbs grow. It changes from a fish-like creature to a tiny frog.

Amphibians feed on insects, earthworms and small fish. They are protected from their enemies by their colouring which usually matches their surroundings and by their ability to produce poisons in their skin.

There are three kinds of amphibians – tailed, tail-less and the worm-like caecilians.

Tailed amphibians
The tailed amphibians are the newts and salamanders. They look like lizards except that instead of having scales they are smooth skinned. They are found largely in Europe and North America and are usually small, though the giant salamander of Japan grows up to two metres long. The eggs of some salamanders hatch inside their mother's body.

Above: This vividly coloured arrowpoison frog lives in the jungles of South America.

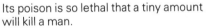

Its poison is so lethal that a tiny amount will kill a man.

A male newt courts a female by beating water at her with his tail.

The male drops his sperm in small packets for the female to pick up using her cloaca.

The female newt lays her eggs one at a time on a leaf. She then folds the leaf round each egg.

The egg sticks firmly to the leaf.

The newt tadpole breathes through gills.

The tadpole develops a second pair of legs, and its gills will soon disappear.

Tail-less amphibians

Tail-less amphibians include frogs and toads, and are found in almost all parts of the world. They hatch with tails, but lose them when they become adults. In the tropics, they can be hard to distinguish from one another but in northern Europe it is usually easy. European frogs have a smooth shiny skin and long hind legs which enable them to move quickly. Toads, on the other hand, have dry rough skin and short hind legs which means they move more slowly.

During winter, European frogs hibernate under damp leaves or mud, and toads hide under logs.

Frogs in the tropics can often be quite strange. Tree frogs, for example, have toes with suckers, which enable them to climb, while flying frogs in Malaysia and Borneo have large webbed feet which help them to glide through the air.

The loudest frog is the American bullfrog which has a large vocal throat sac.

Caecilians

The last and most primitive category of amphibians are the caecilians. They are legless and usually blind. Looking like small worms or even snakes, they bury themselves into mud or damp ground. Some species lay eggs while others produce their young alive. They are found in the wet, tropical regions of Africa, Asia and South America.

Reptiles

Below: Female sea turtles will travel long distances to lay their eggs on special breeding beaches. They lay their eggs in a pit which they dig out of the sand with their flippers. About 100 eggs are laid in ten minutes.

This group of animals includes snakes, lizards, crocodiles, alligators and turtles. They evolved about 350 million years ago. Their predecessors were the amphibians. The latter were only partly adapted to life on land, but the reptiles were the earth's first true land animals. As the dinosaurs, they dominated the land for over 100 million years. Today's reptiles are small compared with the massive monsters of the past, though some crocodiles and snakes may be up to nine metres long.

Cold-blooded

Like amphibians, reptiles are cold-blooded animals so they are never found in very cold climates where their blood would freeze. Even in the moderate climate of northern Europe they must hibernate in winter. They all have scaly skins, and their young resemble the parents, though some may be born a different colour.

Some reptiles give birth to live young, as mammals do, and some lay eggs, which may be either soft or hard.

Reptiles such as turtles or alligators cut their way out of hard shells using a horny growth on the end of the snout. Reptiles once hatched fend for themselves. Parents take little or no notice of their young once they are out of the shell.

There are four basic groups of reptiles – alligators and crocodiles, turtles and tortoises, snakes and lizards and the tuatara, a lizard-like reptile from New Zealand.

Alligators

Alligators and crocodiles, along with their close relatives, the cayman and the gavial, are long creatures covered with scales or plates on their skins. They have powerful tails to propel themselves through water and their eyes, ear-slits and nostrils are all on the top of their flat heads. They can thus use these while the rest of their

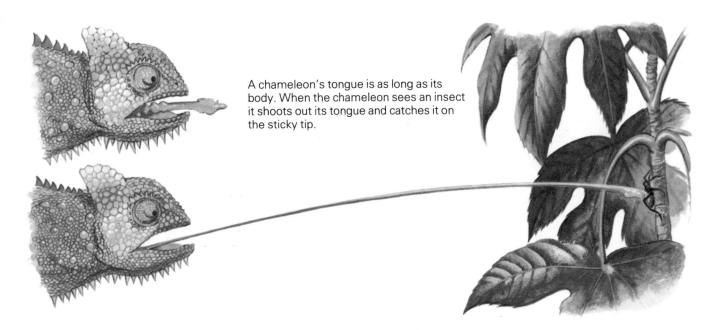

A chameleon's tongue is as long as its body. When the chameleon sees an insect it shoots out its tongue and catches it on the sticky tip.

bodies are submerged. Their four short legs are used only for walking and running. The alligator is usually heavier than the crocodile, and has a broader head. Both crocodiles and alligators live in either fresh or salt water and eat fish, birds and small mammals.

Turtles

Turtles, tortoises and terrapins all have protective shells and their protruding head and four legs can all be drawn back underneath this covering. They may be found in either fresh or salt water and also on land. The land animals are usually vegetarian and the sea animals are carnivorous. Even those who live their lives in water breathe through lungs. The names

Below: The anaconda kills its prey by coiling itself round its victim's body. It then tightens its coils so much that the victim cannot breathe.

turtle, tortoise and terrapin are used in different ways in different countries. In Britain, a turtle is the marine creature, the tortoise the land animal and the terrapin the freshwater animal. But in America the whole family are called turtles.

Snakes and lizards

The largest order of reptiles is the one that includes lizards and snakes. There are over 2,500 kinds of lizards and 2,300 kinds of snakes. Most lizards have four legs while snakes have none. Snakes have no eyelids and their ear openings are concealed under the skin. Though many snakes are poisonous, only two lizards are – the American gila monster and the Mexican beaded lizard. Lizards can discard their tails to help escape from an enemy.

The snake sheds its skin a number of times a year, once a new one has grown underneath. Some snakes are very colourful. The scarlet king snake, for example, is a vivid red, yellow and black arranged in horizontal stripes, and the rhinoceros viper is red, blue, yellow and green with a geometric pattern.

Tuatara

The final order of reptiles is the smallest one – it consists only of the tuatara, found in some islands off New Zealand. This primitive lizard-like creature is the only surviving member of the order of Rhynchocephalia which originated about 200 million years ago.

Birds

American robin

Blue jay

Below: The graceful flamingo with its long, stilt-like legs, curved bill and neck, and beautiful pinkish plumage, lives in marshy or wet regions of the world. The birds comb the mud and sand with their "toothed" bills for shellfish. All wading birds, like flamingos, have long, featherless legs and spreading toes on their feet.

Above: Well known North American birds include the friendly American robin; the mischievous blue jay; the seed-eating, rose-breasted grosbeak; and the great crested flycatcher with its musical call.

The American robin is found all over North America, where it inhabits cities and forests alike. The grosbeak has a stout beak for cracking seeds.

Birds are quite unmistakable because they are the only animals with feathers. Scientists believe that birds are descended from reptiles. Birds still have scales on their legs as evidence of this. But birds, unlike reptiles, are warm-blooded creatures, and their feathers help to keep them warm. They also have backbones and wings, but not all birds can fly. Their wings are actually their forelimbs, so birds have had to learn to walk on their hind legs, like human beings. Birds have no teeth but rely on their bills (beaks) to do much of the work of our teeth.

There are about 8,600 kinds of birds, and they live in all parts of the world.

A bird's body

The long, hollow bones that form the skeleton are small, thin, and light, but very strong. Strutting often reinforces the bones. The powerful muscles of flying birds are anchored to the breastbones by means of a thin keel of bone, like a boat's keel, that sticks out underneath.

To ensure a plentiful supply of oxygen, birds have small air sacs attached to the lungs. These provide extra breathing capacity and keep a constant supply of fresh air to the lungs. The sacs also help to keep the bird buoyant in flight.

The miracle of feathers

Weight for weight, the feather is

Great-crested flycatcher

Rose-breasted grosbeak

much more efficient and far in advance of anything yet designed by man for flight. It is made up of a strong central shaft to which the small, soft barbs are attached. The barbs are firmly linked together by hundreds of smaller barbs called barbules. These are connected by means of tiny hooks.

A bird grows various kinds of feathers. These differ according to their function. The strong flight feathers are found on the wings. Fluffy, insulating down makes up the lower layers next to the skin.

How a bird flies
Anything that flies through the air makes use of two forces – lift and thrust. In birds these are provided by the shape and movement of the wings. As soon as a bird runs or jumps forward with wings outspread, a stream of air flows over and under the wing. Because of the wing's curved shape, the air moving over the upper surface has to travel farther and faster than the air moving underneath. As a result, the pressure underneath the wing is greater and produces lift.

Thrust, the power that pushes the bird forward, is provided by the wing tips which twist and turn, driving the air backwards. The rigid leading edge of the wing acts as a knife blade cutting through the air ahead.

Digestion
Because birds are so active, they burn up an enormous amount of energy, which they get from food. Many birds, especially seed-eaters, have a balloon-like bag at the base of the neck. This is called the crop, and hastily swallowed food can be stored, moistened, and softened there before being digested. This allows some species, such as wary game birds, to snatch food when and where they can, and digest it later in peace.

Birds have no teeth. But they make up for this by having hard, horny mouths. In addition, part of the stomach called the gizzard has extremely muscular walls with tough ridges. Food that reaches the gizzard is ground into a soft, digestible mass, with the help of grit and small stones deliberately swallowed by the bird.

Bills and feet
You can usually tell what kind of food a bird eats by looking at its bill. Birds of prey, such as eagles and owls, have hooked bills for tearing flesh. Hummingbirds have long, thin, tube-like bills for taking nectar from flowers. Seed-eaters, such as finches, have strong, cone-shaped bills for cracking nuts.

Similarly, a bird's legs and feet will show its way of life. Birds of prey have sharp talons (claws) for grasping and · killing. Swimming and wading birds, such as ducks and grebes, have webbed or partly webbed feet to help them in the water. Perching birds, such as

sparrows and canaries, have three toes pointing forwards and one pointing backwards to give them a firm grip on their perch.

Choosing a mate
In courtship, if the sexes are very different, it is usually the male who has the brighter colourings, while the female may be quite drab. The male woos his prospective mate with a gorgeous display of plumage, aerobatics and acrobatics, and often a pleasant song. The peacock has one of the most spectacular displays using his wonderful fan-shaped tail feathers. The bower bird goes to the trouble of building and decorating an ingenious bower (den) for his mate in the depths of the forest. Most birds find different mates each season but some, such as swans, pair for life.

Nests and nest-building
Birds build nests for laying their eggs in and rearing their chicks. Either or both parents may do the building. Birds seem to know instinctively what to do but their technique improves with age and experience.

Nests vary widely according to species and materials available. All kinds of materials are put to use – wool, feathers, paper, straw, and sticks being common. Some nests, such as that of the long-tailed tit, are elaborate and built with great care. Others, such as that of the ostrich, are holes in the sand.

Nesting and breeding in birds

Eggs — large and small

All birds lay eggs. An egg is perfectly enclosed and protected by a hard, chalky outer shell. Within this are two thin skins surrounding the albumen (egg white). The yolk – yellow, reddish, or orange-coloured – lies inside the albumen. An egg will not develop into a chick unless it is fertilized. The fertilized egg has a tiny white spot (embryo) on the surface of the yolk. As the chick grows from the embryo it feeds on the albumen and yolk.

The time needed for eggs to hatch varies according to the species. But during that period the eggs must be incubated (kept warm) by one or both parents.

The ostrich lays the largest eggs of any living bird. They are 15 centimetres long and weigh nearly 1·5 kilograms each. In contrast, the hummingbird's eggs are so tiny that two of them will fit comfortably inside a walnut shell.

Where birds live

Most birds live in trees, because it is probably safer for them there. But, in addition to finding somewhere safe, a bird usually makes its home close to where it can find its favourite food. Fish-eating birds such as gulls and kingfishers live near to water. Sandpipers, which thrive on worms and shellfish, haunt beaches and estuaries.

Songbirds

Bird song is one of the surest signs that spring has arrived. This is because the loudest and most musical songs 'are produced in spring, the mating season.

The voice box of a bird is located at the lower end of the windpipe. This is why birds with long necks have deep voices. The ostrich, for example, emits a kind of hissing roar.

Not all bird song sounds sweet. Some sounds are harsh and sharp. These are usually threats or warning cries when danger looms. True song is produced only by the songbirds. These include the nightingale, blackbird and thrush. The sound of each species is so distinctive that an unseen bird can almost always be identified by its song alone.

Migration

Migration is a term meaning the mass movement of birds or other creatures from one home to another and back again. Most birds migrate in winter from cold climates to warmer ones, and then return to their old homes when the warmer weather arrives. But some birds mysteriously leave at the height of summer.

Some birds migrate singly; others fly in flocks of tens of thousands that darken the sky. Some birds fly huge distances over land and sea. The record is held by a little bird called the Arctic tern, which flies almost from Pole to Pole and back again.

Scientists are not yet quite sure how young birds that have never travelled before manage to find their way over such vast distances

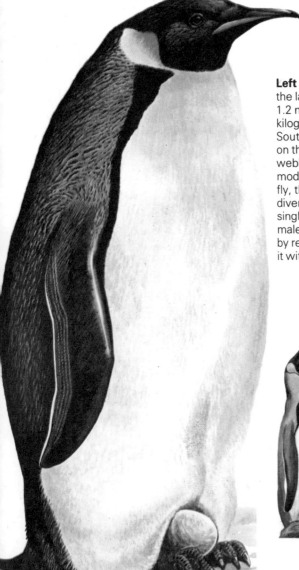

Left and **below:** The emperor penguin is the largest of all penguins, standing about 1.2 metres high and weighing about 45 kilograms. Penguins are found only in the Southern Hemisphere, several kinds living on the ice of the Antarctic. Penguins have webbed feet and flippers (which are modified wings), so although they cannot fly, they are excellent swimmers and divers. The female emperor penguin lays a single egg on the ice and then leaves the male to incubate and hatch it. He does this by resting the egg on his feet and covering it with his loose skin.

longer rise into the air.

The ostrich, rhea, emu and cassowary are all flightless, but they can run swiftly on their long, strong legs. Ostriches live in Africa and are found on the grassy plains where they live alongside huge herds of gnus and zebras. The rhea of South America looks rather like the ostrich but it is smaller and has three toes on each foot, while the ostrich only has two. The emu is an Australian bird; the cassowary lives in Australia and New Zealand.

The kiwi, about the size of a domestic hen, hides itself in New Zealand's forests. Penguins are another group of flightless birds. When danger threatens they take to the water, where their stubby wings make excellent paddles.

without getting lost. But they are convinced that many birds navigate by means of the sun and the stars.

Flightless birds

The wings of some birds are so small and stubby that they are useless for flight. The ancestors of such birds could all fly, but after living for thousands of years in places where they had no enemies (usually remote islands), they eventually found no use for flight and stayed on the ground. After a while their descendants could no

Above: An eagle's nest is called an eyrie and is usually built in the tops of tall trees or on cliffs or mountain tops. Eyries are made of sticks and decorated with fresh leaves. Some eyries are very large.

Below: In the bird world, a parent's job is a demanding one. Young chicks have a constant need for food that usually keeps both parents flying for hours on end to maintain the supply.

Unusual mammals

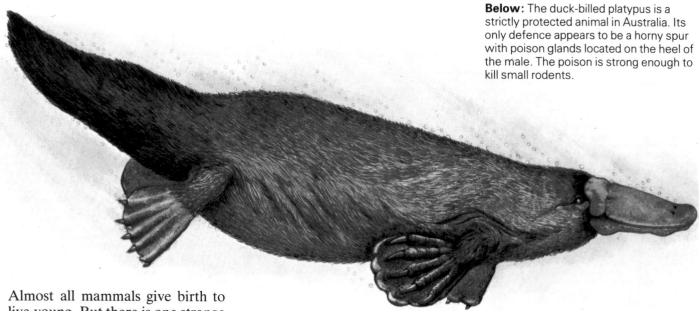

Below: The duck-billed platypus is a strictly protected animal in Australia. Its only defence appears to be a horny spur with poison glands located on the heel of the male. The poison is strong enough to kill small rodents.

Almost all mammals give birth to live young. But there is one strange group – the Monotremes – that lays eggs. The Monotremes all live in Australia and there are about six or seven different kinds living today. They are the most primitive of all the mammals and they inherited their egg-laying habits from their reptile ancestors many millions of years ago.

There are two families of Monotremes: the platypuses and the echidnas, or spiny ant-eaters. The duck-billed platypus is an extraordinary, small water mammal, with dense, dark brown fur, a fleshy bill like that of a duck, a broad, flat tail and webbed feet with five clawed toes. It is an excellent diver and swimmer, and the entrance to its river bank burrow is under water. When the mother suckles its young, milk seeps through its skin onto the hairs of its belly, where the young lick it up. Adult platypuses eat worms, insects, shrimps, and slugs, which they feel for in the mud with their sensitive bills.

The echidna or spiny ant-eater is closely related to the platypus and looks very like a hedgehog. Its

Marsupials

Marsupials are mammals whose young are reared in a pouch in the mother's body. There are more than 250 kinds of marsupials living today, most of them in Australia and Australasia. But some, the opossums, are found also in the Americas.

Marsupials are very small and undeveloped at birth. As a result, they need looking after in their mother's pouch for a long time before they are able to take care of themselves. The baby kangaroo,

Above: The pygmy flying phalanger leaps and glides from branch to branch in its never-ending search for insects and nectar. It is the smallest of all the flying marsupials, measuring about 12.5 centimetres from nose to tail.

flattened body is covered in coarse hair and spines. It feeds by night on ants and termites, which it digs out with its strong claws. It licks up its meal with a long, sticky tongue that emerges from a beak-like mouth. Its dense fur protects it from bites.

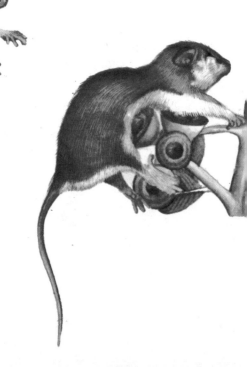

for example, as soon as it is born crawls through its mother's fur and straight into the pouch. There it hangs onto a nipple (milk gland) and never lets go until perhaps several weeks later. Kangaroos have two nipples, but some marsupials have as many as 27.

Marsupials vary enormously in size and appearance. The smallest are as small as tiny house mice, and the biggest, the red kangaroo, reaches a height of 2.1 metres and may weigh as much as 68 kilograms. Some kinds of marsupials look like squirrels and live almost continuously in the tree tops. Some, the "flying" phalangers, glide to earth from the trees by means of a parachute-like fold of skin that joins their front and hind legs together. The big, bear-like wombat has claws so strong that it can dig through concrete in minutes. The teddybear-like koala often miscalled "koala bear", is not a bear but a tree-dwelling marsupial that lives exclusively on eucalyptus leaves. Some marsupials eat only plants, others eat only meat, and still others eat anything they can catch or find.

Bats

Bats belong to an order called the Chiroptera. They are unique in the animal world in that they are the only mammals that can truly fly. Other so-called "flying" mammals, such as certain kinds of marsupials and squirrels, merely glide with the aid of folds of skin.

A bat's wing is made up of a fine stretch of skin that covers the forearm and all the fingers of the hand except the thumb and joins these to the body and the hind limbs. Bats hang upside down by day in various hiding places or from tree branches, and then fly out at dusk.

Most bats are insect-eaters, but some of the largest tropical bats live only on fruit. A particularly unpleasant and dangerous bat is the vampire bat that sucks its victim's blood while the victim is asleep. Its danger to humans is that it can easily transmit the fatal disease of rabies in this way.

Another characteristic of bats is their use of a system of echolocation to locate prey and avoid obstacles while in flight.

Below: Bats are able to locate prey and obstacles in the dark. They emit short, shrill bursts of high-pitched sound whose echoes bounce off an object in their path. The bats pick up the echoes with their big sensitive ears.

Above: The great grey kangaroo of Australia is one of the largest kangaroos. Even when sitting it is as tall as a standing man. It has been so ruthlessly hunted by sheep farmers that today it is an uncommon animal.

Meat-eating mammals

Meat-eating mammals form an order called the Carnivora. There are more than 250 kinds of these animals living today. They range in size from the tiny pygmy weasel (which may weigh less than 30 grams) to the enormous brown bear (which can weigh almost 700 kilograms).

Carnivores are built to hunt for their food. They have well developed canine teeth, and most of them also possess strong, shearing, blade-like teeth for tearing meat off bones. They have heavy skulls and powerful jaw and face muscles. They have a keen sense of smell and hearing, but usually only the cats have outstanding eyesight. Most carnivores are also fast over the ground, especially for short distances.

Many meat-eaters have scent glands under the tail. From these they spray a strong-smelling liquid to mark the boundaries of their territory, and often as a recognition signal for others of their kind. In some species, such as the North American skunk, the scent glands produce such a foul-smelling liquid that it is a highly effective means of defence.

Some meat-eaters, such as lions and tigers, kill their own prey. Others, such as jackals and hyenas, prefer to feed on prey which has already been killed by another carnivore. Some, such as bears and raccoons, eat plants and meat.

Carnivores live in all parts of the world except for Antarctica and some small islands. Most of them are found on land but some, such as the polar bear and the otter, spend much of their lives in water.

Right: The red fox has long been a symbol of cunning and resourcefulness both in fable and fact. Hunted for sport and persecuted as a pest, it still manages to survive and rear its cubs even near cities.

Carnivores and man

Man has waged war on carnivores for many thousands of years. Those that he cannot harness to work for him, he has tried to kill. Many, such as mink and leopards, have been slaughtered for their beautiful skins. Some, such as the fox, are hunted and killed purely for sport. Others are killed because they are regarded, often quite mistakenly, as pests. The weasel, for example, kills hares and game birds such as pheasants and partridges. As a result, the gamekeeper traps and poisons it. But the weasel also kills hundreds of mice, rats and voles each year which would otherwise destroy the farmer's crops and spread diseases.

Kinds of carnivore

There are seven families of carnivore. The most perfect killing machines are the big cats. These include lions, tigers, leopards, jaguars, cheetahs, pumas, lynxes, ocelots, servals, and various wildcats. Our domestic cats also belong to this family.

Another family is made up of civets, genets and mongooses. They are small animals with long bodies and short legs. Civets are the oldest types of carnivores living today. Mongooses are efficient snake killers.

Hyenas form a small family of medium-sized animals of dog-like appearance, although they are more closely related to the cats and civets. They have powerful jaws and their forelegs are longer than their hindlegs.

Wolves, foxes, coyotes, dingos and other kinds of wild dogs make up the dog family. These animals can usually run fast and strongly, and have sharp muzzles and jaws full of teeth.

Another family consists of stoats, weasels, martens, polecats, ferrets, mink, ratels, badgers, skunks and otters. These small to medium-sized animals are usually slender with short legs.

The raccoon family includes the ring-tailed cat, coati and the giant panda. It is the smallest of all the carnivore families, and its members are like small bears with bushy tails.

The last of the carnivore families is made up of bears. They are known as plantigrade animals because they walk on the whole sole of the foot. They include brown bears, black bears, sun bears, sloth bears and polar bears.

Below: The jaguar is the largest carnivore in the Americas, where it assumes the role of the leopard in Africa. It has a larger head and shorter legs than the leopard and the spots are slightly different. It jumps, climbs and swims well.

Below: The tiger is the largest living cat. The Siberian tiger is the largest species, with specimens weighing up to 300 kilograms and measuring four metres from nose to tail. The tiger's stripes help to hide it among the undergrowth.

Siberian tiger

Hooved mammals

Mammals that have the last joint of the toes covered with a hoof are called ungulates. The term comes from a Latin word meaning "hoof". Elephants, deer, zebras, horses, cattle and pigs are all hoofed animals. Hoofed animals are divided into those with an odd number of toes, such as the rhinoceros, with three, and those with an even number of toes, such as the hippopotamus, which has four. All mammals with horns are ungulates, but not all ungulates have horns.

Odd-toed ungulates

The odd-toed order is made up of three families: horses, tapirs and rhinoceroses. They are all large, vegetarians, and good runners. The horse came originally from Europe and Asia. It was later introduced into the Americas. The only truly wild horse, the Przewalski horse, still survives in Asia. The family also includes asses and zebras.

At first glance, tapirs look much like donkey-sized pigs. But they are not related to these animals any more than they are related to elephants, although they have a short trunk. Tapirs have four toes on their front feet but three on their hind feet. They are found only in Central and South America, East India and Sumatra. They are strong swimmers and divers and live on leaves, fruits and grasses.

There are five kinds of rhinoceroses alive today, and they all live either in Africa or Asia. Most of these lumbering, tank-like creatures are harmless if left alone. Some carry one horn on their snout, others carry two. The "horn" is made up of compressed fibrous hairs.

Even-toed ungulates

There are more than 80 families of even-toed ungulates. One or more of their representatives can be found in every continent except Australasia. (Deer were introduced into New Zealand by man.)

Most even-toed ungulates are sociable animals that live together in herds. They have strong scent glands between their hooves and on other parts of their bodies to enable them to keep in touch with each other. The females have milk glands, called udders, located usually between the hind legs, for feeding the young. The young are well developed at birth, and some can run within a few hours.

Some even-toed ungulates have extremely complicated digestive systems, and are called ruminants.

Above: Stags use their antlers for attack and defence. In the rutting or mating season, which usually takes place in the autumn, stags fight each other for mates. But such struggles rarely end in serious harm being done.

Top: Horses are among the best known of all hoofed animals. By a process of selective breeding they vary today in size and function from the tiny Shetland ponies to enormously powerful Shire horses. These Arab steeds, belonging to Bedouin tribesmen in Morocco, are famed for their speed and endurance under harsh conditions.

the mouth where it is chewed and passed into a third chamber. It is then passed into the fourth and last chamber where digestive juices break it down still further before it goes into the intestine. The whole system is really a clever device for allowing grazing animals to snatch a bite, move quickly out of danger, and then digest the meal later.

In addition to the domestic animals already mentioned, ruminants include deer of various kinds, giraffes, okapi, pronghorns, antelopes, yaks, buffaloes, wild sheep and wild goats.

The non-ruminants include pigs and hippopotamuses, but even their so-called simple stomachs are complicated compared with those of other mammals. Camels, llamas, alpacas, guanacos and vicuñas form a group between the ruminants and non-ruminants, with three-chambered stomachs. Chevrotains are among the smallest of living hoofed mammals. They have stomachs that are incompletely divided.

Cattle, sheep and goats are among the ruminants, and they are said to "chew the cud". The food (grass or leaves) is mixed with saliva and goes straight down to the stomach, but without being chewed.

The stomach has four separate parts. Food enters the first chamber where it is stored before being passed into the second chamber where it is softened and formed into masses called cuds. From there the food is returned to

Top right: Though the pronghorn is sometimes called the North American antelope, it is not a true antelope. It ranges over the prairies in herds.

Above: A stag belling. This is a peculiar noise made by stags in the rutting season.

Below: Water is scarce on some of the great African plains. Gnu, giraffe and zebra practically rub shoulders in their eagerness to drink at a waterhole while keeping a wary lookout for predators such as lions and leopards.

Gnu

Giraffe

Zebra

Sea mammals

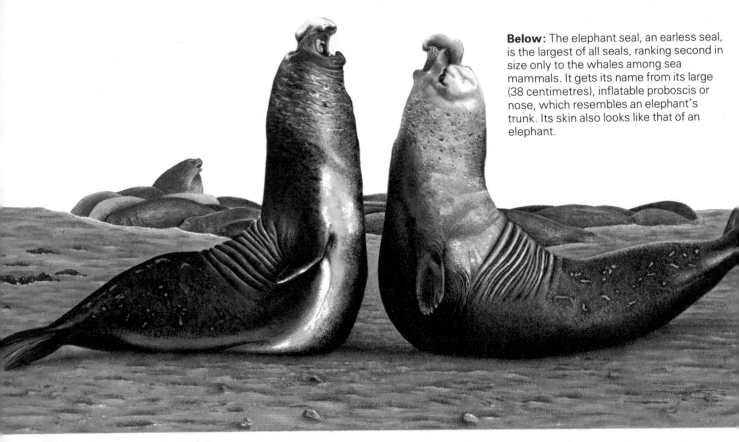

Below: The elephant seal, an earless seal, is the largest of all seals, ranking second in size only to the whales among sea mammals. It gets its name from its large (38 centimetres), inflatable proboscis or nose, which resembles an elephant's trunk. Its skin also looks like that of an elephant.

Apart from being the home of countless fishes, crustaceans, and other smaller creatures, the sea also contains the world's largest mammals, the whales. There are also two other important groups of sea mammals: the pinnipeds or fin-feet (seals, sea-lions, and walruses), and the sirens (manatees and dugongs).

Whales and whale-like creatures

The cetaceans or whales were once land mammals that became adapted to living in the sea. Their huge, streamlined, fish-like bodies enable them to swim far and fast and dive deep. Their skin is hairless and backed by a deep layer of fat called blubber. Their forelimbs have become paddles in the water while their hindlimbs have disappeared entirely. All whales can feed underwater and may remain up to an hour submerged. When a whale spouts it is releasing compressed air through blowholes, or nostrils, on the top of its head. This breath condenses in the colder air and forms a kind of fog which becomes visible.

Whales have been mercilessly hunted for their oil, meat, and other commercial products, and some nations ignore all pleas for their protection and conservation. There is a real danger that these giant, harmless, intelligent crea-tures may soon become extinct.

The finback whales have flat, fairly short heads and a number of grooves which run down the throat, along the breast to the belly. They have a fin on the back. This group includes the great blue whale which, with a length of 30.5 metres and a weight of 120 tonnes, is the largest animal that has ever lived. Other kinds in this group are the rorqual, a light grey and white whale; and the humpback, with its extremely long breast fins.

The right whales have no grooves and no fin on their backs. They have been so mercilessly hunted that they are now extreme-ly rare. They include the Green-

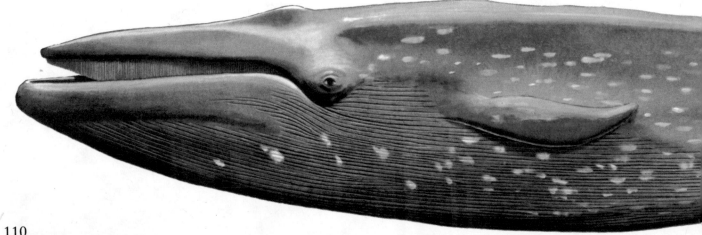

land right whale which has a head that is over 30 per cent of the length of its body; and the smaller black right whale which travels on the Gulf Stream. The Californian grey whale is medium-sized with few throat grooves, a small head and no back fin. The sperm whale is a huge animal with a large, square head. Its skull yields a light oil called spermaceti.

Beaked whales have one or two pairs of teeth in the lower jaw and none in the upper. The group includes the bottlenose whale that lives on cuttlefish in the North Atlantic. The narwhal and the beluga, or white whale, are small-ish animals with a small back fin or none at all, and few teeth.

The dolphins are excellent swimmers and highly intelligent. Many of these small whales have been tamed and trained to perform tricks and carry out complicated manoeuvres. Some reports indicate that they are as intelligent as human beings. The killer whale or grampus has gained a reputation for unmatched ferocity, but recent

research shows that it may be a rather gentle creature in captivity.

Porpoises are small whales that are often seen leaping gracefully out of the water as they escort passing ships. The common or harbour porpoise lives in the North Atlantic.

There are also a few freshwater dolphins (also called long-beaked dolphins) that inhabit Asian and South American rivers. They have small, slender beaks full of teeth.

Seals and sea-lions
The seals and sea-lions are small to medium-sized beasts of prey that have adapted perfectly to their watery environment. Their bodies are torpedo-shaped and their limbs have become flippers. They are well protected by soft fur over a layer of fat. They are able to dive deep in the hunt for fish, which forms their main diet.

There are three families of seals. The eared seals are the only ones that have external ears. The largest of these is Steller's sea-lion, the bulls of which may reach nearly

four metres in length. The California seal-lion is the one most frequently seen in zoos and circuses. The Alaska fur seal is highly valued for its fur but is now strictly protected.

The second family is made up of seals that have no external ears. Their rear flippers point backwards, and on land they are clumsier than the sea-lions. The best known species is the common or harbour seal which is about two metres long.

The third family is made up of the walrus. Bulls may weigh up to 1.5 tonnes. They have deeply wringled skin, no external ears, and curved, ivory incisor teeth that are elongated into tusks up to 50 centimetres long.

Below: Whales range in size from the porpoise to the giant blue whale. They may be divided into two main groups: toothed whales, which have peg-like teeth; and baleen or whalebone whales, which have no teeth but instead have horny plates in their mouth through which they strain their food from the water. The narwhal has a spiral ivory tusk.

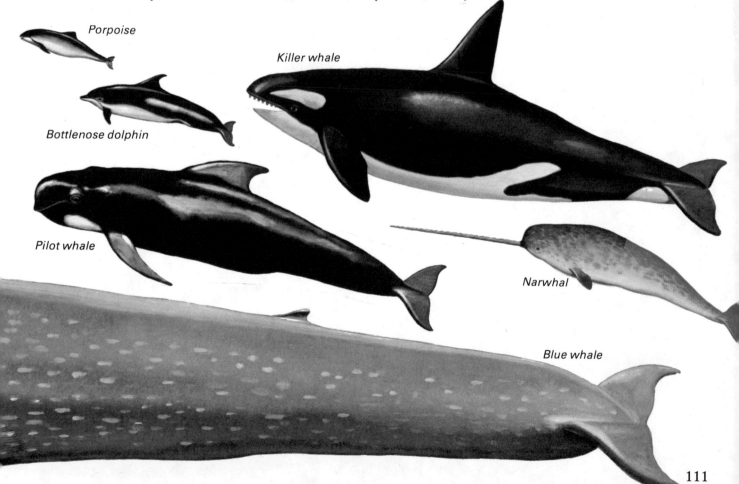

Porpoise

Killer whale

Bottlenose dolphin

Pilot whale

Narwhal

Blue whale

Primates

Below: The picture shows some typical central African monkeys in their natural surroundings. They are: (**1**) red colobus also known as red guereza; (**2**) the gorilla, the mightiest of the apes; (**3**) de Brazza's monkey; (**4**) white collared mangabey, a large, tree-dwelling baboon; and (**5**) the mandrill, the most powerful and fearsome of the baboons.

The order of primates is a large one, with some 193 species spread over 11 families. The word primate comes from a Latin word meaning "first". It is used to describe the highest order in the animal kingdom. Lemurs, tarsiers, monkeys, apes, and man belong to this order. Almost all its members have nails rather than claws or hooves. They all have five-toed feet, and in nearly every case the thumb is placed opposite the fingers to enable them to grasp branches and other objects easily. Most primates live in trees. They have good eyesight, with eyes that look straight ahead. They also have highly developed brains.

Individual families

The tree shrews form a family of what are known as semi-apes. They are a halfway stage between insect-eating animals, such as moles and hedgehogs, and the primates. They look rather like squirrels, with slender bodies and long, bushy tails.

The curious, ghostly lemurs are another family of semi-apes that live in Madagascar. They have large, luminous, yellowish-red eyes and wailing voices and they roam through the trees at night.

The members of the indris family, which also live in the forests of eastern Madagascar, have bare, dog-like faces and stunted, stubby tails. Unlike lemurs, they hunt by day, eating plants and small animals.

The aye-aye, with its bushy tail, big ears, and rodent-like teeth was for many years thought to be a kind of squirrel. But a nail on its big toe and the opposable thumb both show that it is a true primate. It also lives in Madagascar and moves through the trees by night.

Perhaps the most endearing family is made up of lorises, bushbabies, and pottos. The lorises, found in South-East Asia, are cat-sized with fur like that of a teddy bear. They have a very long claw on the second toe of the hind foot which they use as a comb when grooming, and also to dig out insects. The bushbaby or galago has a long, bushy tail, huge eyes, and outstanding, sensitive ears. The potto is similar to the loris but its coat is yellower and it is found only in Africa.

The tarsiers of South-East Asia are rare animals about the size of small dogs. They have a very long instep on their hind feet, almost no neck, hairless ears, and huge eyes. They have adhesive pads on their fingers, like a tree frog.

Monkeys

A sub-order of the primates is made up of the anthropoids. This word means "man-like", and it is used to describe the 400 or so living species of monkeys. There are five families to consider: the marmosets, New World monkeys, Old World monkeys, gibbons and great apes.

Marmosets are the smallest of all monkeys. They look and behave like squirrels and are found only in the Amazon Basin. Instead of nails they have claws on their feet which give them great climbing ability.

New World monkeys, as their name implies, are found only in the Americas. Most of them live in trees and are active by day. They differ from Old World monkeys mainly in having prehensile (grasping) tails, flat noses with nostrils set wide apart and directed sideways, and three premolar teeth. Species include the douroucouli or night monkey, a small animal with

owl-like eyes. It is the only monkey that is active at night. The howler monkey has a howling call that can be heard four kilometres away.

The Old World or narrow-nosed monkeys are found only in Asia and Africa with one exception. They have nostrils close together and only two premolar teeth. Some also have cheek pouches. They include the so-called Barbary apes which, apart from man, are the only primates to live in Europe. There is a small colony on the rock of Gibraltar.

The gibbons are the smallest of the apes and the most athletic. Like the great apes, they have long arms and no tails. They swing through the branches hand over hand or balance upright on their hind legs like a tightrope walker.

Apes

Then there are the three great apes: the orang-utan, chimpanzee and gorilla. These are the largest of all monkeys and man's nearest relatives. The orang-utan is the only Asian anthropoid. It is covered in rust-red hair and its long arms almost reach the ground. The chimpanzee, from the jungles of Africa, is possibly the most intelligent of the great apes and is a favourite in circuses. The gorilla is the largest of all the primates. A male may reach a height of nearly two metres and may weigh up to 350 kilograms. In spite of its massive bulk, the gorilla is an extremely gentle animal.

Left: The grivet monkey (**6**) also called the vervet, is a ground-dwelling guenon of the savannas; and (**7**) the Guinea baboon, a small, reddish, maned baboon, is restricted to a very small region in Africa.

Wildlife in danger

In 1600, it is estimated that there were 4,226 species of mammals. Since then, 40 have become extinct and at least 120 are threatened. Over 80 birds have also become extinct and 210 are threatened.

Extinction itself is a natural process. However, man is now speeding up the rate of extinction in a variety of ways. Traditionally, he has killed other animals for food and clothing. Some animals are also killed for sport and others because they are vermin. Modern technology has enabled man to kill more efficiently and in greater numbers. When whale hunting began in the 800s, for example, the hand-held harpoons he used were primitive and the number killed did not badly reduce the whale populations. In recent years, however, sonar has been used to locate whales. Large factory ships have been established at sea and modern harpoons, loaded with lethal explosives, are used. As a result, the bowhead right whale is already extinct, the sperm whale is threatened and the numbers of the blue whale, the world's largest animal measuring up to 30 metres long, have been drastically reduced.

Poisons that were meant to kill pests have also killed millions of other animals. D.D.T., a poisonous agricultural spray, has been found in Antarctic penguins thousands of kilometres away from where the spray was used. Seas, lakes and rivers have been polluted by industrial waste and millions of creatures have died and their breeding grounds have been destroyed.

Other animal habitats have also been destroyed by man's need for land for agriculture and building. In Malaya, the felling of trees for timber has destroyed the environment and it is believed there are only about 20 rhinoceroses left in the entire Malayan peninsula and about 300 seladang, which is a type of wild ox.

Fortunately we now know how easily a species can become extinct and greater care is taken to preserve animals and their environment if an area is to be exploited. The North Americans, for example, realized in time that the buffalo was on the verge of extinction and have managed to restore herds to about 20,000. There are other ways too in which man is working to undo the harm already done.

Conservation organizations

Most countries have a number of conservation organizations which do a great deal of valuable work. Most important, however, are the two international organizations, the International Union for Conservation of Nature and Natural Resources (I.U.C.N.) and the World Wildlife Fund (W.W.F.), which collect information on en-

Above: The tiger is an endangered species with its numbers falling all over the world. It was feared that there might be none left by the end of this century, so Operation Tiger was launched to protect the animal and save it from extinction.

dangered species and prompt world action to prevent any further loss.

Both organizations have worked closely to launch one of the most ambitious programmes yet undertaken – Operation Tiger. It was feared that the tiger would be extinct in the wild by the end of this century, with numbers already down all over the world. Many countries have taken part in the tiger conservation programme and new laws have been brought in to protect the animal.

Protected areas

Man has also created a large number of zoos, nature reserves and parks where animals are protected. Nature reserves may be as small as a pond where a particular animal has its breeding ground, while national parks often cover hundreds of square kilometres. National parks have a great advantage over zoos because the animals can roam freely and both habitat and animals are preserved. Some of the most famous of them are to be found in Africa, such as the Serengeti National Park in Tanzania and the Kruger National

The great auk was a big flightless bird that nested on the shores of North America, Greenland, Iceland and the British Isles. It was hunted to extinction in the 19th century.

Below: Before Europeans arrived in North America, over 60,000,000 buffalo are thought to have lived there. By 1875 only a few hundred were left. These were protected and there are now herds in many parts of North America.

Park in South Africa. Wild animals in Africa have recently become threatened as man competes with the animals for territory. In the 1930s in Uganda, for example, elephants roamed over 75 per cent of the country; now they are confined to little more than 20 per cent of it.

Zoos were in the past largely responsible for much of the destruction of wildlife as hunters competed for new animals to stock them. Today, however, attitudes have changed and a great deal of valuable research is done in zoos. There have been notable successes in breeding animals that otherwise would have died out. The wisent has been extinct in central Europe since 1921 but there are now 800 of these European bison in zoos.

Right: The giant redwood is one of the tallest trees in the world. Forests once stretched along the Californian coast, but now the tree only survives in reserves.

The past and the present

History is what happened both yesterday and at the beginning of time, and everything in between. It is about people and their problems, ordinary people and extraordinary people.

History is not just about wars and kings but about how much a servant was paid in 1900 and how Julius Caesar and Davy Crockett died.

War and peace

Some have claimed that the happiest nations have had no history, meaning that their stories have been about peace and prosperity and little else. Since 1815, Switzerland has been guaranteed her neutrality by the great European powers and therefore has seen very little excitement. Admirable of course, but being human most people prefer something racier. It does not have to be about war, though the great English novelist, Thomas Hardy, had a point when he wrote: "War makes rattling good history; but Peace is poor reading."

History through books

As long as history is properly taught and people read the right books, this need not prove true. One can get totally riveted by a good diarist like Samuel Pepys, or appalled by reading what happened to women and children in coal mines and factories in the 19th century. And now that so many more people travel abroad, it is so much better to know something about the country that one is

Below: The civilization of Ancient Egypt is the one that tends to catch people's imagination. Great monuments like the pyramids and the Sphinx, pictures and stories of the pharaohs and their treasures, help bring Ancient Egypt to life.

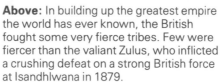

Above: In building up the greatest empire the world has ever known, the British fought some very fierce tribes. Few were fiercer than the valiant Zulus, who inflicted a crushing defeat on a strong British force at Isandhlwana in 1879.

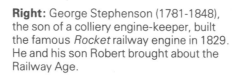

Right: George Stephenson (1781-1848), the son of a colliery engine-keeper, built the famous *Rocket* railway engine in 1829. He and his son Robert brought about the Railway Age.

visiting. Anyone going to, say, Naples, can read in advance about the history of Pompeii, before visiting the ruins. Anyone visiting the *Victory* in Portsmouth without knowing anything about Nelson in advance would miss much of interest on board.

Various people have insulted history, including some historians. Thomas Carlyle said it was a distillation of rumour, and indeed, a lot of "history" is mere guesswork. Carlyle also said that history was the biography of great men, but it is far more than that. It is the story of China and chess and cavalry and chemistry, as well as of Churchill, Custer and King Canute.

Henry Ford, the car-manufacturer, once said that history was bunk. He was in a witness box at the time and was no doubt under pressure.

Some would flatly contradict him and say we can learn from history. Things do repeat themselves, including man's mistakes, but never in quite the same manner.

So why should we read history, for few of us are statesmen who have to study the past? There are two reasons. The first is that the better informed we are, the more complete a person we become and the second, even more important reason, is that reading history can be fun.

People of the dawn

Every man, woman and child on earth is included in a single species known as *Homo sapiens*. This means wise or intelligent man in Latin, and reflects the fact that the size of his brain is larger and supposedly more developed.

Man is a primate, one of the highest orders of mammals that also includes the apes and monkeys. Just how closely he is related to them is still unclear. What is certain is that by about 30,000 years ago a modern-looking man had appeared, having slowly evolved over the previous 500,000 years.

What is a man?

If set against his near-man ancestors "man" and "human" are usually taken to mean someone who could make, and not just use, tools.

Scientists date early man's progress by various methods. Fossils can be dated by their position in the earth's rock strata. The amount of radioactive carbon in organic remains can be dated up to 50,000 years ago. The potassium-argon method reveals the age of volcanic rock strata and can go back 20 million years. Naturally, any find of ancient remains causes a sensation in scientific circles.

Early man appeared in a period we call the Pleistocene. The near-men of those days stood almost erect, were short, and had small brains. That was about a million years ago. *Homo erectus* (upright man) appeared about 500,000 years later. The new men knew about tools and fire and almost certainly could speak. Remains of this type of man were found in Java in the 1890s and in China in the 1920s.

Experts believe that some of the most important advances made by certain types of early man took place as they adapted to the huge changes in climate that were then occurring. In a harsh world only the fittest of the species survived while the weaker, less adaptable members died out.

Peking man

Neanderthal man

Cro-Magnon man

Above: The development of man's ancestors, from Peking man to Cro-Magnon man, took about 800,000 years. The Neanderthalers died out only 30,000 years ago.

Neanderthal man

The best known of all the early men are the Neanderthalers. Their name comes from the valley in Germany where their remains were first found in 1856.

Nowadays, "Neanderthal" is sometimes used, somewhat unflatteringly, to describe a person who looks ape-like and rather unintelligent, but that is an insult to the Neanderthalers, who might well have inherited the earth. Admittedly, they look brutish to us, but their brains were large and they ranged over Europe, Africa and Asia.

They lived in dangerous times, from around 300,000 to 30,000 B.C., by which time their distant cousins – ourselves – had replaced them. Neanderthal man had to

Above and **below:** Many early houses had strong walls and thatched roofs.

Below: One of the greatest discoveries in humanity's long history was how to make fire. Rubbing sticks together must have been the classic way, though many soon learnt to use a fire drill.

Below: A prehistoric man painting on the wall of a cave, and painting with great skill. The discovery of cave paintings, such as those at Lascaux in France, caused tremendous excitement.

contend with great mammoths and other huge creatures of the Ice Age. Why he died out remains a mystery.

Stone Age cultures

There are still people today who live like early *Homo sapiens,* though soon there will be none. A new tribe is sometimes discovered deep in the heart of Amazonia in South America, still living in the Stone Age and never having seen a white man. The Tasaday tribe were discovered a few years ago in a remote cave in the Philippines. Red Indians had a Stone Age culture before Columbus and his successors reached the New World.

The Old, Middle and New Stone Ages, the Bronze Age and the Iron Age are the simple and vivid ways of describing the progress of man. Even in the Old Stone Age, beginning about 500,000 years ago, when simple stone tools were made and fire was used, some men had learnt to paint on the walls of caves. While by the New Stone

Age animals were being tamed and crops grown.

The New Stone Age flourished in the Middle and Near East from about 6000 B.C. and in Europe some 3,000 years later. And it was in the east that the Bronze and Iron Ages started. Iron was being used in parts of Europe from about 1000 B.C.

The first real communities date from the New Stone Age where, as usual, the Near East and the Middle East led the way and the rest of the world finally followed.

The oldest walled town that is known to us may possibly have been the Biblical city of Jericho. It is thought to have had some 3,000 inhabitants nearly 10,000 years ago. The village of Zawi Chemi Shanidar in Iraq is about 1,000 years older. It was found only in 1957.

These two amazing facts make a fitting prelude to our look at the world's first civilizations. That little village had perhaps 150 inhabitants, yet ancient Rome was to top the million mark by 100 B.C.

The first civilizations

While Europe was still in the Stone Age, the first civilizations began in the Near and Middle East. They arose on the fertile lands beside rivers in warm climates. The towns and cities that grew up there were based on settled agriculture and trading in the surplus crops that these regions produced.

These changes began around 4000 B.C. in Egypt and Sumer, which is now part of Iraq, and is the rich farmland between the rivers Tigris and Euphrates, which flow into the Persian Gulf. The Greek name for this area was Mesopotamia – "between the rivers".

The Sumerians cultivated grain and built irrigation canals. They made fine jewellery and pottery and invented a form of writing. They were ruled by priests and built large temples called ziggurats, walled cities and many smaller towns. But around 2500 B.C., fierce tribesmen from the north overwhelmed them.

Egypt

Meanwhile, a far greater civilization had been growing along the River Nile. It was to last for 3,000 years. Ancient Egypt was blessed by her river. On each side was a strip of rich and fertile soil, gradually merging into desert. For about 100 days every year, the Nile overflowed her banks and deposited rich, fertile mud over the surrounding area.

Around 3100 B.C., when Egypt was first united into a single nation, the people had learnt to irrigate and to use the plough.

Despite periods of bitter civil wars and unrest, Egypt, under her succession of god-kings, or Pharaohs, was to remain a nation until the death of the last ruler, Queen Cleopatra, in 30 B.C. No empire in history has lasted longer.

The key figures in the land were the scribes. Having been taught to read and write at school, along with law, mathematics and other subjects, all the key jobs were open to them: priest, engineer, architect, lawyer and diplomat.

Sports included archery and hunting and horses were used after they were introduced to Egypt around 1500 B.C. The Egyptians were not particularly warlike except when they had to be, though some Pharaohs boasted of their triumphs. In fact, it was partly due to the hiring of too many foreign mercenaries that they were finally overrun by other powers.

Though the splendid towns of Ancient Egypt have vanished, there are many monuments left to astound us. The amazing pyramids were tombs of the Pharaohs, the biggest being the Great Pyramid of King Cheops consisting of about 2,300,000 blocks of stone. Contrary to legend, it was not built by millions of slaves, but mostly by workers when their fields were flooded by the Nile and had become therefore, unworkable.

The pyramids were filled with all a Pharaoh would need in the next world, but tomb-robbers wanted the treasures too, so later rulers were buried in secret in tombs in a place now known as the Valley of the Kings. Even there the robbers struck, but they did not find the tomb of the young Pharaoh Tutankhamun. His tomb treasures were discovered only in 1922.

While Egypt flourished, Sumer, as we have seen, fell. A king named Hammurabi set up the Babylonian empire in 1792 B.C. and ruled it brilliantly. Next came the warlike Assyrians, who toppled the Babylonians and captured Thebes, Egypt's capital.

The Assyrians fell to the Babylonian Chaldeans, whose king Nebuchadnezzar transported the Jews to Babylon. But the Chaldeans were overrun by the Medes and Persians under Cyrus the Great, and by 525 B.C. the Persians ruled the Middle East.

Above: The magnificent golden funerary mask of Tutankhamun.

Left: The inside of the tomb of the young Pharaoh Tutankhamun.

Below: At the height of her power, Assyria had one of the finest armies in history, and certainly one of the most terrifying. Lord Byron's famous line, "The Assyrian came down like a wolf on the fold", describes what it must have been like for their less warlike enemies. They had a special corps of engineers, who came into their own when a walled town was being besieged. Chariots were another Assyrian speciality, the prowess of the charioteers making them greatly feared. The capital of Assyria was Nineveh, a huge, strongly fortified city. Nineveh – and Babylon – fell in 612 B.C.

Greeks and Romans

"The glory that was Greece and the grandeur that was Rome" — that was how the American writer, Edgar Allan Poe, summed up the two greatest civilizations of the ancient world.

Greece's story began some 3,000 years ago on the island of Crete and at Mycenae on the mainland. By around 1000 B.C. Greek-speaking tribes had covered the region around Mycenae. Because of the mountainous landscape, small settlements sprang up in each valley, each cut off from the other. These became city-states.

The Greeks were a quarrelsome lot. Most of them went through periods of rule by kings, nobles, tyrants, then government by a few citizens or democratic government.

Sparta was the odd city out. From around 600-370 B.C. it was the most military nation-state in history. If a baby boy was weak in any way he was abandoned on a mountain at birth. If fit, he joined the army at seven and left at 60!

From 500-449 B.C. the Greeks were threatened by the Persians, but the city-states combined to defeat them in a series of land and sea battles.

Now began an age of glory for Athens, with leaders like Pericles, thinkers like Socrates, and play-wrights, sculptors and architects. Alas, the iron men of Sparta conquered them. Then all Greece fell to the half-barbaric Macedonian Greeks under their king Philip.

His son was Alexander the Great, whose conquests ranged as far as Egypt and India. But when he died in 323 B.C., his empire

Above: The Roman legion was a very well organized force of 5,000 men led by a legatus and six tribunes. The men were divided into ten cohorts each. These were divided into centuries of 100 men. Each century was led by a centurion *(above left)*. On the march a legionary *(above)* carried his equipment on a long staff. He put his armour in a bag and slung his helmet on a thong. The block diagram shows a legion in battle order. The legion lay in a slight semi-circle and the cohorts were arranged in two rows. The bravest and more experienced soldiers were stationed on either flank.

Right: The theatre at Epidaurus in Greece, where plays are still put on. Greek dramatists such as Sophocles, Aeschylus and Euripides gave the world its first great comedies and tragedies.

collapsed. Rome easily swallowed Greece in 146 B.C. but, happily, absorbed her culture too.

The Romans

The Romans expanded from a small settlement on seven hills above the River Tiber to become masters of the ancient world. By around 500 B.C. they had freed themselves from the clutches of a notable people called the Etruscans and had begun to build their great republic.

Hard-working, patriotic and wise, good farmers and fine soldiers, the Romans had conquered all Italy by 275 B.C. The people had some power, but the real rulers were the senators, who were nobles and leading citizens.

To gain mastery of the Mediterranean, the Romans fought three wars against Carthage in North Africa, finally razing it to the ground in 146 B.C., long after the great Carthaginian general Hanni-

bal was dead. It was he who had crossed the Alps during the second of the wars, complete with elephants.

Alas, Rome became so rich from her victory that her standards declined. Too much luxury, too many slaves, too many hired soldiers who supported generals, not the state, weakened her.

However, Rome was at the height of her power and there was peace and efficient government. Finally, Christianity was adopted as the official religion but only after much persecution of the Christians.

It failed to stop the rot. Wild German tribes began to invade the empire, which was in sharp decline. The Emperor Constantine moved his capital to Byzantium, later called Constantinople and today Istanbul. Back in Italy the wild tribes ravaged the countryside and took Rome more than once. The great city became a mere shell, although it had once housed a million people. But, as we shall see, Rome's influence was too strong to be wiped out altogether.

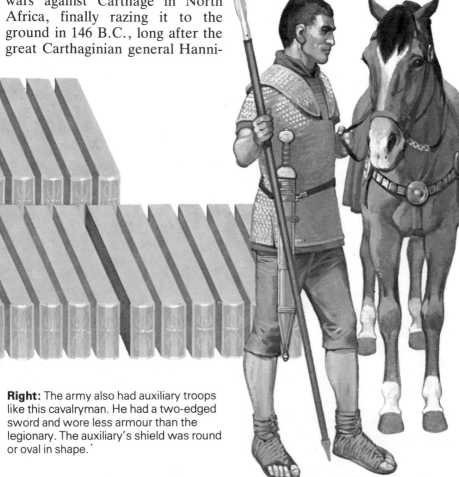

Right: The army also had auxiliary troops like this cavalryman. He had a two-edged sword and wore less armour than the legionary. The auxiliary's shield was round or oval in shape.

China through the ages

China is Asia's largest country and she has had a continuous civilization longer than any other nation. Her recorded history goes back more than 3,000 years and, despite periods of chaos and barbarism down through the centuries, she has often emerged as one of the world's great powers, as she continues to be today.

This great survivor is also the world's most populous nation. Its population passed the 1,000 million mark in the 1980s.

The heartland of early China was the area between the Yellow River (the Hwang-Ho) and the Yangtze to the south.

Before China's true history began, there was a half legendary period when emperors called Hsai ruled from around 2900–1523 B.C. During this period the Emperor Huang Ti is said to have taught his people to rear silkworms and grow mulberry leaves for the worms to feed on.

Left: *Homo sapiens* was an early example of our own species. He is known as Peking man because his remains were found in a cave near Peking in China.

Right: Early in their history, the Chinese became expert artists and craftsmen. This striking bronze piece dates from the Shang dynasty.

Shang, Chou and Ch'in dynasties

In 1523 B.C. the Shang dynasty of rulers came to power in China. The Shangs were both emperors and high priests and their people were divided into classes of priests, nobles, peasants and craftsmen working in a number of city states. Ancestors were worshipped and sacrifices made to nature gods. Examples of writing have been found from this period.

Next came the Chou (1122–256 B.C.). They were ferocious invaders from the north, but they settled down, and though their long reign finally ended in chaos, it was also a golden age of thought and learning.

The most famous thinker was Confucius, who urged people to revere their ancestors and parents and be moderate in all things. He preached charity and love at a time when most of the rest of the world

Left: Confucius (551-479 B.C.) was a great Chinese thinker and scholar who preached the importance of tradition and hierarchy.

was at war.

After the chaos came the Ch'in (256–207 B.C.). The Emperor Shih Hwang-ti was something of a superman, who is remembered for three things. He extended the empire; he built the amazing Great Wall of China to keep out the wild barbarians; and he ordered all historical documents to be burnt to stop his subjects thinking about the glorious past and so concentrate on him. Happily, he did not completely succeed, and when his son was killed, a great new dynasty began.

Han, Sui and T'ang dynasties

This was the Han dynasty (202 B.C.–A.D. 221). China prospered in both war and peace, and in the arts and literature. The writing brush, ink and paper were widely used. The teachings of Confucius were revived and the worship of Buddha came to China from India. Fine porcelain was now being made.

A brilliant civil service ran the nation. You had to be good at exams to get into it, and the exam system lasted until the 19th century!

This great age ended in a period of chaos resulting from an internal civil war. But at last the Sui dynasty (A.D. 589–620) reunited the land and people and the T'ang (620–907) completed the process.

The T'ang dynasty was founded by the great Li Shih-min. While Europe was still in the Dark Ages, China, with her scholars honoured above all others, was the most advanced civilization in the world. The Silk Road, a long caravan route that ended at the eastern Mediterranean, linked her with the West.

Mongols

Alas, civil war broke out yet again, though the Sung (960–1269) finally re-established order in the south. Chinese culture was saved, but it did not advance. Her scholars resisted all change, and this was to harm their country in the future.

Now barbarians whose names are still famous attacked China. The cruel Genghis Khan overran the

Right: A memorial dedicated to Sun-Yat-Sen who died in 1925. He overthrew the Manchus and became president of China in 1911.

north, while his grandson, Kublai Khan, became emperor of all China in 1279.

Yet these were brilliant barbarians, as the Italian explorer Marco Polo found when he visited Kublai in 1275. At last Europeans were free to visit the fabulous country and trade with her freely.

Around 1350 the Mongols (Genghis Khan had come from Mongolia) lost control. The Ming under Chu-Yuan-Chang reigned from 1368 to 1644. Under them, Peking became one of the world's great capitals.

Europeans appeared in increasing numbers. They were considered barbarians, and many were just that. Only Catholic priests were welcome because they behaved and brought scientific knowledge.

The 20th century

The Ming fell to the Manchu dynasty (1644–1912) and more "foreign devils" moved into the country. The Manchus began to lose their grip and were unable to contain the grasping Europeans, who set up outposts on the coast. A rebellion against the whites failed in 1900, while the growing might of Japan cut into China's territory.

The Manchus tried to modernize but it was too late. In 1911 a revolution broke out and Sun-Yat-Sen became president the year after.

His successor, Chiang-Kai-Shek, led the fight against the Japanese in the 1930s and 1940s, but now a new force, communism, was on the march. In 1949, Mao-Tse-tung was able to proclaim the People's Republic of China a communist state.

China's history still continues to be startling. Since Mao's death in 1976 this vast nation has reopened real links with the West. The Chinese people have absorbed more outside influences and more Westerners are able to visit the country to form their own impressions of it.

Left: The Workers' Stadium in Peking crammed with soldiers holding copies of their leader Mao's "Thoughts". China today is less rigid in style.

The Dark Ages

Below: Peaceful coastal and inland communities in many parts of Europe were devastated when the terrible Norsemen erupted among them. Strangely, many of these barbaric invaders settled down and had become townsmen and traders within two generations.

Nowadays, historians object to the phrase "Dark Ages", used to describe European history from the fall of the Roman Empire in the west to around 750. Archaeologists have proved that the barbarians who overwhelmed Rome had a culture of their own and that European civilization did not collapse completely. The Christian Church kept it alive.

Of course, the experts are right. Yet things must have seemed dark enough to civilized Roman Britons confronted by bloodthirsty bands of Angles, Saxons and Jutes after the Roman legions had left to defend Rome in the 5th century.

Some of the barbarians who invaded Italy were already half-Christian and partly under the powerful influence of Rome even as it declined. It is no accident that Latin, the Roman language, is the basis of many languages, including Italian, French and Spanish.

By 597, St. Augustine was preaching to the new pagan rulers of what had been Roman Britain. Wales, Scotland and Ireland had been converted to Christianity earlier.

The eastern Roman Empire still flourished at Byzantium (Constantinople). Their empire stretched from Greece to Egypt. Barbarians laid siege to the great city, but it survived.

The Franks and the Arabs

In the west, the greatest of the Germanic tribes were the Franks, who gave France their name. Their fierce ruler Clovis (465–511) was an important convert for Christianity and really founded the Frankish kingdom. The kings that followed him conquered most of what are now the Common Market countries, excluding Britain. Charles the Great (Charlemagne) ruled over a huge empire from 771–814. In recognition of his role in winning new lands for the Christian faith he was crowned Holy Roman Emperor by the Pope in 800.

His empire collapsed at his death, splitting into different kingdoms. Far worse, Europe was attacked by

Above: The Battle of Puig in Spain between Moors and Christians in 1237. According to legend, St George, riding on horseback, came to the Christians' aid. The last Moors were driven out of Spain in 1492. Yet by then many had settled down to become law-abiding citizens.

two ferocious enemies.

A new religion, Islam (*see page 136*) preached by the prophet Mohammed, was on the march. It was more than a way of life it was a fighting creed. Constantinople lost its empire to the Arabs while the followers of Islam converted the fierce Moors of North Africa into Muslims. The Moors overran Spain and poured across the Pyrenees into Frankish territories. They were halted in 732 by Charles Martel in a ferocious battle at Poitiers which saved Europe from being overrun.

In fact, the Arabs were far more cultured at this time than the Europeans. They excelled in learning and the arts, and their great city of Baghdad was the centre of a true civilization. They were the contact zone between the Greeks in the west and the Chinese in the east.

Scandinavian invaders

Meanwhile, from the 8th century onwards, daring raiders were sailing from Scandinavia in their powerful "long-ships". They raided countries as far afield as Ireland and Russia. Known variously as Vikings, Norsemen or Danes, each of their names spelt terror in the lands they invaded.

Left: A bronze Celtic wine flagon.

Right: A mosaic of Charlemagne.

Overcrowding, love of adventure and squabbles at home caused them to set out in ships which could even brave the Atlantic Ocean. They reached Iceland in 863 and probably America around 1000. They set up the first Russian state called Novgorod in 862. They sailed up the major rivers of Europe, plundering and murdering. They ravaged England, Scotland, Ireland, Wales and the Isle of Man. They menaced the Mediterranean. But they, too, failed to take Constantinople.

It seemed they would conquer all England, but Alfred the Great halted them in 878 at Edington. Yet in England and elsewhere within a generation or two, the terrible Norsemen had settled down to become excellent colonists, traders and townsmen. They accepted Christianity and brought their strong rule to Europe. This showed most of all in Normandy in France where the grandchildren of Norse raiders became the Normans, one of the most disciplined and strong-minded races in the world.

They had another triumph in England, where in the 11th century King Canute ruled over an Anglo-Danish empire. This, while it lasted, made England the southern tip of Scandinavia. But the Norse cousins of Canute and his men, having settled in Normandy, had other ideas.

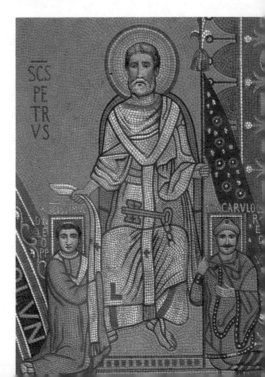

Europe takes shape

In 1066, a date that is familiar to many English people, William the Conqueror defeated King Harold at Hastings.

Total disaster appeared to strike the English. Their nobles lost their lands and powers to William and his Normans. The poor became near slaves of foreign masters. Yet in the long run Norman blood, discipline and strength proved a blessing. Meanwhile, in the grim aftermath of the conquest, the English had become part of Europe because William was still Duke of Normandy.

He brought the feudal system with him. His lords were given

Above: In the course of a siege in the Middle Ages, archers kept up a steady attack on the castle. If necessary, they used wooden shields to protect themselves. Meanwhile battering rams, catapults and scaling ladders were used to try to penetrate the castle defences. This siege is taking place in the 13th century. Later, gunpowder transformed siege warfare.

lands in return for military service and the system laid down the position of all classes including the serfs.

As well as powerful castles, the Normans built glorious cathedrals in Normandy and England. Gradually, the nightmare of the Conquest was forgotten. The English language survived and was finally used by the Normans.

Ireland was invaded and partly subdued, and the valiant Welsh were conquered by Edward I, who died in 1307. Neither he nor his successors could subdue the Scots. England was not yet Britain.

Charlemagne created a body known as the Holy Roman Empire, as we saw on page 127, but his empire died with him. In 962, Otto I revived it with the Pope's blessing. It lasted until 1806.

However, papal power often clashed with imperial power. Otto's empire included basically Germany and Italy, but his successors were not his family: they were elected by clergy and nobles. Church and State clashed continually over the election of officials. Even the greatest emperor of the period, Frederick II (1194-1250), could not dominate the Pope.

France and England at war

As for France, held back by the power of Normandy and England, she did not come into her own until the reign of Philippe Auguste, who drove out the Norman English. By his death in 1223, he had made France a European power.

From 1095-1272, the leading European powers launched Crusades to free the Holy Land from Islam. Many went mainly for adventure and loot. Each side had its heroes, including Richard the Lionheart of England and Saladin, the Muslim ruler of Egypt.

France now seemed poised for greatness, but its prosperity was ruined by the Hundred Years' War with England (1339-1453). Edward III claimed the French crown and at first all went England's way, especially after Crécy (1346) where English longbowmen defeated the mounted French nobility. Eighty years later the French found a champion in Joan of Arc, and finally England lost all her French territories. After the long wars only Calais remained hers. Only for a brief period under Henry V, the victor of Agincourt, had English arms triumphed in the last years of the war. Now it was England's turn to be ravaged by the civil war known as the Wars of the Roses.

This struggle was between the rival houses of Lancaster and York and finally ended when Richard III was defeated in 1485 and Henry VII became the first Tudor king.

Eastern Europe

When the Vikings fought and traded their way into Russia in the ninth century, they were welcomed by the barbaric Slav peoples there as allies in the fight against invaders from the east.

The newcomers set up duchies in Novgorod and Kiev, and the Slavs became Christian. Their religion was Greek Orthodox not Catholicism.

From the 13th century, the terrible Tartars and Mongols poured out of Asia, where Genghis Khan and his descendants (*see page 124*) had established a mighty empire. They cut deep into Europe, then fell back, but not from Russia, whose leaders were forced to pay them tribute. The whole of southern Russia was part of the Tartar Empire and not until the 1550s were the Tartars finally driven out. By then Moscow had long been the country's chief city.

Moscow's rulers were influenced more by the east than by the west at this time, not least because a terrible blow had befallen Christendom. Constantinople had fallen to the Turks in 1453.

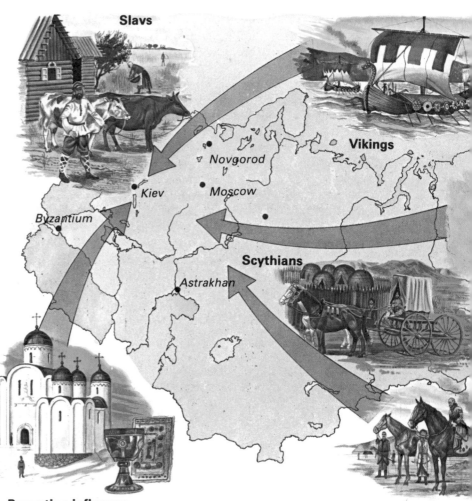

Slavs

Vikings

Novgorod

● *Kiev* ● *Moscow*

● *Byzantium*

Scythians

● *Astrakhan*

Byzantine influence

Above: One of two Turkish pirates, known as Barbarossa (red-beard), who terrorized the Mediterranean early in the 16th century. Suleiman the Magnificent made Barbarossa his Grand Admiral, and he won much treasure for Suleiman.

Right: The donkey as a means of transport is a common sight in central Turkey today.

The Ottomans

The Turkish Empire had started to invade Europe in 1355 using, as well as Muslim Turkish soldiers, a picked force called the Janissaries. These were Christian youths, taken from their parents who were prisoners-of-war, converted into Muslims and trained as soldiers who were almost as ruthlessly disciplined as the Spartans (*see page 122*).

The peoples of Eastern Europe faced the Turkish threat valiantly, but their sheer numbers and determination beat them back to the River Danube. Fortunately for the future of Europe, the Tartars chose this dangerous moment to sweep down on Turkey from the rear, and a mighty Christian force was raised to fight the Turks, or the Ottoman Empire as their domains were then called.

But Constantinople, the most fabulous city in Europe, possessor

Golden Horde

Tartars

had let him down. Naturally, he suffered a crushing defeat. Hungary thus fell to Turkey and the road to Austria was now open.

Suleiman was a great ruler and a fine general and Turkey prospered under him. But luckily for Europe, Turkey declined after his death. The Spanish and Austrians smashed her sea power at Lepanto in 1571 and a century later John III of Poland saved Vienna from a huge Turkish army in 1683. Other victories followed and the Turkish Empire, vast as it still was, was never the same again.

Left: A succession of invaders stormed into Russia during the Middle Ages. The Golden Horde were the Mongolian Tartars, the name coming from the splendour of one of their leader's tents.

Above: Suleiman the Magnificent of Turkey (1494-1566) conquered much of what is now called the Balkans. This miniature painting shows him hawking, a favourite sport of the sultans.

of unimaginable riches, could not this time be saved. After a siege lasting eight weeks, the city fell to Sultan Mahomet II. Now indeed the Roman Empire had finally fallen.

The sultans of Turkey took over the great city and made it a Muslim one. It had a different splendour and was renamed Istanbul. Meanwhile, where would the Turks strike next?

Their target was Vienna and if Vienna fell, Western Europe would face a grave threat. A great battle was fought at Mohacs in Hungary in 1526 between Louis II of Hungary and Bohemia and Suleiman the Magnificent. Louis had a mere 28,000 soldiers against Suleiman's 200,000, for his allies

Right: The spectacular Cathedral of the Assumption in Moscow, which was built in the 15th century as a private church for the ruling tsars.

The Renaissance

Above: A portrait of Queen Elizabeth I, when she was 25, by an unknown artist. She is wearing her robes of state.

Below: A picture of the Italian city of Florence, the artistic heart of the Renaissance, and still a breathtaking sight.

The Middle Ages was a period when religious thought dominated everything – when the finest achievements were glorious and majestic cathedrals. A reaction was bound to follow.

What began as a revolution in art and literature in Italy around 1350 later spread to plays, architecture, science, politics, religion, medicine and exploration.

Immortal figures like Leonardo da Vinci, Shakespeare, Columbus and Raleigh were just some of the great names in an age that lasted until around 1600. Leonardo was an engineer, architect and scientist as well as a painter and sculptor, while Sir Walter Raleigh was a soldier, sailor, explorer, poet, scientist, writer, courtier and statesman. Theirs was a many-sided genius.

Anything seemed possible in that glorious period when the emphasis was on life and the living, rather than the next world and death. It was called the Renaissance. The word means re-birth in French and it is not too fanciful to say that the spirit of European man was being reborn in the Renaissance.

Renaissance men

The age began when Italian writers and poets started rediscovering the literature of Greece and Rome. The poet Petrarch and the writer

Above: A detail from Michelangelo's marvellous series of paintings in the Vatican's Sistine Chapel in Rome. The portrait is of the prophet Isaiah.

Boccaccio, whose *Decameron* placed him as "the father of the novel", led the way in the 14th century. The movement grew as scholars fled to Italy from Constantinople which, as was related on the previous page, fell to the Turks in 1453. The scholars brought with them priceless ancient manuscripts.

Meanwhile, a number of artists and sculptors were flourishing, many of them based in Florence. Botticelli, Leonardo da Vinci, Donatello and Michelangelo were just some of them. They, too, were influenced by Greece and Rome, especially their myths.

The artists were helped by the fact that a new rising class of Italian merchants had money to spend on beautifying their houses and becoming patrons of the arts. This made the artist freer, as did commissions from the great nobles. Previously, he had normally been hired by the Church and had not been free to express himself. In fact, the Church itself no longer demanded such a formal artistic style, and became a patron of the new artists. Some of the period's crowning glories were Michelangelo's paintings in the Sistine Chapel in Rome.

The spread of culture was transformed by the development of printing, which dates in Europe from the 15th century. Printed books became available to all literate people, although they were not cheap. One book that had special influence was *The Prince* by the Italian Machiavelli. It was a tough, often cruel age and the book told nobles how to retain power even by wicked and unscrupulous methods.

Science had been virtually dead in the Middle Ages but now brilliant scientists also appeared. This was perhaps the most far-reaching aspect of the age. For centuries science had been discouraged by the Church, largely through fear and ignorance. Copernicus, the father of modern astronomy, discovered that the earth went round the Sun. The great astronomer-physicist, Galileo, faced trouble with the Church authorities for his Copernican beliefs because they went against the Church's teachings. So did the remarkable Vesalius, the father of modern anatomy, who became professor of surgery at Padua, which was to become the centre of European medical research.

Religion was affected by the Renaissance and the spread of new thought that led to the Reformation *(see page 136)*, when many people left the Roman Catholic Church. There were religious as well as artistic explosions in those turbulent times when the questioning of beliefs was the order of the day.

The age of exploration, as can be seen overleaf, was another expression of the Renaissance in action. No longer were the confines of Christendom enough for man. This new freedom had to be expressed and each country expressed it in its own way.

The Renaissance in England

England's Renaissance period came later, after the country had settled down from the Wars of the Roses in the 15th century and the storms of religious controversy in Henry VIII's reign. The amazing flowering of talent came in the second half of Elizabeth I's reign. William Shakespeare, England's and some would say the world's, greatest poet and playwright, was the crowning glory of the age, but he could not have existed alone. There were poets such as Edmund Spenser and Philip Sidney, musicians such as William Byrd, and playwrights such as Christopher Marlowe and Ben Jonson.

So it was that the spirit of the Renaissance conquered Europe.

Below: Another painting by Michelangelo, who was equally famous as a sculptor. So famous did he become that in his own time he earned the title "divine".

New worlds

In 1295 the Italian traveller Marco Polo had returned from his epic journey to China, bringing news of the splendours he had seen. How to get at these treasures of the East became the great question. By the 15th century, however, it had become vital to find a sea-route, for the Turks and Arabs had blockaded the land routes.

Columbus and America

Christopher Columbus wanted to reach the Indies (India) by sailing west at a time when most people still believed that the earth was flat. It was therefore feared that he would sail over the edge. He may have known about the Viking voyages westwards, but he had no idea that America was in the way.

Failing to get Portuguese help, Columbus, who was a sailor from Genoa in Italy, persuaded Queen Isabella of Spain to back him, and he set out with the *Santa Maria* and two other small ships in 1492. It was a famous year in Europe's history, for that year Spain was finally freed from the Moors. Some might find that description unjust, for the Moors were hard-working and artistic and a great loss to Spain.

Columbus reached a small island in what is now called the Bahamas on 12th October 1492, imagining he had reached Asia.

Spanish and Portuguese conquests

In less than 50 years, Spanish conquerors, bearing the Cross and eager for gold, had conquered Mexico and Peru and had built up a huge empire in the New World. Central and South America, apart from Brazil which Portugal colonized, belonged to Spain and she took parts of North America, such as Florida, soon afterwards.

It was a Spanish expedition that first sailed round the world, though its leader, Magellan, was killed on the voyage in 1521. He pioneered the route around Cape Horn, the southernmost tip of South America. Portugal pioneered the eastern sea-route to Asia. The Portuguese learnt to brave the Atlantic in tough craft called caravels. Sailors were trained in a special school set up by Prince Henry the Navigator,

Below: The Incas of Peru were ruled by a god-king, seen here travelling about his kingdom. The Incas, though advanced in many ways, did not have the wheel. In 1532, the Inca Empire was conquered by a handful of Spaniards under Pizarro, who came searching for gold.

notably Sir Francis Drake, played havoc with Spain's treasure fleets. Drake led the second expedition to go round the world, returning with vast riches. Religion had by then entered into the struggle, with Protestant England set against Catholic Spain, and there was also a Catholic queen in Scotland with Mary, Queen of Scots, on the throne.

The climax of these stirring times came when Philip's "invincible armada" was utterly defeated by a combination of English seamanship and the weather in 1588.

England's first successful colonies in North America were established at Jamestown in Virginia in 1607 and at New Plymouth in Massachusetts in 1620, where the Pilgrim Fathers landed.

From these two settlements and others that followed there grew a freedom-loving British race who would one day rebel against Britain. In New France (Canada) the French were building an empire. Other races were interested in North America, too, including the Dutch who built New Amsterdam, which later became New York.

though the prince never left home himself. Finally, in 1498, 28 years after Henry's death, Vasco da Gama reached the west coast of India. Portugal set up colonies there and in Africa. The setting up of a sea-route to the Far East was of great importance to the Western European economy.

The 16th century seemed destined to belong to Spain. Charles V, the Holy Roman Emperor, who was crowned in 1520, ruled a colossal empire that stretched from Germany to Spain and was rapidly embracing more and more of the New World. But his son Philip, who was married for a time to Henry VIII's daughter Mary, found himself later in the century up against the England of Elizabeth I, Mary's sister.

England's contribution
Elizabeth's sea-dogs (sailors), most

Above: When the Spanish Armada took shelter in Calais Roads, the English sent in fireships, causing havoc. The Armada took to sea again, and the English seamen and the weather utterly destroyed it.

Below: William Penn (1644-1718) was given a grant of land in America which he made a haven for Quakers. He signed fair treaties with the Indians, unlike most of his fellow countrymen.

Religious rivalries

A German miner's son grew up to be a priest, but not an ordinary one. He became a revolutionary who changed the world. His name was Martin Luther (1483-1546) and he challenged his own Roman Catholic church. More than anyone else he founded the great "protesting" religious movement – Protestantism. He was also the founder of the Reformation.

Reform was badly needed. There had been churchmen who had agitated for reform earlier, but to no avail. Popes were political as well as religious leaders and many men went into the church simply to gain power.

As we saw on pages 132-3, the Renaissance not only changed the arts, but thought as well. Thus religious attitudes had begun to change, too. Europe was in a turmoil which was bound to spill over into the sphere of religion. Luther gave it the decisive push in 1517.

A friar arrived in Wittenberg where Luther lived and began peddling indulgences. For enough money, the sins of his listeners and their dead relations would be forgiven. Officially, the money went to build St Peter's in Rome and fill the church coffers, though there were plenty of chances for pocketing some. Many were appalled by indulgences, but only Luther acted. He nailed up 95 theses (arguments) against them on the church door. Each one struck at the heart of the all-powerful Catholic Church.

Religious wars in Europe

Luther was denounced and was lucky to survive many dangerous moments in his life. Controversy raged like a forest fire across Europe. Tragically, it led to bitter wars between Catholics and Protestants, so fierce were the feelings on each side. Tudor England escaped without a religious war, though a few hundred were executed for their rival faiths. France was torn apart by civil war and many thousands of Protestants

Above: The Catholic Church instituted the Spanish Inquisition to stamp out heresy, burning and torturing victims who did not repent. The Inquisition was by far the most ruthless in its early days. It lasted from 1478-1820.

Above: Martin Luther was the man who, more than any other, started the Reformation, and was the founder of the breakaway faith of Protestantism.

Below: A typical battle scene of the English Civil War between the Cavaliers (the King's men) and the Roundheads (Parliament's). It was a religious as well as a political struggle.

died. In 1598 the Edict of Nantes gave the French Protestants, known as Huguenots, freedom to practise their religion in peace. Alas, in 1685, King Louis XIV banished them and many fled to England.

Germany suffered appalling civil wars until, in 1555, the various German states were allowed to choose whether they would be Catholic or Protestant. The north became mainly Protestant, the south mainly Catholic.

The Netherlands suffered terribly for their Protestantism. Their Spanish rulers started up the horrifying Inquisition. Those who would not give up the new faith were tortured or burnt.

Meanwhile, the Catholic Church, faced with such a massive rebellion, set about putting its house in order. In a way, the Reformation was its salvation.

Without it, the Roman Catholic church might have gradually declined. As it was, it recovered and remains the largest Christian faith.

The 17th century saw Germany ravaged by the 30 Years' War, which was both political and religious. King Gustavus Adolphus of Sweden came to the aid of the Protestants and, finally, in 1648, the war ended with the divisions remaining much as before. Now the Holy Roman Empire was centred on Austria.

England's great civil war in the mid-17th century was mainly political, with Parliament set against Charles I. The result of Parliament's victory was that the king was beheaded in 1649.

The early 18th century
When Charles II was restored to his throne he proved as sensible as his brother James II, a Catholic, was foolish. James lost his throne, through trying to restore Catholicism, to his daughter Mary and her husband, the Dutch William of Orange. When Mary's sister, Queen Anne, died in 1714, a descendant of James I, George of Hanover, became George I. The nation was now Great Britain, for England and Scotland were linked politically in 1707, and firmly Protestant.

Things were very different in France where Louis reigned as an "absolute" monarch. He was the most powerful man in Europe until, in the first years of the 18th century, his troops were defeated in four great battles from 1704 to 1709 by Britain and her allies under the Duke of Marlborough.

In Eastern Europe, Russia retained her Orthodox faith whilst Poland remained Catholic. Though a Polish king had saved Vienna from the Turks, Polish power was declining due to internal squabbles and Swedish invasions. This enabled Russia to expand westwards. When Peter the Great (1672-1725) came to the throne, the stage was set for Russia to become a modern European power.

Mighty monarchs

The French Revolution of 1789 began a new chapter in European history. For the first time there was an attempt to give equality and freedom to the majority of the French people.

The nightmarish religious wars between Catholics and Protestants were over. Composers like Bach, Handel and Mozart, painters like Watteau and Fragonard and great thinkers like Voltaire brought glory to the age.

Agricultural methods improved, especially in Britain. The open field system gradually disappeared, enabling farmers to create separate farms with fields enclosed by hedges and fences. The improvements helped all classes, while the nobility and the middle classes prospered.

Then there were the rulers. Several deserved the rather grand title they have been given: benevolent or enlightened despots. They were very powerful rulers who genuinely cared for their people. The most famous were Maria Theresa of Austria – the best of them all – Frederick the Great of Prussia and, to a lesser extent, Catherine the Great of Russia. Catherine, like Peter the Great before her, helped to make Russia into a modern state by copying ideas from kingdoms in Western Europe.

Was this, then, something of a golden age? In many ways yes, but after a period of peace, there were two major wars.

War of the Austrian Succession

The first major war since Louis XIV had been humbled by Britain and her allies broke out in 1740. Young Maria Theresa (1717-80) succeeded her father, the Holy Roman Emperor, Charles VI, in that year. Though Europe's leading powers had previously promised to acknowledge his daughter, greed changed their minds. Britain, already at war with Spain, came to Maria Theresa's aid. Aligned against them were Prussia and France.

Prussia was the rising power in Europe. Her young king, Frederick II (1712-86), later called the Great, had been mainly interested in culture, to the despair of his father, Frederick William. This iron-willed ruler had made Prussia into a military state. Once his son became king, he developed an interest in the army himself and proved to be a very good military commander.

The result of all this was the War of the Austrian Succession (1740-48). The heroic Maria Theresa rallied her Austrian, Hungarian and other peoples together, while the British under George II defeated the French at Dettingen in 1743. It was the last time a British monarch was to lead his troops into action. The French attempted to invade England, but a storm shattered the invasion fleet. Revenge for the French came with the Battle of Fontenoy. Peace came leaving Maria Theresa on her throne, but she lost the province of Silesia to Frederick.

Meanwhile, the last attempt of the Stuarts to regain the throne had ended in 1746 when Prince Charles Edward (Bonnie Prince Charlie) and his Highlanders were defeated by an army of English and Lowlanders at Culloden. The Highlanders were punished savagely for this uprising.

Below: Louis XIV of France made the Palace of Versailles near Paris the most magnificent in Europe. Many thousands of workmen laboured for years to build it for Louis and his Court.

Above: A statue of Frederick the Great of Prussia, who loved not only military glory but also music and literature. He made Prussia a major European power.

Below: Catherine the Great, the German-born princess who became Empress of Russia, was a brilliant ruler who made her country powerful and a leading European nation. She died in 1796.

Seven Years' War

The peace of 1748 was hardly observed by Britain and France, who were both eager to gain two supreme prizes, North America and India. When the Seven Years' War broke out in 1756, India and North America had already seen plenty of action.

In India, the English had set up the trading East India Company in 1600. The French and English played tug-of-war with the loyalties of the many native rulers. They both thus built up spheres of influence. A major setback to the French occurred in 1751 when a young clerk turned soldier, Robert Clive (1725-74), won a remarkable victory at Arcot.

Things were going less well in North America. Britain now had 13 colonies along the Atlantic coast. The French in Canada had fewer settlers, but were used to forest warfare and got along better with the Indians. The French had explored southwards beyond the English colonies down to the Gulf of Mexico and hoped to box their rivals in with a line of forts.

To make matters worse colonies squabbled amongst themselves and also with the British government over taxes. They also had to provide men and supplies for the British troops fighting the French.

In 1754, an expedition set out to take the French Fort Dusquesne (now Pittsburgh, Pennsylvania). It was a mixed force of British Redcoats and colonists, with General Braddock in command. In 1755, deep in the forest, the expedition was ambushed by Indians and Frenchmen and almost wiped out. One of the survivors was a young American named George Washington, who was to lead the fight against the British a little over 20 years later (*see page 146*). For two years after this defeat, the French won virtually every battle in North America.

War officially broke out in Europe a year after this disaster. Austria, now hoping to recover Silesia, had allied with France and Britain allied with Prussia, thus reversing the previous alliance. Everything went wrong for the British at first, but once William Pitt, later Earl of Chatham (1708-78), became this nation's prime minister, things began to go right. By sheer strength of personality, he imposed his will on the Cabinet, Parliament and king. His policy was to hit France as hard and often as the country's resources would allow. Colossal victories were won on land and sea. Indeed, 1759 was christened the Year of Victories. In that year French Canada suffered a mortal blow when Wolfe defeated Montcalm at Quebec; the French were also beaten at Minden in Germany, at sea at Quiberon Bay, and in sugar-rich Guadeloupe in the West Indies. India had been virtually won from France in 1757 by Clive's great victory at Plassey. When peace came in 1763, Britain had a great empire.

Prussia was not so lucky, for most of Europe had been ranged against her. Only the military genius of Frederick the Great and the valour of his army saved their nation, which would one day come to dominate the many other German kingdoms.

The age of revolutions

Above: Marie Antoinette, the Austrian-born Queen of France, was never popular with the French people. They blamed her extravagance for much of their country's problems. She was guillotined in the French Revolution in 1793, some months after her husband, Louis XVI, had suffered the same fate.

Below: On 4th July 1776, the American Declaration of Independence was signed by the Congress at Philadelphia. Though their fight against Britain dragged on until 1783, Americans date their nation's birth from that historic July day.

When General Wolfe and his men defeated the French on the Heights of Abraham outside Quebec in 1759, it was only a matter of time before all French Canada fell to the British. As the bells of victory rang out in Britain and her American colonies, no one could foresee that within a few years those same colonies would rebel against the mother country.

With the French threat gone, however, the freedom-loving Americans began to resent being governed from a parliament in London in which no Americans sat. They also resented trade restrictions and taxes. When a new tax on tea was imposed in 1773, Americans boarded ten ships in Boston harbour and threw the cargo overboard. In 1775 war broke out.

Many Americans remained loyal and few Britons wanted to fight their cousins. Besides which it was very hard to wage a war across the Atlantic. The British won many battles but lost the ones that mattered, including the key one at Yorktown in 1781.

Meanwhile thousands of Americans loyal to the Crown went to Canada and formed a new British nation alongside the many French that lived there under British rule.

The French Revolution

The French, having supported the American revolution, soon had one of their own to deal with. Unlike Britain which was a comparatively free nation peopled by a lively, vigorous race without much class hatred, France was seething with discontent. It was badly governed, almost bankrupt, and had a wretched peasant class with virtually no rights at all.

In 1789, the French Revolution broke out in Paris, and liberal-minded people everywhere rejoiced. The Bastille was stormed and feudalism was abolished. At first it was a moderate affair and the king, the well-meaning Louis XVI, was not threatened.

Gradually, as in most revolutions, extremists got the upper hand. This was after the king and queen had tried to escape and Austria and Prussia prepared to invade France. The monarchy was abolished and armies of ill-trained but patriotic citizen soldiers hurled back the invaders.

Now, with France in arms against much of Europe, including Britain, a reign of terror began. Not only were the king and queen executed on the notorious guillotine, but anyone else who dared to oppose the new extremist rulers called Jacobins. Very many innocent people died without a trial. Then the Jacobins started butchering each other. In 1794 the terror ended with the Jacobin leader Robespierre following his victims to the guillotine. So a truly freedom-inspired revolution had turned into a blood-drenched shambles.

Napoleon

Yet France herself had survived, and now began the rapid rise to fame of one of the most brilliant men in history, Napoleon Bonaparte. He was a Corsican,

born in 1769, and he first made his name by his brilliant victories in Italy against the ruling Austrians. By 1799, he was master of France.

A great general and a great statesman and organizer, he had many admirers outside France who saw him as a champion of freedom who would overthrow Europe's all powerful rulers. And there was also something to be admired about a leader in those class-bound times, whose generals had almost all risen from the ranks to high command. This, surely, was a fine outcome to the French Revolution?

Alas, Napoleon's ambitions were unlimited and in the end proved his downfall. After a short peace from 1802-3, during which time he concentrated on reorganizing and reforming France, he made himself emperor, a move which shocked many. He was all set to invade Britain, but Nelson's great victory at Trafalgar in 1805 put paid to that plan. So he proceeded to become master of Europe.

To help his plans, he closed all European ports to British ships, realizing how much Britain depended on trade. At first, his plans looked like succeeding, as his armies conquered all they came up against. But he became too ambitious. In 1812, when his troops were being driven out of Spain by the British under Wellington, he invaded Russia. Though the French captured Moscow, they had to retreat. An icy winter and constant attacks by Russian cavalry almost wiped out Napoleon's army. By 1814, he had lost his empire and was in exile on the island of Elba.

He escaped, and for 100 days had Europe in a turmoil until his final defeat at Waterloo on 18th June 1815.

After the wars, European rulers took no chances and many ruled their people too harshly. As we shall see, though, they failed to stifle the spirit that France and Napoleon had stirred up.

The first crack in the peaceful surface was the breakaway of Spain's Central and South American empire soon after Waterloo, and Brazil soon became independent of Portugal. It could only be a matter of time before Europe, too, saw more revolutions.

Above: A portrait of Napoleon Bonaparte. After his defeat at Waterloo the revolutionary leader was exiled on the tiny island of St Helena where he died in 1821.

Below: The Battle of Aboukir in Egypt in 1798 was one of Napoleon's first great victories. Although Napoleon won the battle, his fleet was soon afterwards destroyed by Nelson in Aboukir Bay.

The Far East

Above: The memorial to Queen Victoria at Calcutta.

Left: A striking Indian hunting scene which dates from the reign of the Mogul Emperor, Akbar the Great (1542-1605).

Below: The Indian patriot Gandhi (1869-1948) was chiefly responsible for India gaining her independence from Britain in 1947. One of the finest things about him was that he sought independence by peaceful means, such as publicly breaking unjust laws to focus attention on them. Tragically, he was murdered at a prayer meeting in New Delhi.

India's ancient civilization dates back about 5,000 years. In the valley of the Indus River in the north-west a remarkable people built cities, palaces and temples. They could read and write and were fine artists.

Around 1500 B.C. the Indus people were invaded by a lighter-skinned race, the Aryans. These barbaric conquerors settled down to become civilized farmers and craftsmen, and adopted the Hindu religion.

India met Greek culture when Alexander the Great led his army there in 327 B.C. Not until the reign of Asoka, who died in 232 B.C., was the country united. His bloody victories finally sickened him and he became a devout Buddhist.

More invaders came, including Muslim followers of Islam. From 1525 the Muslim Moguls ruled India. Their greatest king was Akbar the Great (1542-1605), who tried to reconcile Hindus and Muslims. Later Moguls were less able and India was split by its two religions.

The European trading nations had arrived by now, the first being Portuguese in 1498. Then came the British, Dutch and French. All of them set up trading posts to exploit the riches of the vast sub-continent. Britain's East India Company became the most important of them, and by the 1760s Britain controlled Bengal (north-east India) whereas other European powers had barely a foothold.

The East India Company continued to rule in Britain's name and gradually took over all India except areas ruled by Indian princes with British blessing.

In 1857, the Indian Mutiny erupted among Indian troops in the Bengal army. It was mainly caused by British inability to make allowances for Indian religious beliefs. Although confined to northern India, Indian atrocities were more than repaid by avenging British troops and a legacy of bitterness was left.

The British Crown took over from the East India Company and ruled India through a fine civil service. Roads and railways were built and much progress was made. But, naturally, many Indians longed for self-rule, not least because the British, though honest and just, mostly looked down on

Above: The samurai were the military class of old Japan and were highly privileged. The shogun, who ruled the country, depended on them for support.

the Indians. A freedom movement was set up but this did not stop Indian troops fighting valiantly in two world wars.

Freedom came in 1947, but at a price. The country had to be split in two because of religious hatred. Hindu India and Muslim Pakistan came into being after considerable bloodshed. Finally, peace, if not friendship, came, though there have been conflicts since. Now

there are three nations, East Pakistan having broken away to become Bangladesh. India's long history is still a troubled one.

Above: *The Wave,* a beautiful wood-block print by the Japanese artist, Hokusai (1760-1849). Japanese art has always been admired by foreigners. Today, the Japanese admire Western arts.

Japan

Japan's early history is lost in legend for the earliest records only date from A.D. 400 and strong government from around 800, by which time the Chinese influence was strong.

The Japanese religion, Shinto, has countless gods and is very patriotic. The emperor was regarded as divine.

The country was torn for centuries by civil war between families of military lords. The most powerful nobles of all from the 12th century onwards were the shoguns. Under these warlords were the samurai, a warrior class.

Virtually no Europeans were allowed into Japan from 1542-1853, Japan's rulers forcing her to remain medieval and isolated. But when times changed and people wanted to modernize, Japan's advance was incredible. An Ameri-

Right: A Japanese Shinto priest. Shinto is a patriotic as well as a religious creed. Indeed, until 1946, the Japanese regarded their emperors as gods. Shinto rules of moral behaviour have something in common with those of Buddhism and Confucianism.

can fleet visited her in 1853 and forced the country to open itself up to the west. By 1905 she had become an advanced industrial power able to defeat Russia in a naval battle. What Japan did in World War Two is related on page 153.

Today, Japan is one of the world's most advanced industrial nations. Less than 150 years ago she was, as it were, locked firmly in the Middle Ages.

New nations and ideas

After Napoleon's exile to Elba, the great powers met at Vienna to settle the future of Europe. When news of his escape from Elba reached them, the meeting broke up in order to raise an army. The Allies under the Duke of Wellington met Napoleon's forces at Waterloo and defeated them. Napoleon himself was exiled to St Helena in the Atlantic.

A new age dawns

Most of the work of the Congress of Vienna, as it is called, was already done. As we have seen, the French Revolution and Napoleon had given Europe's rulers a fright and they were determined to put the clock back.

It was not that easy. For all the misery and bloodshed the revolution and Napoleon had caused, millions had been given a glimpse of freedom.

The Congress also upset countless thousands, speaking many different languages, who suddenly found themselves under new rulers because of boundary changes. Belgium and Holland were forced together; much of northern Italy was taken over by Austria; and Poland, which had suffered from its powerful neighbours in the previous century, was divided up between Russia, Austria, and Prussia. Norway and Sweden were forcibly joined and the Austro-Hungarian Empire became a giant mixture of peoples. Germany, now called a Confederation, was dominated by Prussia.

To add to this restlessness, the effects of the Industrial Revolution increased the feeling of frustration. The Industrial Revolution had begun in Britain in the late 18th century. Its ill-effects, some of which are still felt, included overcrowded new industrial towns and ill-planned factories where men, women and children worked far too long hours. Machines could do the work of many people. The resulting unemployment caused an anti-machine backlash. But there was a bright side too in the form of

Above: Nearly every town in Italy has a statue of the great Giuseppe Garibaldi (1807-82), who did so much to free Italy from foreign domination. In 1860, with 1,000 men, all volunteers, he freed both Sicily and Naples.

Right: Garibaldi pictured in action.

sensational progress. Industry, agriculture and transport were transformed.

Even before Waterloo there had been steamboats, but the real revolution was the coming of the railways. The first, from Stockton to Darlington, opened in 1825, and by 1830 the Railway Age had begun. Travel speeded up enormously. The actual work of building tracks, tunnels, bridges and embankments was carried out very quickly. By 1838, there was a commercial electric telegraph and by 1851 England and France were linked by undersea cable. By 1870 there was a railway network of 20,000 kilometres.

Revolutions in Europe

In the years after Waterloo, this new, swiftly changing age, plus the suppression of ordinary people's hopes, caused unrest and finally triggered off more revolutions. Even Britain barely escaped one in the 1840s over the reform of Parliament.

France threw out her king in 1830 because he tried to restore the hated old ways, and replaced him with a monarch who was more of a figurehead, like Britain's. Belgium broke away from Holland, but Spain, Russia and Austria crushed their revolts.

Meanwhile, Greece had freed herself from the Turks with French and British help. Britain in particular was willing to aid others gain their independence, and, happily, had abolished slavery in her empire in 1833. The new nations which emerged in Europe were all hastily given kings by the leading powers.

The year 1848 became known as "the year of revolutions". They were caused by every sort of unrest including bad harvests, but most of all by the lack of political freedom. France acquired a president, Napoleon's nephew, to replace King Louis Philippe. He later became the Emperor Napoleon III. (Napoleon's son never reigned.) Italy, Germany, Austria,

Hungary and Spain all had uprisings during this year, but they all failed and were brutally suppressed. Yet after it all, things were getting a little better for the general population.

Between 1854-56, Britain, France and Turkey fought Russia in the Crimean War. The Russians had wanted to capture the Turkish city of Constantinople (Istanbul) and thus have a port and outlet to the Mediterranean. Though Russia was defeated, the British campaign was ill-managed. Little of credit came out of the war except for the heroic work of Florence Nightingale and her nurses.

Now it was Italy's turn to win her freedom and become a single nation. The statesman Cavour, helped by the French, had removed the Austrians from the north in 1859. The next year, the great patriot and guerrilla fighter, Garibaldi, who had fought in 1848, invaded Sicily and the Kingdom of Naples, and in 1861, King Victor Emmanuel of Sardinia and Piedmont became king of almost all Italy.

Meanwhile, Prussia was reaching new heights of power under Europe's most brilliant statesman, Count Otto von Bismarck (1815-98). He wanted German unity, with Prussia's king as Germany's king. He believed in short wars to gain his ends. Austria was defeated in seven weeks to reduce her superpower status. Then in 1870 he took on France, which seemed at the time to be Europe's leading military nation. The French were rapidly defeated and Paris itself fell after a long siege.

That was in 1871, and though no one could know it, the seeds of the First World War (1914-18) were now sown. France had lost territory to Germany and wanted revenge. Britain would soon be locked in naval rivalry with her. And, as we shall see on pages 148-9, the scramble for empire was to cause yet more rivalries.

Above: "Not by parliamentary majorities are the great questions of the day settled, but by iron and blood," said Bismarck, the first Chancellor of Prussia.

Left: Thanks to Bismarck, William I became Emperor of all Germany.

America's first century

The rise of the United States of America is a staggering success story. In 1783, when their long fight for freedom from British rule was finally over, the 13 colonies-turned-states were anything but united. A century later the U.S.A. was well on its way to becoming a major world power.

Back in 1783, the urgent task was to invent a form of government that would keep the rival states happy but give the new nation strong leadership. Leading citizens drew up the remarkable American Constitution. This gave each state its own law-making body and the nation a central government.

The new republic had a President, a Congress and a Supreme Court, all keeping an eye on each other. Naturally, the President, especially a strong one, was very powerful, but Americans, having had their fill of kings, wanted no tyrannical rulers, monarchs or otherwise, so they ensured that their leaders were restricted in many ways. The first President was George Washington, who had led his country to victory.

Above: Plains Indians depended on the buffalo for food, shelter and clothing. The destruction of the great herds by whites helped them defeat the Indians.

Below: Sitting Bull was a famous Sioux war chief and medicine man. He was one of the leaders at the Battle of the Little Bighorn in 1876. He was killed in 1890.

Early history

The other great task was to expand the nation and fill it with people. The infant republic was still confined to the Atlantic seaboard, though dauntless pioneers like Daniel Boone, and many women and children, had already begun to head westwards.

In fact, the U.S.A. had officially gained all the land to the Mississippi River by the Peace Treaty of 1783, but ownership means people on the ground. And already men with vision saw America stretching to the Pacific.

The pioneers helped make America great. They were helped at the start through a colossal land deal by President Jefferson called the Louisiana Purchase. In 1803 this gave the U.S.A. all the land between the Mississippi and the Rockies. The French sold it for a mere 15 million dollars. No one, of course, consulted the first Americans, the Red Indians.

In 1848, a war with Mexico was won and that added Texas and California to the growing number of states. This happened just before gold was found there. The nation was thus becoming richer and richer.

The Indians in the east had been killed or forced westwards. Once the plains, too, were found to be fertile, their days here were numbered as well. The buffalo they used for food, shelter and clothing were almost wiped out by whites. Railroads criss-crossed Indian lands from the 1870s onwards, and settlers poured in like a never-ending flood from the eastern states. The Indians fought valiantly but in vain. The survivors were put on reservations. This was mostly land that was too poor to farm or which nobody else wanted.

Civil War

Meanwhile, the most devastating war in American history had been fought between North and South. This was the great American Civil War of 1861-65.

The mainly agricultural Southerners grew cotton using slave labour, and wanted to spread their way of life by basing the new emerging states on slave labour. The Northerners, many of them traders and manufacturers, objected to slavery and wanted a strong Union. The Southerners believed in "states' rights" more than the Union. Eleven Southern states broke away and formed the Confederacy in 1861 and war broke out with the capture of Fort Sumter in Charleston.

The South had most of the best leaders and her troops at first nearly won, but Northern numbers, industrial might and armaments triumphed in the end. The war lasted four years and cost over 500,000 lives. The man who led the North, Abraham Lincoln, was murdered by a mad Southerner a few days after the terrible war ended, but he had saved the Union. During the war he had proclaimed that all slaves in the rebel states should be free.

After the war business boomed and industry with it. Millions of immigrants from all over Europe arrived to swell the population.

By 1900 America was expanding, having fought a war with Spain that gave her a Pacific empire of islands. Her navy was growing fast, and when she joined Britain and France against Germany in 1917 in World War One, victory was certain. She was a world power indeed.

Above: From the 1840s pioneers headed westwards across plains, deserts and mountain ranges to settle in the far west. The crossings were very rugged and many people died on the way.

Below: The Battle of Gettysburg in the American Civil War took place in 1863. It was the biggest battle fought on American soil. Though a draw, the South withdrew.

Empires

Above: Sleek and swift, the clipper ships sped like greyhounds across the world's oceans in the last century, the final age of sail. Some of the most famous clippers were the ones which brought tea from the east to Britain.

Below: The scene at Botany Bay, New South Wales, in 1770, when Captain Cook took possession of Australia for Britain. Later, he charted the coast of New Zealand. Both were to become leading members of the British Empire, and afterwards the Commonwealth.

There used to be a saying that the sun never set on the British Empire and it was true. At its height from the late 19th century until the 1940s it covered 25 per cent of the globe and 500 million people were under British rule in both the Northern and Southern Hemispheres.

Today, with just a handful of colonies left, the sun never sets on the slightly smaller Commonwealth, the free association of nations which once formed the Empire.

North America

The first British Empire ended with the loss of the American colonies in 1783. Though this made many Britons suspicious about the value of colonies – they forgot that it was Britain's own fault that she lost America – a new empire soon sprang up. This was born out of trade and profit motives and, in some cases, a Christian desire to convert the natives from pagan beliefs. The main areas of empire-building were Canada, Australia, New Zealand, Africa and India. (The story of Britain's Indian empire is on pages 142-3.)

The United States hoped to get Canada and tried to conquer it in the War of 1812 with Britain. British troops and Canadians, many of them Loyalist Americans who had settled in the north after the War of Independence, kept the Americans out.

The Canadian colonies became a united self-governing dominion in 1867, although British Columbia in the far west only agreed to join when the Government promised to build a transcontinental railway. Canada's "West" was very different to America's. A few hundred "Mounties" kept law and order out there and protected Indians and settlers alike.

Australia, New Zealand, Africa

Australia's first white settlement was a penal colony founded in 1788 on the site where Sydney now stands. From this unhappy beginning a great nation arose. The mainly farming community was transformed from 1851 onwards by the discovery of gold. The gold rushes that followed brought thousands of new settlers. In 1901 the six states combined to form the Commonwealth of Australia.

Like Canada, Australia and New Zealand rallied to the Allied cause in both world wars. The settler history of New Zealand really dates from the 1840s. For a time it

Above: Bombay was the gateway to the British Raj, as the Indian Empire was called. Raj means rule. Pictured is the imposing railway terminus.

Above right: Part of the spirit of colonialism were the many men and women who believed in and preached the values of Christianity and the British way of life. This missionary is in the Sudan.

seemed that white New Zealanders would avoid the mistakes of other colonies and live peaceably with the native race of the country, the Maoris. However, it was not to be. There were bitter wars.

The first fruits of colonial rule here were seen when the first cargo of frozen New Zealand lamb reached Britain in 1882. In another ten years the country had introduced the first "welfare state" and given women the vote.

Meanwhile, Britain had joined the "scramble for Africa" in the 19th century and had come out best. The only real opposition came from the Boers (settlers of mainly Dutch origin) in South Africa. The British were humiliated many times in the Boer Wars (1899–1902) before they finally won.

There were British colonies all the way along the sea route to India via the Suez Canal (opened in 1869) and there were many others dotted over the globe. The British navy ruled the waves between Waterloo (1815) and 1914.

Yet not until the late 19th century did Britons as a whole become empire-minded, though the empire had helped make it the richest nation at the time.

Other European nations built big empires, notably the Dutch in what is now Indonesia, the French in Africa and South-East Asia, and Spain, Portugal and Belgium in Africa, where Germany, too, had a stake until 1918. Some were harsh rulers, others were fair. Like all empires, they were a mixture of good and bad and their passing still affects the world to this day.

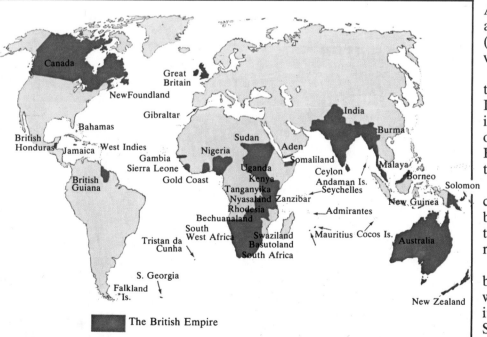

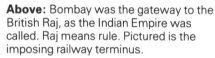

The British Empire

Above: At the beginning of the 20th century, the British Empire extended into all corners of the globe, backed up by wealth earned in trade and industry, and a powerful navy. It was at its height in 1919, soon after the death of Queen Victoria. However, during her reign, the Empire received one or two shocks, as for instance when British colonies in South Africa were attacked by the Boers.

The world at war

Looking back more than 60 years, World War One seems sheer insanity. Yet many welcomed it in 1914, not knowing that modern war would be a nightmare of a bloodbath.

In the early 1900s, Europe had divided into two armed camps. After centuries of enmity or uneasy friendship, France and Britain became allies, with France wanting revenge on Germany for her defeat in 1870. Meanwhile, Britain and Germany were locked in naval rivalry, and Germany envied Britain's empire. The Austro-Hungarian Empire was Germany's natural ally and Turkey sided with them too. Russia allied herself to Britain and France. Europe was like a powder keg.

Europe goes to war

The murder of the heir to the Austrian throne, Archduke Franz Ferdinand, was the fuse that set fire to Europe. The assassination took place at Sarajevo in what is now Yugoslavia on 28th July 1914, and the countdown to war took less than a week.

Germany declared war on Russia on 1st August and on France on the 2nd. The same day the Germans invaded Belgium, which brought Britain in on the 3rd. Italy and Japan joined the Allies later, and the U.S.A. came in after 1917.

The main and most horrifying war zone was the Western Front in France and Flanders. After a swift German thrust on Paris was halted, rival trench systems were dug from the Channel to the Swiss border. So began the nightmare of trench warfare, which has haunted the imagination of mankind ever since.

Meanwhile, the Russians were knocked out of the war when the 1917 revolution broke out and the nation's new rulers, the Bolsheviks, made peace. Bitter fighting continued in the Balkans until late in 1918.

The Dardanelles campaign in the Near East was meant to come to the aid of Russia by knocking Turkey out of the war. The scheme was a costly failure but the Turks were eventually defeated two years later. The small German empire in Africa and the Pacific was taken.

Below: A vivid impression of a German attack on a British trench in 1917. Trench warfare had many quiet moments between the big offensives. For weeks at a time, the main enemies were often the weather, mud, dirt and disease. The stalemate of trench warfare was finally broken in 1918, after the British had invented the tank.

Naval and air warfare

The war at sea, the first modern naval war, saw only one great sea battle, off Jutland in 1916. It was a draw. The British lost more ships, but the German High Seas fleet never really ventured out again. However, German submarines, the dreaded U-boats, caused such havoc to British shipping that Britain was brought to the brink of starvation. Ships started sailing in convoys protected by warships, and this cut down losses. The invention of the depth charge helped in the fight against the submarines.

The first air war took place high above the trenches and bombs were soon dropped on civilians and troops alike. Air warfare did not win the war, but it was a sign of things to come.

The nightmare ended on 11th November 1918. People believed it to be the war to end all wars. A million British and Empire troops had perished and far more Frenchmen, Germans and Russians. But the lesson was not learnt.

A new Europe was born, including the world's first Communist power, the U.S.S.R., under the dynamic leadership of Lenin. The age of kings was over.

World War Two

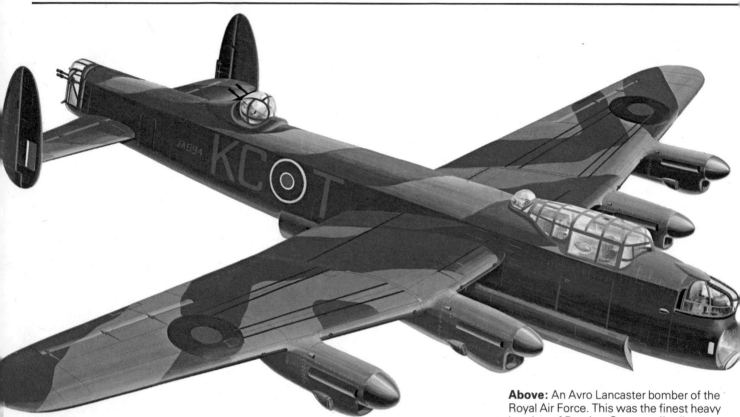

Above: An Avro Lancaster bomber of the Royal Air Force. This was the finest heavy bomber of Bomber Command's all-out attack on Germany. One of its raids was the "Dambusters" epic in 1943.

Twenty years after World War One had ended, Europe was on the brink of war again. It was the summer of 1939.

Germany had bitterly resented the Peace Treaty of Versailles in 1918 which had stripped her of money, overseas possessions, and parts of what she considered her homeland. However, for much of the 1920s she was in no position to do anything about it.

The rise of Hitler

A leader for Germany appeared in the terrible form of Adolf Hitler, the leader of the Nazi Party, which came to power in 1933. The war-weary nations allowed him to prosper, to build up the country's armed forces with forbidden weapons, including tanks and war-planes. Under Hitler, Germany recovered her self-respect, but with wicked side-effects. The Nazis preached racial superiority of the German race and hatred of the

Jews. Hitler demanded more "living room" for his people.

The result was the take-over of a willing Austria, the grabbing of Czechoslovakia in 1938, and the invasion of Poland on 1st September 1939, complete with dive bombers and the finest tank force in Europe.

Britain and France declared war, but could not save Poland, which fell before the German *Blitzkrieg* (lightning war). There was now a lull, which lasted until spring 1940.

War in Europe

In April, Denmark and Norway were attacked. In May, it was Holland and Belgium's turn. The German success was total and France itself surrendered in June, the month that the Italian dictator Mussolini joined forces with Hitler.

The British army had evacuated Europe via the beaches of Dunkirk

in naval vessels and a flotilla of small boats.

There followed the epic Battle of Britain in which the outnumbered Royal Air Force defeated the German *Luftwaffe* at a time when it looked as if Britain would be invaded.

Beaten, the Germans switched to night attacks on British cities. They also continued to overrun Europe. By April 1941, they had

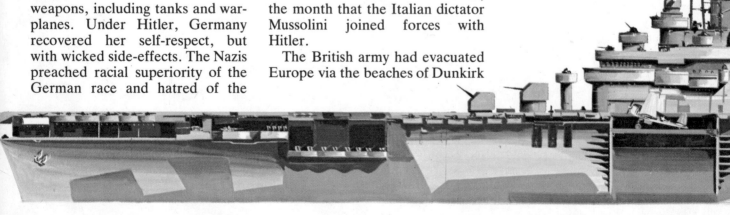

Below: The World War Two weapons pictured are (*top left*) a 32 round MP 40 (*top right*), a 7.9 millimetre rifle (*bottom left*), a standard hand grenade and (*bottom centre*) a Walther P-38 pistol. All are German weapons.

Below: Though battleships proved a liability in World War Two because they could be sunk by bombers, aircraft carriers more than proved their worth. This monster is an American carrier, the *Wasp*. The carrier's chief enemy was the submarine, and a Japanese submarine sank *Wasp* in 1942.

added Yugoslavia and Greece to their conquests.

Hitler now made Napoleon's mistake. He invaded Russia on 22nd June 1941. Not that it seemed a mistake at the time, with the Germans masters of Europe. Their U-boats were sinking so much shipping that Britain was in danger of starving.

World-wide conflict

On 7th December 1941, the war became truly a world one, when the Japanese launched an air attack on the American naval base at Pearl Harbor in Hawaii. Soon they were conquering Malaya, seizing Singapore and Hong Kong, and occupying key islands in the Pacific. Even Australia and New Zealand were threatened.

The next year, 1942, saw the tide turn against the Axis powers (Germany, Italy and Japan). The sleeping giant (America) was now aroused. American and Australian troops started the long battle to beat the Japanese in the Pacific, and in great air-sea battles the power of Japan began to wane.

Meanwhile, in the Western Desert of North Africa, the famous Eighth Army led by General Montgomery, having saved the Suez Canal from Rommel's Afrika Korps, won the Battle of El Alamein. And in Russia the German advance ended at Stalingrad in 1943.

Sicily and Italy were invaded that year by American and British forces. Mussolini was deposed and Italy surrendered.

On 6th June 1944 (D-Day), American, British, Canadian and Free French forces invaded France to begin the reconquest of Europe under the command of General

Above: German airmen enjoying a few moments of relaxation in the desert war in North Africa. Finally, the Allies drove the Germans out of Africa in 1943.

Eisenhower. It was to take nearly a year to defeat Germany despite the devastation of her cities from the air. Finally, on 8th May 1945, she surrendered.

The war against Japan was being won the hard way in the Pacific, the fanatical Japanese having to be forced out of their island strongholds one by one. And the British 14th Army had driven the Japanese out of Burma and were poised to reconquer Malaya. Suddenly it was all over. Atomic bombs were dropped on the cities of Hiroshima and Nagasaki, and on 2nd September 1945 Japan surrendered to the American General MacArthur.

It had been by far the most costly war in history in terms of human sacrifice, not least because so many civilians died.

The world since 1945

Above: Though there was television before World War Two, the Television Age really began when the war ended in 1945. The picture shows a B.B.C. television announcer in 1950.

Above right: A grim scene from the Vietnam war. The Americans, supporting South Vietnam, lost the war, though they used everything except atomic weapons. The war deeply divided America.

Above: The Beatles were by far the most famous pop group of the 1960s. Their records sold in millions. They are seen here with medals awarded to them for services to music and the export trade.

When World War Two ended in 1945, there seemed to be three "super-powers": the U.S.A., U.S.S.R. and Britain. In fact, there were two. Britain, the only one to have fought right from the start, was tired and, after two great wars, her riches had been drained away. Also, although she had been the first industrial power, her industries had not modernized as much as the newer industrial nations.

Nevertheless, Britain cannot help being an influence on the world. Her huge empire has changed into a Commonwealth of nations. London remains one of the major world cities, especially in the field of international money, while the English language is spoken throughout the world.

U.S.A.

America is now the world's most powerful nation. In the 1930s, she went through a "depression" and millions were out of work. The boom years seemed over. The war changed all that, and America's huge natural resources made sure she stayed at the top.

She generously poured money into Europe, including the defeated Germany and Japan. With this they were able to build up a very modern industry out of the wartime ruins.

U.S.S.R.

The other super-power, the U.S.S.R., suffered terribly in the war. Her sheer size and her resources enabled her to recover, even though her hard-working people's standard of living is not yet as high as that enjoyed by the West.

Almost as soon as the war ended, the Allies started to disagree. Russia had reached deep into Europe to help defeat Hitler and she was staying put. Nations such as Poland, Czechoslovakia, Rumania, Bulgaria as well as East Germany are now Communist-ruled and the rulers are backed up by Russian tanks. However, they are beginning to try and show themselves independent of Russia. The amazing Marshal Tito showed the way as far back as 1948. Yugoslavia is Communist yet independent. Meanwhile, since the

death of the ruthless dictator Stalin in 1953, Russia has tried to come to some sort of relationship with the West.

Atomic age

America and Russia could destroy each other in a few minutes. This is the central fact of our age. The atom bomb that destroyed Hiroshima in 1945 was much less powerful than today's nuclear weapons. The odd thing is that this fact has probably prevented another world war. But the high cost of making arms has created economic problems. This factor was involved in a nuclear disarmament treaty signed by the U.S.A. and the U.S.S.R. in 1987.

The Third World

China has become a major world power. Meanwhile, the Third World powers, nations that are neither "East" nor "West", do their best to survive. America helps some, Russia others, still more are grateful for help from anyone. Some are rich, some poor, some dictatorships, others democracies. Most of them suffer from one of our century's greatest problems, over-population. Starvation is a constant threat.

The United Nations, founded in 1945, tries to keep the peace, but is not strong politically. For instance, Israel, founded as a Jewish home-land in 1948, has been at war or in a state of armed truce ever since, although Israel and Egypt agreed a peace treaty in 1979. The Middle East has become increasingly powerful in international affairs. Money from oil sales has enabled Muslim nations to build up modern armies.

Africa, too, once carved up by European empire-builders, is a continent full of flash points and tensions. The movement towards African nationalism, started in the 1950s, still exists. The speed of the colonial withdrawal from Africa has posed many problems for emerging nations. Few of the countries are stable, politically and economically.

Life-styles

Yet for more and more people life gets easier. Trade unions have improved working conditions. Air travel has opened the world to millions. Television is the universal entertainment. Medical advances are staggering.

What the future holds none can tell. We read in the papers of new conflicts occurring every week. Some are major, others minor, but they are all a threat to world peace and prosperity. The Victorians believed in progress totally and that things must get better. But they could get worse. It is up to us to see that they do not.

Above left: President John F. Kennedy, whose tragic assassination in 1963 stunned the entire world. His brother Robert was assassinated five years later at an election meeting.

Above: Both the Russians and the Americans were eager to be the first to get a man on the Moon. In the end, the Americans won the race. The first man on the Moon was Neil Armstrong, who set foot on it in 1969. The very first man in space had been the Russian Yuri Gagarin in 1961. He made a single circuit of the earth in 108 minutes.

Above: Is this the shape of towns and cities to come? This urban landscape is San Francisco in California. Many people fear that the pollution from such cities may upset the balance of nature.

155

World events I

B.C.	
4000	Civilizations emerge in Egypt and Sumeria.
3200	About this time Egypt becomes a single nation.
3000	Earliest Cretan and Greek civilizations.
2700-2180	Major pyramids being built in Old Kingdom of Egypt.
850	Traditional date of founding of Carthage.
776	First Olympic Games held.
753	Traditional date of Rome's foundation.
745	Assyria at its most powerful.
612	Chaldeans capture Nineveh, Assyria's capital.
551	Birth of Confucius.
538	Persians take Babylon.
490	Athenians defeat Persians at Marathon.
480	Greeks defeat Persian fleet at Salamis.
431	War between Athens and Sparta.
404	Sparta supreme in Greece.
371	Spartans defeated by Thebans.
338	Macedon supreme in Greece.
334	Alexander the Great invades Persia.
332	Alexander occupies Egypt.
330	Collapse of the Persian Empire.
327	Alexander invades India.
323	Death of Alexander.
275	Rome master of all Italy.
264	Rome at war with Carthage (First Punic War).
241	War ends with Rome master of Sicily.
218	Second Punic War, in which Hannibal crosses Alps.
216	Hannibal's victory at Cannae.
214	Great Wall of China started.
202	Hannibal defeated at Zama.
201	End of Second Punic War.
149	Third Punic War.
146	Carthage destroyed.
73	Spartacus the gladiator leads a slaves' revolt in southern Italy.
71	The revolt is finally suppressed with extreme cruelty, thousands being crucified.
60	Rome ruled by Triumvirate: Pompey, Julius Caesar, Crassus.
55	Caesar invades Britain, leading a second expedition there the following year.
49	Civil War: Caesar versus Pompey, ending in the following year with Pompey's defeat at Pharsalus.
44	Caesar murdered in Rome by conspirators led by Brutus and Cassius.
43	A second Triumvirate formed: Mark Antony, Octavian (Caesar's great-nephew and heir) and Lepidus.
42	Battle of Philippi. Brutus and his army defeated. Death of Brutus.
31	Battle of Actium. Death of Antony and Cleopatra. Triumph of Octavian, now master of Roman world.
27	Octavian becomes the Emperor Augustus and proves a magnificent leader.
4	The date suggested by scholars for the birth of Jesus Christ.

A.D.	
14	Death of Augustus, who is succeeded by Tiberius.
30	The assumed date of the Crucifixion of Jesus Christ.
43	The third invasion of Britain by Rome ends in her becoming a Roman province after much fighting.
60	Rebellion of Boudicca (Boadicea) who burns Londinium, but is finally defeated and kills herself.
64	Great Fire of Rome for which the Christians are blamed and brutally persecuted.
66	Rebellion of Jews against Rome. In 70 Jerusalem falls and the revolt is savagely put down.
79	Pompeii and Herculaneum destroyed by the eruption of the volcano Vesuvius.
83	Agricola defeats the Caledonians at Mons Graupius, establishing Roman rule in Scotland.
122	Hadrian's Wall started to protect Britain from the warlike tribes in Caledonia (Scotland).
313	Christianity permitted by the Emperor Constantine in the Roman Empire.

395	With the death of the Emperor Theodosius, the Empire is split into East and West.
410	Alaric the Goth sacks Rome. The Emperor Honorius warns the Britons to defend themselves.
415-419	Visigoths conquer much of Spain and France and set up kingdom of Toulouse.
432	St. Patrick begins his mission in Ireland, whose patron saint he later becomes.
452	Attila the Hun invades Italy. The city of Venice founded by refugees.
455	The Vandals (from the Baltic area) capture and ravage Rome, destroying many treasures.
476	The last Roman Emperor in the West is dethroned by the German Odoacer.
515	Saxon advance across Britain is halted at Mount Badon, perhaps by a Romano-British chief called Arthur.
570	Birth of Mohammed in Mecca – the founder of Islam (Mohammedanism).
597	St Augustine lands in Kent to preach the gospel to the Saxons.
643	Alexandria in Egypt taken by Muslims (Mohammedans), who take the rebuilt Carthage in 698.
711	Muslims successfully invade Spain, where they are known as Moors.
732	Muslims defeated at Tours (in France) which halts their advance.
793	Vikings launch large-scale attacks on many parts of Scotland, Ireland and England.
800	Charlemagne crowned Holy Roman Emperor in Rome.
827	Invasion of Sicily by Muslims.
862	Vikings found a state in Russia.
871	After triumphs and disasters, Alfred defeats Danes at Ethandune, saving south and west England.
899	Death of Alfred the Great, whose son Edward recovers part of England under Danish rule.
982	Greenland discovered by Norsemen. Viking long-ships able to brave Atlantic waves.
991	More Viking raids on England.
1000	The Norse seaman, Leif Ericsson, almost certainly discovers America around this date.
1014	The Irish under BrianBorú defeat the Vikings at Clontarf.
1016	The Christian Dane Canute becomes king of England.
1060	Normans (descendants of Norsemen) invade Sicily.
1066	William the Conqueror, Duke of Normandy, invades England and defeats Harold at Hastings.
1075	Turks capture Jerusalem.
1086	The Domesday Book, a census and survey of England, compiled on the Conqueror's orders.
1099	The First Crusade to the Holy Land. The Crusaders capture Jerusalem.
1169	English invade Ireland for the first time and claim "overlordship" of the island.
1170	Thomas à Becket, Archbishop of Canterbury, murdered in his own cathedral.
1192	King Richard the Lionheart captured and held to ransom, returning from Third Crusade.
1215	English barons force King John to sign *Magna Carta* at Runnymede.
1227	Genghis Khan, Mongol ruler of much of Asia, dies and his huge empire breaks up.
1237	Mongols, known as the Golden Horde, invade and dominate much of Russia.
1265	Ordinary people sit in the English parliament for the first time on orders of Simon de Montfort.
1281	Mongols fail to capture Japan. Kublai Khan now Mongol ruler of China and much of Asia.
1281	Edward I completes conquest of Wales. He is to be less successful against the Scots.
1314	Defeat of English by Scots at Bannockburn under Robert the Bruce. Scotland independent.
1338	The Hundred Years' War between England and France begins.
1346	English victory at Crécy. Triumph of English longbowmen over mounted French nobility.
1348	The terrible Black Death reaches Europe from Asia. Around 25 per cent of population wiped out.
1369	Tamerlane, the Mongol ruler, begins a series of conquests in Asia.
1380	Russians win a victory over the Golden Horde.
1381	Peasants' Revolt in England led by Wat Tyler.
1399	Richard II deposed by Henry Bolingbroke who becomes Henry IV, first Lancastrian king.
1410	Poles and Lithuanians crush Germanic Teutonic Knights at the Battle of Tannenberg.
1415	Great Victory of the English under Henry V over the French at the Battle of Agincourt.
1429	French under Joan of Arc raise the siege of Orleans. Joan burnt at the stake at Rouen in 1431.
1453	End of Hundred Years' War in France's favour. Turks take Constantinople.
1454	First book wholly printed by movable type, the Mazarin Bible, produced by Gütenberg.
1455	Start of the Wars of the Roses in England. First battle fought at St Albans.
1469	The marriage of Ferdinand of Aragon and Isabelle of Castile unites most of Spain under one crown.
1485	Richard III defeated at Bosworth Field by Henry Tudor (Henry VII). End of the War of the Roses.
1488	Cape of Good Hope rounded by Portuguese seaman, Bartholomew Diaz.
1492	Granada, the last Moorish area in Spain, falls to the Spaniards. Columbus reaches the West Indies.
1494	Agreement by Spain and Portugal to divide unexplored parts of the world between themselves.

World events II

1497	John Cabot, an Italian seaman serving Henry VII, discovers Newfoundland.
1498	The Portuguese seaman, Vasco da Gama, reaches India by sea, the first navigator to do so.
1499	Amerigo Vespucci, after whom America is named, explores the South American coast.
1513	Spanish explorer Balboa discovers the Pacific Ocean. English defeat Scots at Flodden.
1517	Martin Luther nails up his 95 theses on church door, thus starting the Reformation.
1519	Magellan sets out on the first circumnavigation of world. A success, despite his death.
1521	Hernando Cortes conquers Mexico for Spain. Turks take Belgrade.
1532	Conquest of Peru by the Spaniard Francisco Pizarro and less than 200 men.
1534	Henry VIII makes himself supreme head of the Church of England in defiance of the Pope.
1535	Execution of Sir Thomas More for his refusal to recognize Henry.
1540	Coronado leads the first expedition out of Mexico into what later was called the American West.
1558	French take Calais, England's last foothold in Europe. Elizabeth I succeeds to the English throne.
1562-98	Religious wars in France, Catholics v. Huguenots (Protestants).
1564	Birth of William Shakespeare, one of the world's greatest playwrights.
1571	Turks defeated at sea by Don John of Austria at Lepanto, and their sea-power broken.
1572	Massacre of St. Bartholomew's in France. Many Huguenots perish.
1577-80	Circumnavigation of the world by Drake, who returns home laden with Spanish treasure.
1579	Seven Dutch provinces unite, thus beginning the Dutch Republic.
1587	Execution of Mary, Queen of Scots, around whom plots to overthrow Elizabeth have centred.
1588	Destruction of Spanish Armada by English fleet aided by the weather.
1603	Death of Elizabeth I. Succeeded by James VI of Scotland as James I of England.
1607	England's first colony founded in the New World at Jamestown, Virginia.
1620	Pilgrim Fathers land in what later becomes the colony, then state, of Massachusetts.
1642	English Civil War breaks out. First battle fought at Edgehill.
1649	Charles I executed and England becomes a Commonwealth. Cromwell ruler of all Britain by 1651.
1660	Restoration of Charles II to throne.
1666	Great Fire of London, a year after the Great Plague. Newton's discovery of gravitation.
1688	The Glorious Revolution. James II deposed. William of Orange and Mary become joint monarchs.
1701	Grand Alliance formed against Louis XIV of France.
1704	British take Gibraltar and Marlborough wins first great victory against French at Blenheim.
1707	Act of Union between England and Scotland, the two parliaments being united.
1714	With death of Queen Anne, George I ascends throne as first Hanoverian king.
1715	Death of Louis XIV of France. Despite defeats by Britain, France still the major European power.
1740	Frederick the Great, King of Prussia, attacks Maria Theresa, Queen of Austria.
1746	Battle of Culloden ends Bonnie Prince Charlie's attempt to regain throne for the Stuarts.
1756	Seven Years' War breaks out: Britain and Prussia v. Austria and France.
1757	Clive's colossal victory at Plassey in India wins Bengal for Britain.
1759	Britain's "Year of Victories", most notably at Quebec, which brings about fall of French Canada.
1775	Outbreak of the American War of Independence.
1776	Americans declare themselves independent on 4th July. Their war leader is George Washington.
1781	Final major battle of war at Yorktown won by Americans and French.
1783	End of war with Americans independent.
1789	Storming of the Bastille Prison in Paris is the start of the French Revolution.
1793	Louis XVI of France executed. France in arms against much of Europe.
1796-97	First great victories of Napoleon Bonaparte. Britain alone left in the field.
1798	Napoleon invades Egypt. French fleet defeated by Nelson at Battle of Nile.
1802	Peace of Amiens. War breaks out again with France the following year.
1803	Louisiana Purchase gives U.S.A. the whole of the Mississippi Valley to the Rockies.
1805	Nelson's supreme victory at Trafalgar. Napoleon defeats Austrians at Austerlitz.
1808	Peninsula War begins. French driven out of Spain by Wellington in 1813.
1812	Napoleon's disastrous invasion of Russia, which ends in the retreat from Moscow in mid-winter.
1815	Final defeat of Napoleon by British and Prussians at Waterloo.
1821	Death of Napoleon on the island of St Helena to which he was banished after Waterloo.
1829	Greece wins independence from Turkey.
1830	French depose king. Belgium freed from Holland. Russians crush Polish revolt.
1832	Great Reform Bill passed giving the vote to far more people. By 1884 all British males have the vote.
1836	Boers make their Great Trek from British South Africa to Transvaal. Texas freed from Mexican rule.
1837	Queen Victoria ascends throne. She reigns until 1901. The Victorian Age begins.

1848	Year of revolutions in Europe. Gold found in the state of California, newly acquired by the U.S.A.
1851	Great Exhibition in London attracts worldwide interest. Gold found in Australia.
1853	Commodore Perry visits Japan. After centuries of isolation, Japanese welcome the West.
1854-56	Crimean War: Britain and France fight to prevent Russian designs on Turkish Empire.
1857	Indian Mutiny. After early disasters it is harshly put down by British, Sikhs and Gurkhas.
1859	Charles Darwin's *Origin of Species* published. His ideas cause a sensation.
1860	Much of Italy united by Garibaldi's forces and Cavour's statesmanship.
1861	American Civil War breaks out over states' rights and the question of slavery.
1863	Battles of Gettysburg and Vicksburg make defeat of South in Civil War almost certain.
1865	Civil War ends. Assassination of President Lincoln. Salvation Army founded by William Booth.
1866	Prussia defeats Austria in Seven Weeks' War. Venice freed from Austrians.
1867	Canada united as a Dominion. U.S.A. buys Alaska from Russia.
1869	Suez Canal opened. The engineer in charge was Ferdinand de Lesseps.
1870	Franco-Prussian War ends in disaster for France. Italy now totally a free nation.
1871	William I of Prussia becomes emperor of all Germany. Triumph for Prussian leader Bismarck.
1876	Custer's last stand at Little Bighorn. Telephone invented by Alexander Graham Bell.
1881	First Boer War results in independence of the Transvaal.
1885	Khartoum falls to the Mahdi. Death of General Gordon at Khartoum.
1895	Röntgen discovers X-rays. Sigmund Freud, founder of psychoanalysis, publishes his first work.
1898	Spanish-American War won by U.S.A., thus gaining an empire.
1899-1902	Second Boer War won by British after many defeats and setbacks.
1901	Commonwealth of Australia comes into being. Death of Queen Victoria.
1903	Wilbur and Orville Wright achieve first manned powered flight at Kitty Hawk, U.S.A.
1904-5	Russo-Japanese War won by Japan, which becomes a world power.
1906	San Francisco almost destroyed by earthquake. First Labour M.P.s in British Parliament.
1907	New Zealand becomes a dominion.
1909	Union of South Africa formed. Blériot flies across the Channel.
1911	Norwegian Roald Amundsen leads first expedition to South Pole.
1912	S.S. *Titanic* sunk on maiden voyage. War breaks out in the Balkans.
1914-18	World War One. Britain declares war on Germany on 4th August.
1917	America joins Britain and France against Germany. Russian revolution begins.
1919	Peace conference. Alcock and Brown fly the Atlantic.
1924	Death of the Russian leader Lenin.
1926	Britain's General Strike.
1929	American slump leads to worldwide depression.
1934	Hitler becomes dictator of Germany.
1936	Spanish Civil War. Abdication of Edward VIII.
1939-45	World War Two. Britain declares war on 3rd September.
1940	Fall of France and the Battle of Britain.
1941	Germans invade Russia. Japanese attack Pearl Harbor.
1942	Tide begins to turn against Germany and Japan.
1943	German disasters in Russia. Italy surrenders.
1944	D-Day: 6th June. Paris liberated.
1945	Germans surrender in May, Japan on 14th August.
1947	India independent. Pakistan created.
1948	State of Israel created.
1949	People's Republic of China formed.
1950-53	Korean War.
1953	Stalin dies. Everest climbed.
1958	Common Market formed.
1959	Castro comes to power in Cuba.
1962	Cuban missile crisis.
1963	Assassination of President Kennedy.
1965	Death of Sir Winston Churchill.
1969	Americans land men on Moon.
1975	North Vietnam defeats South Vietnam.
1985	Assassination of Mrs Indira Gandhi.
1987	U.S.A. and U.S.S.R. sign nuclear disarmament treaty.

Freedom to choose

"No man is an island," wrote the poet John Donne nearly 400 years ago. In five words he summed up how much we all depend on one another.

A Robinson Crusoe or a hermit in his lonely cell may be alone because of bad luck or from choice, but few other people are. Certainly few want to be. Loneliness is a terrible condition.

How close we are to our friends and neighbours depends on many things, including who governs us. But closeness does not always bring people together.

Democracy or dictatorship

Closeness is linked with personal freedom. At one end of the scale there is the free man and woman, a cowboy on a horse, a ballerina, a small farmer. All of them and many more are independent figures in a true democracy. At the other end of the scale are the unfortunate people who live under dictatorships. Their every movement, every step in life, has to conform to what their rulers say.

Of course, our free men and women are not completely free. The cowboy is earning a living and the ballerina, too, is part of a team. They are not "islands" even though they are free to do what they want, if they are skilful enough. Even in dictatorships people can remain free in spirit and some – like dancers – are so skilled and popular that they have far more freedom than most people.

Patriotism

Do we owe our neighbours or country anything? Patriotism is not in fashion now. The idea of "my country, right or wrong" has been replaced by a general disinterest in anything other than oneself and one's own environment. Better is what John F. Kennedy said when he became President of the U.S.A.: "Ask not what your country can do for you: ask what you can do for your country."

That can apply to what we can do for the world, what we owe to society. We live in a world which can be destroyed in a few minutes. We are closer together than ever due to television and air travel, despite all the differences that divide us. It is right to love your country, sincerely, not boastfully, but all of us, whether we like it or not, are citizens of the same world.

This does not mean we should brood all the time about its problems. Life is for enjoying and for living, but not as a human island.

The pictures on these pages show the sheer variety of the activities of men and women all over the world, though it would need many more pictures to do full justice to the subject.

Above: On America's tiny Manhattan Island, architects are forced to build upwards due to lack of space. The New York skyline is certainly impressive, but do buildings like this make the kind of city people will want to live in in the future?

Left: What does the orator in London's Hyde Park suggest to you? Democracy visibly at work in Britain? Someone with something to say? British people value their freedom of speech. In some parts of the world, such freedom is severely restricted and people are even imprisoned for not conforming to an official point of view.

Right and **above right:** Throughout history, religion has been a powerful force. It has both united large groups of people, and been the excuse for dreadful wars. Peaceful festivals of all kinds draw people together, as at the religious festivals at Suwa Shrine, Nagasaki in Japan (*right*), and at a mosque in Delhi, India (*above right*).

Farming through the ages

"Man does not live by bread alone" says the Bible, which is, of course, true. There is more to life than food. Yet because food is the basic requirement of humanity, farming is by far the most important industry.

Strictly speaking, agriculture, or farming, means the cultivation of fields, but the words now include the breeding and use of animals.

From gathering to mechanization

The change from just gathering wild plants and hunting wild animals to the organized planting and harvesting of crops, and organized use of animals, was one of the key steps in the making of a civilization. In some parts of the world the change has still not been made and primitive peoples go on gathering and hunting in the age old way.

The development of agriculture must have followed a set pattern in all parts of the world. A start was made with some sort of a digging stick, and sooner or later this developed into the plough. First of all man did all the hard work, but when he invented the animal-drawn plough he had progressed a long way.

Tools for keeping down weeds and for harvesting the ripe crops were invented and the very best times for sowing and harvesting the crops were gradually discovered by

Above: An Egyptian farmer using a wooden plough. Fortunately the earth is soft. It may yield up to five harvests a year if tilled and irrigated continually.

trial and error. The materials used for the tools were improved or replaced by new ones, such as when iron replaced bronze.

The first written records we have about agriculture come from Ancient Egypt and Mesopotamia about 6,000 years ago. The story of those first civilizations is told on pages 120–1.

By 4000 B.C., agriculture in those regions was already highly organized. Not only did Egypt's River Nile and Mesopotamia's two rivers, the Tigris and Euphrates, overflow their banks regularly. When the waters receded, they left behind rich mud, which was just right for cultivation.

The peoples of these regions also developed first-rate irrigation systems so that water could be stored and then distributed during the dry seasons.

Systems of agriculture vary from place to place and also change with time. For instance, crop land has sometimes been changed to grazing land by landowners if it proves more profitable to do so.

The simplest sort of farm is the "subsistence" one. This is a small-holding upon which a family grows

just enough crops to feed itself, using fairly simple tools and farming methods. Often this type of existence is allied to what is termed shifting agriculture or «slash and burn». This involves a semi-nomadic cycle of clearing land by setting fire to it, growing crops there until yields decrease due to soil exhaustion, then moving on.

As technical knowledge grows throughout the world and as communications improve, farms usually become bigger. The farmers grow crops and breed animals for sale. This is known as "commercial" farming and at this stage agriculture becomes an industry. In many non-industrial countries it is the key industry. Even in industrial countries, agriculture is still important because home-produced food is more likely to be cheaper than imported food.

The implements and machines used by farmers today are very complicated, and are also very expensive. Food can now be transported great distances because of refrigeration (cold storage). Meanwhile, much has been learned about how to keep the land fertile by careful land management.

Above: Rice is the staple diet of countless millions of people in China and throughout South-East Asia.

Left: A scene familiar to millions of filmgoers – cowboys branding their stock. Cattle are branded for identification and each owner has a different mark.

Below: The fishermen of Lake Patzcuaro in Mexico use unique "butterfly" nets to catch the delicate white fish that are found in the lake.

The latest developments

As well as natural manures from animals and rotting vegetation, artificial fertilizers are now produced. There are also special chemicals for killing weeds and plant pests. Special foods are now available for animals to add to their natural diet or even replace it altogether, as in the farming of battery hens.

Research is constantly going on into the development of new strains of grain crops, of fruit and vegetables, and of animals. Many governments give money for this research and many universities throughout the world now have departments of agriculture and horticulture.

The United Kingdom has a very efficient farming industry. The vast majority of the food produced is consumed at home. Even so, the country has a sizeable import bill for food.

Some of the countries in which agriculture and stock-raising are very important export industries are the U.S.A. (wheat, maize, soybeans); Canada (wheat); Australia (sheep, mainly for wool); New Zealand (sheep, mainly for meat, and cattle mainly for butter and cheese). Other countries include Indonesia and Thailand (rice); Spain, Israel, Morocco and South Africa (fruit and vegetables); Denmark, Holland and Ireland (bacon, butter and cheese); India, Egypt and the U.S.A. (cotton); France, Italy and Spain (grapes for wine); and Argentina (meat).

Some of these countries' economies depend almost entirely on their agricultural exports, for example Ireland, Denmark, New Zealand and Argentina.

Today, more and more experts are beginning to realize the importance of using nature's manures efficiently, instead of depending on artificial fertilizers. The natural ones are better for the soil and because they are so much cheaper, they can be very useful in poorer countries.

163

Town life

Centuries ago the word "town" could mean a group of houses within a wall or hedge. Today we would call a mere group of houses a hamlet.

Now a town means anything larger than a village. As for a city, it does not always mean, as many think, a town with a cathedral. The word can be applied to any really important town, though strictly, in Britain at least, a city is created by a charter.

Early towns
The earliest known walled town is Jericho, which seems to have been built nearly 10,000 years ago. Like nearly every city and town, it must first have been a farming community. Gradually, surplus food brought about trade. Traders require security in which to work, and thus the farming community was the early focus for a larger settlement. Some towns grew up around castles and monasteries, others built fortified walls around their settlement.

Some early civilizations had very splendid cities. The very names Babylon and Nineveh have a cer-tain glamorous image to this day, just as some towns and cities do now: London, Venice, Rome, New York, Paris. They all have their individual character and attrac-tions for each of us.

Some towns are recognized the world over by a single structure, such as the Eiffel Tower in Paris and the Parthenon on the Acropolis at Athens.

Old towns and cities may seem romantic to us, but we would not like to have lived in many of them. For all the fine buildings of the medieval cities, the back streets

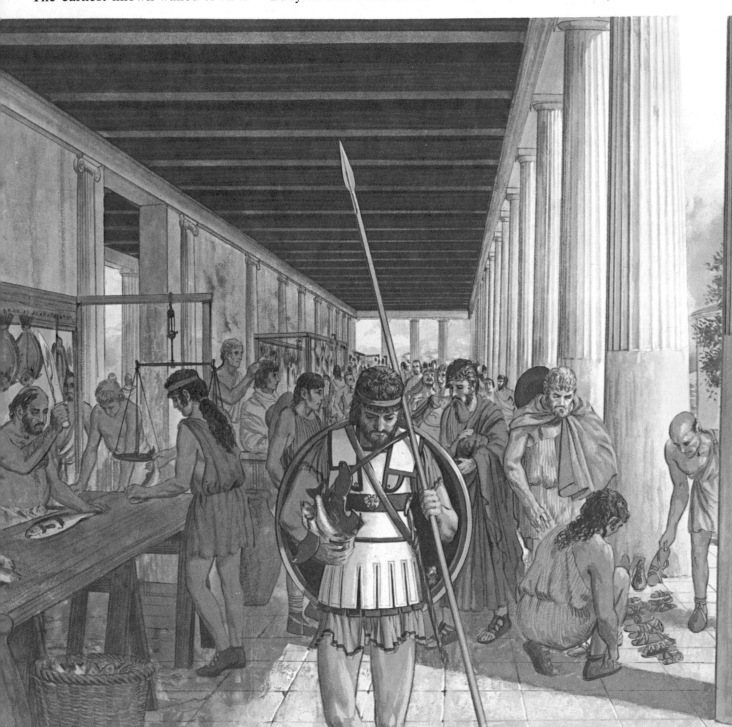

were narrow, dirty and evil smelling. These primitive conditions still exist in some places. People threw their slops out of the windows onto passers-by. Sanitation was generally primitive and the water was often contaminated. It is hardly surprising that disease and regular outbreaks of plague were evils people got used to. With so many wooden buildings in such a small area, there was the constant danger of fire. The Great Fire of London happened in 1666 just one year after the Great Plague.

In those days the country was

Below: Many ancient Greek towns and cities were lively commercial centres. In this market scene, a number of slaves are being sold. After years of good service, some earned their freedom.

still close at hand and people could get out into it easily. Many towns had animals grazing in them.

The cities of the distant past have to be imagined from their remains. Many of ancient Egypt's mighty monuments still survive in quite good shape. The glory that was Greece and the grandeur that was Rome have to be judged by splendid ruins alone. Fortunately there are many, especially at Pompeii and Herculaneum near Naples, which were overwhelmed by the eruption of Vesuvius in A.D. 79. Because of this disaster we know an astonishing amount about the life of those times. The clock stopped when the volcanic lava engulfed Herculaneum and cinders, ashes and stones buried Pompeii. When the towns were

excavated, cakes that were being baked when the catastrophe occurred had been preserved.

Industrial towns

Until the growth of industrial towns early in the 19th century, most medieval towns were centred on a market place. Towns were bustling and exciting places, the social centres of an area.

The Industrial Revolution (*see pages 168-9*) turned some towns into dirty, smoke-blackened places. Overcrowding became the rule, ghastly slums grew up in every new town and old ones as well. Smoke filled the air and the death rate soared. The gulf between rich and poor widened, especially in towns and cities.

As the 19th century progressed, real efforts were made to improve things, but many towns were beyond help. At least the relation between dirt, lack of sanitation, bad water and disease was realized as medical knowledge advanced.

The age of the motor car brought a different problem. Traffic congestion grew as the road system proved hopelessly inadequate. Pollution from exhausts rather than from factory chimneys was the new problem. The one good thing about the car was that it made people mobile and took them into the countryside. They could then appreciate what the towns were turning into. Bombing in World War Two, for all its horrors, at least provided a chance for parts of old cities to be rebuilt.

Today, for all the excitement and entertainment that towns and cities can provide, many are decaying in their centres. The middle classes move out to the suburbs and beyond, and the poorer people and many immigrants are left in the decaying centres.

This sad process started in America and has now reached Britain and other countries. A city, a fine town, a lovely village: all these are part of our civilization. A town must be good to live in, good to look at and good to visit.

The traders

Trading is as old as history itself. Our prehistoric ancestors must have used one basic method of trade long before there was any money. That method is called barter, or swopping, which most young people know all about.

Exchanging goods for money is, of course, the usual form of trading. Trading with another country, importing its goods and exporting one's own, is vital to most nations. Few countries can produce everything their people need.

Some traders make fortunes, being in the right place at the right moment. Most Britons over 45 recall sweet-rationing during World War Two, and how those children who did not eat sweets could make small fortunes by selling their sweet coupons. Similarly, in the Californian gold rush which started in 1848, few would-be miners "struck it rich", but nearly every trader did. They sold much needed goods at a handsome profit. One Italian immigrant to California, who later became a millionaire, started off by selling chocolate to the miners.

Early trade

The first great trading people were the Phoenicians. Phoenicia itself lay on the eastern Mediterranean coast, near present-day Lebanon. But the Phoenicians colonized much of the Mediterranean coastline. Their greatest city was Carthage which was destroyed by Rome during the Punic Wars.

Phoenician sailors had ventured out into the Atlantic around 500 B.C. They traded for tin in Cornwall. Their greatest explorer was Hanno the Carthaginian who travelled all along the north-west African coast.

The more the world was explored by Europeans, the more

trade grew. Sea-borne trade was of course at the mercy of pirates. The Vikings began as raiders, later founded colonies, and became businessmen and traders.

Sometimes natives were given mere trinkets for valuable furs or precious stones – valuable, of course, only in the West. Later natives might want guns. A very important land deal occurred in 1626, though no one realized it at the time. The Indians of Manhattan Island, now the heart of New York, sold it to the Dutch for trinkets worth less than 50 dollars.

Imports and exports

Some countries have to import to survive. Britain cannot feed herself, despite her farming output. In return for food imports, she must export industrial and other goods.

Today's key product is oil and countries which have plenty cannot help being rich. In a more modest way, some countries have products they can sell to others with different climates. The West Indies, for instance, export bananas to colder nations.

There are "visible" and "invisible" exports. A visible export is, for example, an Italian car sold to the U.S.A. A typical invisible

Above: The food market in Ibadan in western Nigeria is one of the biggest markets in West Africa. Standard weights and measures are not always used and goods are often sold in piles.

Below: The Ancient Greeks traded widely in the Mediterranean, and founded many Greek colonies. Wine and olive oil were among the products shipped abroad. Timber and, especially, grain were major imports. Greek craftsmanship was also in much demand.

export is insurance. The Americans may well insure a big ship with the great association, Lloyds of London. This means an export for Britain and an import for the U.S.A.

The largest empire ever known, Britain's, was based on trade. Merchant ships carried manufactured goods to the far corners of the earth and returned with holds laden with sugar, cotton, coffee, tea and other goods. The invention of cold storage greatly helped the process.

The "balance of payments" is vital to a trading nation. That is why it is serious when, for example, Britain's balance of payments reveals that she is importing far more than she exports, even allowing for "invisible earnings" like tourism. A nation can also go broke, just like a small business.

Of course trading in bygone days must seem more romantic than today's, unless pirates looted your cargo. The poet Matthew Arnold conjured up the good old days, describing how a Phoenician from Tyre saw a "merry Grecian coaster come, Freighted with amber grapes, and Chian Wine, Green bursting figs, and tunnies steeped in brine". That was a cargo indeed!

The industrial age

"I hope to . . . astonish the world all at once," wrote the great potter Josiah Wedgwood, to his partner in 1775.

That quotation sums up the brighter side of the Industrial Revolution, which began in Britain in the mid-18th century. The factors that made Britain "the workshop of the world" were many. She had coal supplies, a large labour force, brilliant inventors, a stable government and a large merchant fleet to carry the products all over the world.

Industrial Revolution

The men who transformed Britain mostly knew each other and exchanged ideas. The Scottish engineer, James Watt (1736-1819), father of the modern steam engine, stands out. By 1785 his engine was in use in a cotton factory. With Matthew Boulton he also set up an ironworks at Soho near Birmingham. Iron was the essential material for making the steam engines that were so vital to industry.

Richard Arkwright improved on James Hargreaves' spinning jenny and made a spinning frame, and he and Jedediah Strutt set up a spinning mill worked by water power. Crompton's mule and Cartwright's power loom were other inventions that revolutionized textiles. The textile industry was born in Lancashire where the damp atmosphere, fast-running streams and closeness of coal supplies provided ideal sites.

Industrialization made the country richer, but factory owners needed armies of workers. Too often conditions in the new factories were nightmarish, while around them depressing slums sprang up. Low wages and long hours were felt necessary in order to help industry expand. Trade unions did not exist until the 1820s. Children worked 12 hours a day in filthy conditions in the factories and coal mines.

Conditions began improving

Below: Strikes are very much a part of the industrial age. Here is an artist's impression of a strike in Belgium in the 1920s. The right to strike is one of the basic freedoms.

Right: The agricultural stand at the Great Exhibition of 1851 in Hyde Park in London was full of the latest farm equipment from ploughs to turnip slicers.

Below: An artist's impression of forging iron, the painter being Joseph Wright. The great advance in the mid-19th century was cheap steel. Henry Bessemer found that steel could be made cheaply by applying a hot blast to molten pig-iron in a "converter". Carbon was added after impurities had been expelled. Bessemer was knighted in 1879 and he died in 1898.

from the 1840s, when the Victorians heard the full facts for the first time. Gradually hours became shorter and conditions better, but the battle goes on to this day between employers and wage-earners.

Meanwhile, Britain and her growing empire blossomed. New inventors and inventions appeared almost every year. The Stephensons, father and son, helped start the Railway Age, which transformed world communications. Isambard Kingdom Brunel (1806-59) built great stretches of railway, bridges and Atlantic steamships. Others followed their lead.

Britain soon had rivals, especially the U.S.A. and Germany. Scientific progress, stirred on by men like Michael Faraday (1791-1867), the great physicist, was remarkable. Much of it affected the public directly, such as electric light and decent plumbing in the 19th century, and radio and television in the 20th century.

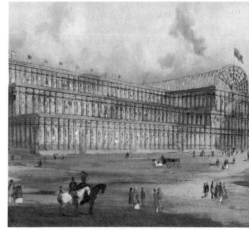

Above: Joseph Paxton was the designer of the remarkable Crystal Palace, where London's Great Exhibition of 1851 was held. It was built entirely of iron and glass. The event was a colossal success.

The 20th century

We are now in the age of electronics and the computer. Silicon chips can store knowledge in an even smaller space. But despite mini-computers like these, the problems continue. Unemployment or underemployment, the proper use of leisure, bad housing, class divisions that began in the Industrial Revolution, are still with us. Of course life is better than it was, especially due to the colossal advances in medical knowledge. This knowledge is still increasing.

Yet the legacy of the Industrial Revolution is a mixed blessing. Machines are here to stay whether we like it or not. Industrialization has had important social and political consequences. It has also given mankind new opportunities to exercise his greed and aggression.

Government

Once a few people formed a group it became necessary to organize the life within that group. Perhaps the chief was the bravest man in the group. Certainly he had to have a strong personality.

Some tribes had war chiefs and religious leaders as well, and sometimes the two jobs were combined. The great Indian Sioux leader Sitting Bull, one of the key figures at the Battle of the Little Bighorn where General Custer and his men were wiped out in 1876, was both a fighting chief and a medicine man.

Some tribes would decide important things in council, though in times of desperate crisis the views of certain men must always have come to the fore. But what if the chief died? Another chief might be elected, or the chief's son might take over. This was the beginning of a hereditary monarchy. The crown, the headdress, or simply the job, would go from father to son.

Gods and monarchs

Some rulers became gods. Two notable examples in historic times were the Pharaohs, the god-kings of Ancient Egypt, and the Inca rulers of Peru. The Inca Empire collapsed like a pack of cards when its ruler Atahualpa was killed by the Spaniards in 1533, because the people felt their god had died. Less than 200 Spaniards were able in this way to conquer an empire of millions.

Early kings were usually "absolute" or all-powerful monarchs; often they were downright tyrants. Monarchy was often linked with religion, and in the Middle Ages the idea grew in Europe that a king was God's representative.

This meant that a rebellion was a very serious matter indeed, for a monarch was crowned and anointed in God's name. Kings are called "God's anointed" in the Bible. In the 17th century, the Stuart kings of England and Scotland promoted the idea of the Divine Right of Kings. Charles I continued this tradition but was

Above: Britain's monarchy is a very ancient one. Queen Elizabeth II reigns but does not rule. She is also queen of many Commonwealth countries and is regarded as Head of the Commonwealth by its members.

beheaded in 1649 after a civil war between royalists and parliamentarians, led by Oliver Cromwell. The blow echoed round the palaces of Europe as a warning.

Charles's son, Charles II, was restored to his throne in 1660, but there was no more nonsense about the Divine Right. When his brother James tried to resurrect the idea, he was forced to flee the country.

Gradually, the idea of constitutional monarchy developed in countries such as Great Britain. Today, Queen Elizabeth II reigns but she does not rule. She is a figurehead and her government rules, though she can advise.

In the 18th century, as we saw on page 138, "benevolent despots"

Above: In Nazi Germany Hitler and his ruthless lieutenants did their best to see that the young were turned into Nazis. The Hitler Youth Movement ended with the total defeat of Germany in 1945.

ruled some parts of Europe. These were powerful monarchs like Frederick the Great of Prussia and Maria Theresa of Austria. They were thoughtful rulers and, in the case of Maria Theresa, very popular. Today, there are only a handful of monarchies in Western Europe, and a few in the Middle and Far East.

Democracy or dictatorship

Britain was the world's first parliamentary democracy. The Greeks invented democracy (government by the people), but did not extend it to include slaves. They had earlier tried the system

Left: One of the sure signs of a true democracy is the right to parade and protest about things that people believe in strongly. If peaceful protests are not allowed, democracy is in danger.

known as oligarchy, the rule of a few select citizens.

The key thing about a democracy is that everyone over a certain age has the right to vote and to re-elect or throw out the government. Democratic countries have various systems. The U.S.A. has a President who rules as well as "reigns", though with a Congress that can keep an eye on him. Italy has a president who is a figurehead and, like Britain, a prime minister who heads the government.

Sometimes a nation has two main parties, as has been the case through much of Britain's history while other democracies have several. These are then often forced to form coalition governments, the power being shared by more than one party.

Alas, much of the world is ruled by dictators. Single party elections, like Russia's, have alternative candidates, but all are members of the only party. There are military dictatorships and civilian ones. A feature of all of them is a lack of freedom, including the lack of freedom to criticize the government. Woe betide anyone who dared criticize Adolf Hitler and his Nazi Party once they held power in Germany in the 1930s. Some of today's Communist countries have an equally harsh way with "dissenters". An ideal Communist state would have everyone free and equal, a workers' paradise without profits being made by anyone. Yet this creed, proclaimed by Karl Marx from the 1840s onwards, has sometimes proved to be more ruthless than any monarchy.

Some dream of no government at all, but in the modern world that is an impossibility. It could only be achieved by an all-powerful civil service, which would in fact be a government.

Left: China has changed since this picture of a group of Chinese was taken. They are all dressed alike, and all hold copies of *The Thoughts of Chairman Mao*. Since Mao Tse-tung's death in 1976, attitudes have altered and there appears to be greater freedom.

171

World religions

Above: A striking statue of Jesus Christ, the Son of God to all Christians.

Left: Lincoln Cathedral is the third largest cathedral in England. William the Conqueror ordered it to be built in 1072 and it was completed in 20 years. After a fire in 1141, it was rebuilt. In 1674 the great architect Sir Christopher Wren added an arcade.

Below: Three holy shrines in Jerusalem. The Dome of the Rock and the Church of the Holy Sepulchre are Christian shrines, and the Western Wall is Jewish. Non-Jews call it the Wailing Wall because of the prayers and lamentations it has seen. It is said to be part of Herod's Temple.

Dome of the Rock

Western Wall

Holy Sepulchre

In the ancient world that our ancestors inhabited, there grew up the belief in gods, some good, some evil. The gods were in the thunder and the rain and lightning, in lakes and mountains, and above and below the earth. Indeed, the earth was a mother figure to most tribes.

Today there are fewer religions. Some say religion is dying, yet the facts suggest otherwise. Even in countries where it is frowned on, such as the U.S.S.R., it survives. And for many, scientific knowledge does not disprove the idea of a God.

Christianity

The most widespread religion is Christianity. Officially, there were some 1,062 million Christians in 1985. Naturally, there is no way of calculating how many of those were truly practising. About 60 per cent of that number were Roman Catholics, whose church goes back to the very start of Christianity.

Jesus Christ lived in Palestine and was crucified around A.D. 30. Such was the strength of his message of love and hope for the oppressed that his followers were able to spread it far and wide, despite appalling persecutions by the Romans. Finally, Rome itself was converted to Christianity in the 4th century.

Though Jesus preached peace and love, many Christians have behaved very differently. Christianity itself was split in two in the 16th century when Catholics and Protestants fought bloody religious wars.

Christianity is an off-shoot of Judaism, the religion of the Jews. They were the first known people to worship a single God. Their early story is told in the Old Testament, which starts as myth and merges into history.

The good Muslim has five duties: to bear witness to one God; to pray up to five times a day; to give money generously; to fast for a month called Ramadan; and, if possible, to make a journey at least once in a lifetime to the holy city of Mecca. There are also strict rules of behaviour.

Hinduism
Hinduism is a way of life as well as a faith. It has many gods and there is a belief in rebirth (reincarnation), not necessarily as a human if the dead man has been a wrongdoer.

The ultimate object of the Hindu is to attain eternal bliss. The creed is an easy-going one in some ways,

Above: The many millions of Muslims in the Middle East and elsewhere turn towards the holy city of Mecca to pray.

No race has suffered more for so long as the Jews, not least from Christian hands. Ironically, Christ and his disciples were Jews. Since 1948, the Jews have had a homeland, Israel, where so much of their history happened.

Islam
The largest non-Christian faith is Islam, a word which also describes the Muslim world. It has at least 555 million followers and the number is growing.

The Islamic god is called Allah. The faith was preached by an Arab merchant named Mohammed (570-632). Born in Mecca, he gave up business after he claimed to have been visited by an archangel. The new teachings were written down and collected in a book, the Koran, which is the Muslim bible. The Arabs thrilled to his ideas, not least because it was a fighting creed.

Above: A remarkable Hindu temple at Kandy in Ceylon, now known as Sri Lanka. The many statues are of Hindu gods.

Below: A group of Buddhists, followers of Buddha, "the Enlightened One", who lived 2,500 years ago in India, but whose influence is strong in Asia and other parts of the world, including Europe.

for there are no compulsory beliefs. However, there is a caste system involved which divides people very strictly into classes. The bottom class is the group known as the untouchables.

Buddhism
Buddhism is named after the Hindu Prince Siddhartha Gautama, otherwise known as the Buddha, or the Enlightened One. The creed has spread far beyond India, where it began. Its founder died around 480 B.C. having preached a way of escaping from the threat of endless reincarnation by living a holy life. Then eternal bliss will be attained.

Buddhism has lost much of its hold in India, but remains widely practised in other parts of Asia.

Art and architecture

Above: African art has a tradition of carving and sculpture. This 16th-century ivory mask comes from Nigeria.

Right: *The Birth of Venus* by the Italian Botticelli (1444-1510) is a marvellous picture of the Renaissance. It is now in the Uffizi Museum, Florence.

Art is a big word. It can apply to any human skill: dancing, fencing, warfare and even living. The "arts" cover everything from sculpture to singing. But here we are concerned with painting, sculpture and the art that affects all of us, architecture.

Architecture is a science as well as an art. Apart from designing skilfully, the architect must know all about building methods and materials. Today's architects use materials unknown a century ago: sheet glass, reinforced concrete, plastics, aluminium and so on.

These have naturally widened the architect's range. Formerly, the materials were wood, brick and stone, but with these the great architects and craftsmen, both known and unknown, worked miracles. Soaring walls, superb arches, wonderful domes, stately columns survive intact or can still be seen as splendid ruins. We can still marvel at European churches, the temples of Greece and Rome, the pagodas of China and Japan and the mosques of the Middle East.

Few architects get such chances to build cathedrals and palaces now, but there is plenty of excitement to be had in designing buildings and whole complexes of buildings. The architect has to consider everything from the lighting and heating to the cost of it all.

Sculpture

The arts of painting and sculpture date back to prehistoric times. They are the painter's and sculptor's way of representing someone or something, or putting over a thought or a feeling.

Above: A wonderful example of Greek architecture, with six statues acting as pillars. No civilization has excelled the Greeks in architecture.

Below: A famous example of early and truly 20th-century art. It is *Les Demoiselles d'Avignon* by the Spanish artist Picasso (1881-1973).

As everyone knows, some people are born artists, some can acquire a certain skill, others are always hopeless! So it must have been in the Stone Age.

This is not guesswork. There is proof in caves in Spain and France, especially at Lascaux in France. The drawings there of animals are full of colour and movement.

Sculpture, both in the round and in bas relief (partly raised from a flat surface), flourished in all the great early civilizations. In Athens nearly 2,500 years ago some of the loveliest statues and bas reliefs of the human figure at rest and moving were achieved.

Later, unknown sculptors filled cathedrals and churches with sculptures in wood and stone. Then came the great Renaissance sculptors (*see page 132*) including Michelangelo, Bernini and Donatello. The Frenchman Rodin, was the greatest 19th-century sculptor, while more modern greats include the British sculptors Epstein, Henry Moore and Barbara Hepworth.

Painting
Painting spans the world even more than sculpture. Paint can wear off all too easily, which is why discoveries are so important, whether in tombs of Egyptian pharaohs or on the walls of Pompeii and Herculaneum, which were both buried when Vesuvius erupted in A.D. 79.

Early religious painting in Christian Europe was anonymous, but then came the Renaissance, which brought out Italian masters, including Michelangelo, Raphael and Leonardo. The 17th century saw Dutch landscape painters, the Dutch master Rembrandt, and the stark figures of El Greco (the Greek who moved to Spain). Eighteenth-century Britain produced the great English portrait painters, Gainsborough and Reynolds.

France dominated the 19th century, including the famous Impressionists who painted out of doors

Above: The spectacular Castle Neuschwanstein, built by King Ludwig of Bavaria in 1867, almost looks like something out of fairyland. Ludwig was a sad and lonely figure. He helped the composer Richard Wagner stage his great operas about German myths and legends, then turned to building. His ideas were so extravagant that he was declared mad.

and were thrilled by the effect of changing light. They included Monet and Renoir. Masters like Cézanne and Van Gogh (who was Dutch) advanced the frontiers of art still further.

Our century has seen an explosion of styles of painting. One entirely new field has been abstract art, which uses line, colour and movement without recognizable shapes to convey an idea or feeling or to appeal to the mind or eye. Yet traditional forms of art still flourish, too.

Above: A poster of the French actress Sarah Bernhardt as the sorceress Medea. She thrilled theatre audiences a century ago as much as Laurence Olivier has thrilled them in our time.

Above: The brilliance of Russian dancers is largely due to the rigorous training they receive at the great ballet schools in Leningrad and Moscow. Nureyev and Baryshnikov were trained in Leningrad.

The performing arts are there to be enjoyed. Of course, if you are slowly struggling line by line through a Shakespeare play for an examination, boredom can set in.

This is understandable, for the truth is that great art, though it can be simple, even at first sight or sound, is often so rich and dense in texture that it cannot be grasped at once. Yet with a little effort the listener or spectator can find more and more to enjoy and even to love for a lifetime.

The performing arts include theatre, opera, ballet, films and music.

Theatre

The theatre covers several types of play. There is tragedy, like Shakespeare's *Othello*, about the downfall of a great man. There are comedies, thrillers, dramas with strong stories, and plays which are a mixture of styles, like tragi-comedies.

There are also farces, in which the comic situations are so appalling for the characters that the result is tragedy turned upside down. And there are musicals, such as *The Sound of Music* and *Evita*. The first great plays, both tragedies and comedies, were written over 2,000 years ago in Ancient Greece. The theatre thus has a long history.

Ballet

Ballet was born in 17th-century France. This elaborate form of dancing can tell a story, as in *Swan Lake*, or can simply be dancing for its own sake, expressing a mood like love, or just delighting an audience by brilliant movements.

The key figure is the choreographer, who invents steps and rehearses the dancers. Russia's dancers have been the most exciting for nearly a century, but some of her finest dancers have left Russia for the West, including

Nureyev, Makarova and Baryshnikov.

Today, the most creative ballet countries are America, Britain, Germany and Denmark. Britain's Royal Ballet and Ballet Rambert are world famous. The first was founded by Ninette de Valois, the second by Marie Rambert, whose company is now an experimental one. The most famous of all British dancers is probably Margot Fonteyn.

Ballet became a great art form 70 years ago when Serge Diaghilev brought his Russian company to Western Europe. Overnight, ballet ceased to be simply a pretty spectacle and became a mixture of dance, drama, painting and music.

Opera

Opera dates from 1597, when a group of poets and musicians in Florence tried to recapture the spirit of Greek drama. They

believed Greek actors intoned their lines, but the operas they created with words being the equal of the music gave way to operas where music and song became the senior partners.

To an Italian or German singing a story is almost second nature, just as the Shakespeare-lover accepts characters speaking verse. In both cases the reason is the same: to heighten moods and feelings.

Listening to or watching opera can be very rewarding. Mozart, Verdi, Wagner, Puccini and Richard Strauss are some of the most popular composers.

Music and films

Few modern operas or symphonies are truly successful in the popular market, although there is no reason why this should be so. Many people are nervous of "serious" music, but they have failed to understand that all music, whether Beethoven or rock, is there to be enjoyed. The symphony orchestra as we know it

Above: The symphony orchestra is a comparatively recent development in the history of music. A modern orchestra comprises first and second violins, violas, cellos, double-basses, flutes, clarinets, oboes, bassoons, trumpets, trombones, horns and percussion.

dates from about 200 years ago, though it was smaller then. Modern "popular" music sees a constant search for new forms of expression in music. Since the 1950s, electronic music has appeared on the scene.

Films have been dominated by America since the silent days earlier this century. The first film superstar was Charlie Chaplin. Occasionally a film becomes legendary, like Orson Welles' *Citizen Kane* and some of John Ford's Westerns. The film's director is the key figure. There have been great, good and bad films made in many countries, including Britain, Italy, France, Japan and Russia. But basically, all films set out to entertain.

Entertain? That is back to the point at which we started.

Above: In Africa, and in many other parts of the world, traditional songs, dances and music play a central part in everyday life. Many of those heard and seen today have ancient origins.

177

The world of books

corde: qm ipi deum videbut. Beati pa
cifici: qm filij dei vocabutur. Beati q
plecutionē patiūtur ꝓpter iusticiam:
qm ipsoꝝ est regnū celoꝝ. Beati estis
cū maledixerint vobis· et plecuti vos
fuerint et dixerūt omē malū aduersū
qm ipsoꝝ est regnū celoꝝ. Beati estis

Above: No one is certain who was Europe's first printer, but it may well have been Johann Gütenberg (1397-1468), who was born in the German town of Mainz. Mainz became a centre of printing, and sent out printers to other towns. Unhappily, Gütenberg died in poverty.

Left: Part of Gütenberg's famous Bible.

Ask a friend to list the most important of mankind's inventions and discoveries and he or she may say the internal combustion engine, the cure for some disease, the aeroplane, television and so on.

Yet none of these, scientific or otherwise, are as important, indeed none of them would have even been possible, without the greatest of all inventions, the book.

Consider what the book or printed word can do. It can give pleasure in the form of stories, poetry and plays. And it can teach anything and everything from how to build a model boat to how to build a skyscraper; from how to cook a three-course dinner to how to ease pain and suffering. An expert's knowledge can now be spread all round the world.

It was not always so. For many centuries books had to be written out by hand. Even advanced civilizations like Ancient Greece and Rome had to do it the slow way.

History of books and printing

The Ancient Egyptians were writing books some 4,500 years ago, written on the reed "papyrus". That is where our word paper comes from. The fibres of the plant, when pressed into a sheet, make a good writing material. In the 1850s it was discovered how paper could be made from wood pulp.

Printing started in the Far East, centuries before it reached Europe. It was in the 15th century that Johannes Gütenberg in Germany and William Caxton in England, started printing, using separate pieces of metal type.

Though modern printing methods are far in advance of Caxton's, he and his contemporaries made the big breakthrough. Whereas printing type had to be put into place by hand, now machines do it. The Bible, which had been laboriously copied by hand and was not widely available, could now be printed and became familiar to countless thousands. It thus came to be translated widely. The plays of Shakespeare, who died in 1616, were first published in 1623. Many of them would have been lost for ever without printing.

A few years earlier, one of the first novels had appeared. This was *Don Quixote* by the Spanish writer Cervantes, about an eccentric knight and his faithful servant, Sancho Panza. By the 18th century novels were all the rage. One of the first great British ones was *Tom Jones* (1749) by Henry Fielding.

Children were not catered for until the 19th century. Books such as Defoe's *Robinson Crusoe* and Swift's *Gulliver's Travels* are now read by children, but they were not written for them. Young people had to make do with books written to "improve" them. Fairy stories began to be published in the 18th century, but the flood of children's books did not start until the 19th century. Space does not permit any sort of list, so here are two ever-popular books that everyone knows: *Treasure Island* (1883) by Robert Louis Stevenson and *Winnie the Pooh* (1926) by A. A.

Right: The splendid library of the Escurial, the palace and monastery that King Philip II of Spain had built in the mid-16th century. He died there in 1598.

Milne, for example.

In the days before radio and television, novels achieved huge popularity. Charles Dickens and Alexander Dumas were read the world over. In our own time, though people lament that too few people actually read books, the facts suggest otherwise. The paper-back has brought the world of cheap books to the masses.

Libraries and publishing

Public libraries help. Though they date back a long way, the turning point came in Britain in the middle of the 19th century, when the first free ones were opened.

Long before then a whole new profession had grown up, the profession of publisher. And another profession, journalism, flourished also. Since early in the 17th century there had been newspapers. The very first seem to have appeared in Germany in 1609. Britain's first successful one, *The Daily Courant,* appeared in 1702 and lasted until 1735. It could be bought in London "next door to the King's Arms Tavern at Fleet Bridge"!

Books continue to pour out from the presses: fiction, biographies, technical books, thrillers, comic books, adventure stories and love stories. If a classic novel is tele-vized, thousands of copies have to be published to cope with the demand. Meanwhile information, scientific or otherwise, can be flashed around the world in an instant. And if it has to be accurate information, the written word is sent or read out. Our modern world would find it difficult to ma-nage without it.

Left: Books mean knowledge as well as fun, as these Australian children are no doubt finding. Books pass on useful information, great literature. even humour.

Sports and pastimes

From archery to yachting, sport is keenly followed or played by hundreds of millions of people. Note that word "followed" however, for many who claim to love sport never get around to playing any.

Use of leisure time
It is not known who invented sport. In the remote human past, everyday activities like hunting and fighting were considered great sport. Red Indians thought horse-stealing the greatest sport of all. The word sport began life as disport, a word commonly used in the Middle Ages.

Sport requires leisure, which explains why the rules of many of the world's most popular sports were drawn up in the Victorian age by the British middle classes, who had a reasonable amount of time to enjoy life. Added to that, the British public school system encouraged teamwork and therefore team games. The result was soccer, rugby football, and cricket as we know them today, and non-team games in the true sense of team, such as lawn tennis, badminton, fives and squash.

Above: A motor race in Italy.

Below: In front is the Russian sprinter Borzov, who won the 100 and 200 metres at the Munich Olympics in 1972. Each year more records are broken as athletes strive to be the fastest man or woman.

Mass football was all the rage in the Middle Ages. The authorities were always banning it because it interfered with archery drill and because it caused riots. There were few rules and many casualties. In Wales the game was called knappan and there were sometimes 2,000 players, some of them playing on horseback with cudgels to hit the wooden ball. The object of the game was to get the ball into

Below: Cycling is universally popular. The earliest known bicycle race was in 1868, and cycling has been an Olympic sport since the modern Olympics began in 1896.

Above: Soccer is the most popular sport on earth, and these British supporters at Liverpool Football Club would no doubt say theirs is the finest team!

Left: Chess is a very ancient game. There have been world championships since the 1880s, and Russia alone has more than 7,000,000 players who take part in competitions. The longest known game lasted 200 hours. It took place in Bristol, in south-western Britain, in 1984.

convince people that sport is sport and not a matter of vast importance and national prestige. What really matters most is the game itself and how it is played. A win should be a cause for rejoicing, not for violence.

Modern popular sports

Two of the most popular sports are angling and golf. The first, even more than most, is something you adore or are bored stiff by. It needs a special kind of patience. The second, though usually expensive to play, is very hard to play well, but very satisfying when you do. Because it is not over strenuous, it can be enjoyed by anyone. So can lawn tennis at an ordinary level, though at the top this pleasant, social game becomes very tough indeed.

Sports have to be attractive to survive because there are so many more things to do with one's leisure time nowadays. Some sports, of course, can only flourish in certain countries. An Austrian soon learns how to ski, whereas the average Briton has few chances to enjoy skiing near home, except for some Scots.

A sport can vary from nation to nation. Cricket, the great game of the Commonwealth, is an example. All the energy of West Indians shows in the way they play the game, while the sense of the timelessness of the Orient seems to result in numerous draws between India and Pakistan.

The most popular sport on earth is soccer. Millions might claim that it is not their favourite game, but its appeal is now worldwide. This is based on two things. First, it is a very exciting game, but so are others. The second reason may explain just why it has conquered the world: it is so easy to arrange a game. Most sports need special equipment, and the right ground. Yet in its basic form all soccer needs is a ball, an open space and goalposts made out of four coats thrown on the ground. No wonder it succeeds!

one's own village, at any cost.

Olympiads

The greatest sporting occasion, the Olympic Games, was revived in modern times after having been one of the glories of Ancient Greece. The games were a period when the rival city-states forgot their quarrels and enjoyed their athletes' prowess. Of course, there was still rivalry both on and off the field. The first games were held in 776 B.C. and the last in ancient times were held in A.D. 393. In 1896 they were revived in Greece, and have been held every four years ever since except during periods of war.

Rivalry in sport is natural and healthy though, as everybody knows, it can lead to violence and hatred. It is not always possible to

181

Today's technological world

Science is the name we give to the process of discovering the laws that govern our universe or, in other words, the exploration of nature. This involves the discovery of everything from distant stars to the working of the human brain, and from the most advanced mathematics to new medicines.

Some science is carried out just to find the answers to new questions or problems. This is often called pure science. The term applied science is used when the discovery is put to some particular use. Applied science is the same as technology, but technology goes further in discovering answers to problems which need resolving as soon as possible, for example, the best way to preserve strawberries or to build a new hospital.

Technology in history

Some people think of technology as something new. Man has, in fact, used technology for thousands of years, and because of this has become one of the most successful of all creatures.

Humans are not especially large, fast or fierce, and we lack the sharp fangs and claws which other creatures have. We have come to rule our planet because our brains are larger, and they have enabled us to find new answers (in science) and put them to use (in technology).

Early technology was concerned with how to make the best fire, how to sharpen stone or wood weapons, and how to make the best use of an animal killed in the hunt. Later technology was concerned with the cultivation of the land and domesticating animals.

Modern technology

As the scope of human knowledge became wider, the rate at which it

Below: Many people think that the Apollo flight to the Moon in 1969 symbolized technology. This, in fact, was a very specialized task not connected with the fields in which most technologists work. Huge sums of money were set aside to carry out the Apollo programme.

was gathered also increased. Though it is difficult to measure, the whole of the human knowledge of 1780 was perhaps less than the amount of new knowledge gained each day in 1980. School-leavers today ought to know a great deal more than the great scientists of 200 years ago.

Some areas in which progress has obviously been very fast indeed are the science of materials, atoms and nuclear power, diseases and their treatment, transport, communications, and most forms of manufacturing. Such fields of activity are often helped by inventions and lucky discoveries that provide unexpected answers.

Problems of technology

The more we discover, the greater our power becomes. Nearly all this power is put to good use. For example, most nuclear research is aimed at finding better ways of providing energy without the pollution that comes from using coal and oil. But nuclear energy can also be used to make bombs, and nuclear accidents, like that at Chernobyl in 1986, can have serious and far-reaching effects.

Even discoveries about our bodies, and how we reproduce and behave, are seen by some people as a threat. We may soon learn how people become criminals, and how they could be reformed to make them useful members of society. Yet "changing" people is often thought to be wrong. There is a danger that we might start to divide people into a top group of those with power and a lower group who are little better than robots.

So far, however, this is not the case – but that is how people used to be. It is largely due to technology that human beings have gradually become more equal.

Below: A later Moon mission, Apollo 15, arrived with a Lunar Rover, a wheeled vehicle driven by electric batteries and designed for travel on the Moon's surface. The Apollo Moon missions provided scientists with fresh information about how the Moon may have been formed.

Astronomy

Above: In 1609 the great Italian scientist Galileo used what was then a new invention, the telescope, to observe the Moon more closely. He found a world of mountains and valleys. At first he thought the great plains were seas and named them as such. He then turned his telescope on the other planets and discovered four moons orbiting Jupiter.

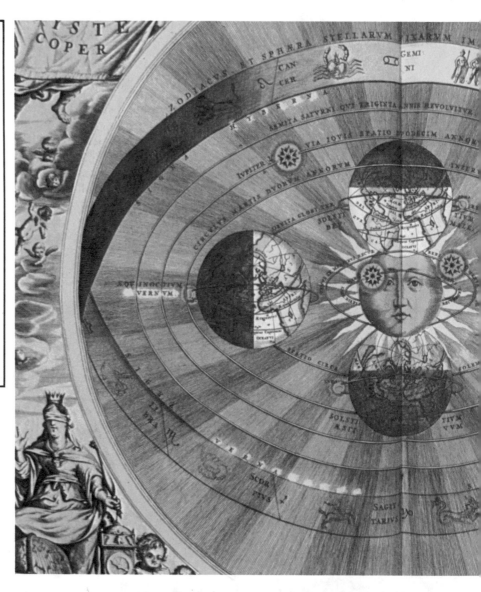

Above: The Greeks were the first to suggest that the earth might not lie at the centre of the universe. But it was left to the Polish astronomer Copernicus in 1543 to publish solid evidence that the earth moves round the Sun. Even then it took 100 years before the theory was widely believed.

Astronomy became the first science many thousands of years ago, when men began to study the Sun, Moon, planets and stars and record their movements across the sky. The heavenly bodies fascinated man, for what they were made of or why they existed was a complete mystery. It was noticed, however, that they moved in predictable, regular ways, which provided a useful and reliable means of measuring the passage of time and dividing up the year.

It was seen that the stars formed a variety of fixed patterns in the sky but it seemed that a few stars did not fit in with these patterns. They appeared to move across the sky from one star group to another and became known as the wanderers. The Greek word for wanderer was *planetes*, from which our word planet was derived.

The ancient astronomers
With no telescopes, and without even the aid of spectacles, the ancient astronomers had no chance of discovering much about the nature of the stars and planets. This meant that for thousands of years, astronomy was concerned mainly with the positions and

movements of these bodies. The star patterns, or constellations, were given names, so that parts of the sky could be referred to easily. Gods, heroes, animals and objects all had constellations named after them. The Babylonians noticed that the planets all moved through the same band of stars. They divided this band, called the zodiac, into twelve equal parts, naming each one after a constellation it contained. We call these twelve names the signs of the zodiac. The Babylonians thought that the positions of the planets in the zodiac somehow affected their lives.

The Egyptians developed a deeper understanding of astronomy than the Babylonians and used their observations as the basis

for an accurate calendar (*see page 188*). Of all the ancient peoples, however, it was the Greeks who made the greatest contribution to astronomy.

Greek astronomy
Thales of Miletus was the first of the great Greek astronomers. He is said to have predicted the eclipse of the Sun in 585 B.C., and may have been the first person to state that the earth is a sphere. Aristotle came to the same conclusion about

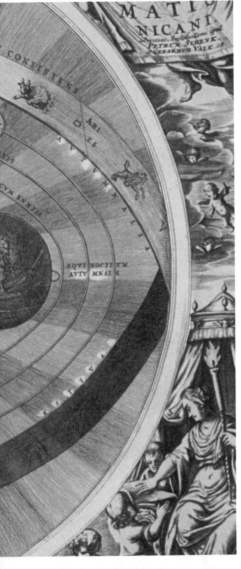

300 B.C., after watching an eclipse of the Moon. He realized that the earth's shadow was passing across the Moon, and he could see it showed the earth's curved profile. The following century, Aristarchus of Samos made an even more startling statement. "The planets", he said, "revolve around the Sun", but most people believed that the earth, being so important, must be at the centre of the entire universe.

Of all the Greek astronomers, the greatest was Hipparchus, who lived in about 100 B.C. His important work included the cataloguing of over 1,000 stars. Some 300 years later, this information was published by another great astronomer called Ptolemy. Unfortunately he supported the theory of the earth-centred universe, and this idea was accepted, almost without question, for many centuries.

Modern astronomy

The turning point in astronomy came in 1543 when a Polish priest called Nicolaus Copernicus declared that the Sun was, after all, at the centre of our planetary system. The Church strongly opposed this teaching, and one outspoken supporter of Copernicus called Giordano Bruno was burned at the stake. However, the idea of a Sun-centred system gradually became accepted.

The invention of the telescope in 1608 finally gave astronomers an opportunity to study the heavenly bodies in more detail. With the new instrument, Galileo soon discovered the dark patches on the Sun called sunspots, as well as Saturn's rings and four of Jupiter's moons.

A new era of astronomy had begun. Today, huge astronomical telescopes in many parts of the world probe the heavens in a continual search for new knowledge about the universe.

Below: The 510-centimetre Hale telescope in California, U.S.A., is one of the world's largest reflectors. The telescope is solely used for taking pictures. Unlike the eye, photographic film can "store" light falling on it and thus show stars too faint to be seen by the naked eye.

Above: The dome of the Hale Observatory at night, in the open position. Observatories are generally sited on hilltops where the air is clear.

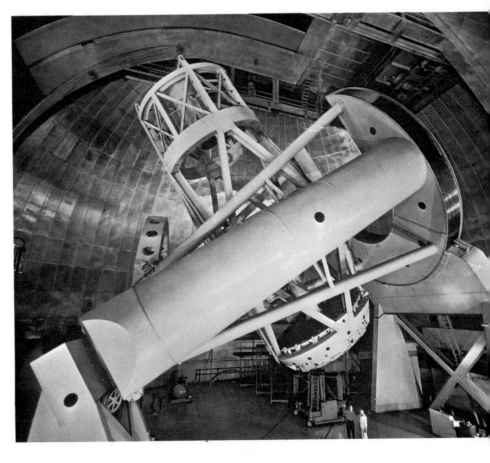

Ways of measuring

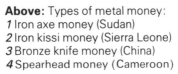

Above: Types of metal money:
1 Iron axe money (Sudan)
2 Iron kissi money (Sierra Leone)
3 Bronze knife money (China)
4 Spearhead money (Cameroon)

Above and **right:** Primitive societies all have their own particular ways in which wealth is shown. To some Pacific islanders, these huge quarried stones were used as a form of money. To a Tibetan it was a brick made out of compressed tea leaves. The economy of New Guinea was dependent on trading in cowrie shells until 1940.

Young children often use their fingers for counting and adding small numbers. Even adults sometimes use their fingers to indicate numbers when talking to someone who does not understand their language.

Thousands of years ago, man adopted this system to count his possessions. Small numbers presented no problems but, for numbers above ten, it was necessary to note the number of tens counted as well as the number of units. A second person could count each completed ten, up to ten tens, and

a third person could count the number of hundreds. In this way, our hands formed the basis of our common system of counting – the decimal (tens) system.

Using a pile of stones for counting proved more convenient when dealing with large numbers. One stone could represent each object counted, but it was simpler to use separate piles of stones to represent units, tens, hundreds and higher multiples of ten. This meant that fewer stones were needed and made the larger numbers easier to recognize. For example, instead of

using 213 stones to represent 213 objects, only six stones were needed. The groups of stones were usually placed between parallel lines marked on the ground or drawn in a layer of sand sprinkled on a table. Later, the stones were often put in grooves carved in a table top. Instead of stones, wooden counters were sometimes used. As they were all the same size, they were easier to handle and count. The next development was to use bead-like counters threaded on parallel rods or wires mounted in a frame.

The calculating devices mentioned above may have been first used in Ancient Egypt or Babylon, but the earliest surviving examples date from the time of the Ancient Greeks. The Romans also used these calculators, and the idea probably spread from them to the Chinese. Although some people could carry out written calcula-

Left: A slide rule and a speedometer are analog computers. These represent figures as physical magnitudes. The milometer and abacus are digital computers. Here quantities are represented by actual numbers.

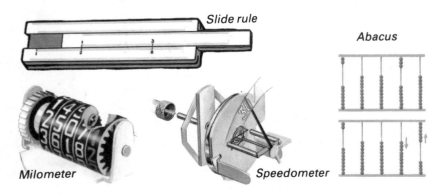

Slide rule

Abacus

Milometer

Speedometer

tions, early writing materials were expensive. For this reason, calculating boards and bead frames remained popular for centuries. The boards survived in Europe until the early 1600s, and the bead frame is still used in some eastern countries today.

The calculating board was called the abacus, from a Greek word meaning slab. The same name became used for the bead frame. Designs vary, but all work on the same basic principle. The Japanese soroban abacus, for example, has five beads on each rod. One of these beads has a value of five, while the other four each have a value of one. A total of nine therefore can be counted by sliding the beads along a rod. A count of ten is registered by returning the beads to their original positions and moving a "one" bead on the next rod. Because it is so cheap and reliable, the abacus may even survive the strong competition from today's pocket-size electronic calculators.

Computers

A computer is a device used to make calculations: there are two types – analog and digital. Digital computers are counting devices, while analog computers are concerned with measurement. We usually associate complex electronic equipment with the term computer, but it can also be applied to numerous simple instruments, such as the abacus, thermometer, milometer and speedometer. The milometer is a mechanical device for counting the number of kilometres or miles a vehicle has travelled. Like the abacus, therefore, it is classed as a digital computer. In a typical thermometer and speedometer, a quantity varies in a similar, or analogous way to the quantity under investigation. This is why these devices are known as analog computers. In a thermometer, a column of liquid rises or falls with temperature. In a speedometer, the deflection of the needle across the dial varies with

the speed of the object.

Electronic analog computers are used mainly in laboratories for making engineering calculations. Electronic digital computers are the high-speed accounting machines of the business world.

Above: A pathology technician checks a blood sample. She is using the counter on her right to keep track of the number of blood cells per square millimetre on the slide under the microscope.

Below: The interior of a modern computer room.

Time

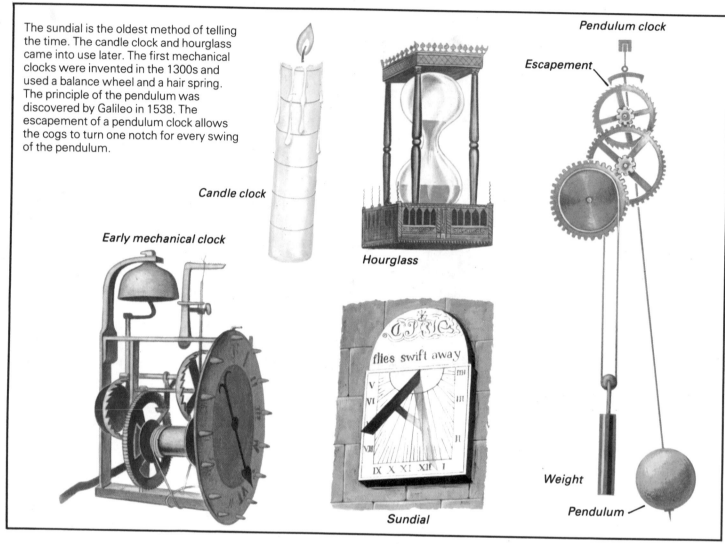

The sundial is the oldest method of telling the time. The candle clock and hourglass came into use later. The first mechanical clocks were invented in the 1300s and used a balance wheel and a hair spring. The principle of the pendulum was discovered by Galileo in 1538. The escapement of a pendulum clock allows the cogs to turn one notch for every swing of the pendulum.

Candle clock

Early mechanical clock

Hourglass

Pendulum clock

Escapement

Weight

Pendulum

flies swift away

Sundial

The heavenly bodies are man's natural timekeepers. Their movements through space cause changes that indicate the passing days, months, seasons and years.

The length of the day is set by the rate at which the earth spins on its axis. It is this motion which causes the apparent rising and setting of the Sun. The lunar (Moon) month is the time taken for the Moon to orbit the earth. This movement causes the regular changes of the Moon's appearance that we call phases. The bright yellow disc of a "full" Moon is seen when the Sun's rays completely illuminate the side of the Moon that can be seen from earth. As the Moon changes its position, less and less of the illuminated part is visible from the earth. Eventually, at "new" Moon, the side facing the earth is in darkness. After this, the

Moon gradually becomes "full" again.

As the earth moves in its orbit around the Sun, a regular pattern of seasonal changes marks the passing of each year. This occurs because the earth is tilted on its axis. During part of the orbit, the north pole is tilted towards the Sun and the south pole is tilted away from it. This period is summertime in the north and wintertime for countries south of the equator. When the earth is at the other side of the Sun, the north pole is tilted away from the Sun, and the south pole is tilted towards it. This gives rise to winter conditions in the north and summer conditions in the south.

When man began to settle and farm the land, he needed to plan when to sow his crops and wanted to know when to expect a harvest.

Calendars were devised for this purpose, but problems arose immediately as the year does not divide up into an exact number of lunar months. Apart from which the year does not happen to be equal to an exact number of days.

The Ancient Babylonians assumed that there were exactly twelve lunar months to the year. As a result, their calendar was about eleven days too short, and the months gradually got out of step with the seasons as the years passed. To prevent this, the Babylonians added an extra month every third year. They also made other, smaller corrections when necessary. They knew that certain stars became visible at particular times of the year and used this fact to keep a check on their calendar. The calendar used in western countries today is based on the system

Above: A mariner's astrolabe, probably of Spanish origin and made in 1585, held in front of an ancient navigational map. The astrolabe measured the angle between the stars and the horizon. This roughly gives your latitude. Astrolabes were probably invented by the Ancient Greeks.

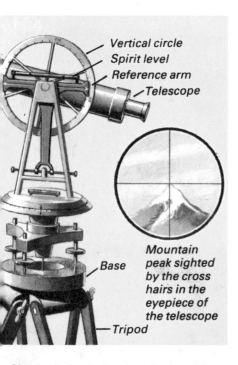

Vertical circle
Spirit level
Reference arm
Telescope

Mountain peak sighted by the cross hairs in the eyepiece of the telescope

Base

Tripod

Above: A simple drawing of a theodolite. A surveyor points the telescope at the object and centres it using the cross hairs in the eyepiece.

devised by Julius Caesar in 46 B.C. He introduced the idea of having a leap year with an extra day every four years. Slight modifications have been made since then to ensure long-term accuracy.

Clocks and watches

Before clocks were invented, the movements of the Sun and stars were used to tell the time. Then the Egyptians invented a form of sundial. This first clock was simply a stick placed upright in the ground. Its shadow varied in length and position as the Sun moved across the sky. The shadow passed over a scale marked around the base of the stick, so the time of day could be seen immediately. The Sun's apparent path through the sky changes throughout the year, which makes the sundial inaccurate, but the fact that the sundial "hour" was actually longer in summer than in winter was of little importance thousands of years ago. The sundial still enabled a community to work or pray together and it did not matter if the actual starting and finishing times varied a little. A much more serious problem was that the sundial became useless when the Sun was covered by cloud. This led to the development of other timekeeping devices that did not depend on the Sun.

Below: The compass is an essential aid to navigation on land, at sea and in the air.

In its simplest form, the Egyptian clepsydra, or water clock, was a container from which water slowly leaked. As the water level went down, its position against a marked scale indicated the time. Later water clocks became more elaborate. Some had a float that moved a pointer to indicate the time; others even had a mechanism to strike the hours on a bell.

Another early timekeeping device was the candle. Provided it was not put in a draughty place, the candle would burn at a fairly steady rate. Its length, therefore, was an indication of the time it had been burning. A scale of notches along the candle showed the passing hours.

The first mechanical clocks appeared in the 1300s. A weight on a cord pulled a toothed wheel around, and a device called an escapement regulated its speed. Spring-driven clocks were first made in the 1400s, and pendulum controlled escapements were introduced in the 1650s by Christiaan Huygens. In 1675, Huygens invented the hairspring and balance wheel regulator system. This enabled fairly accurate portable clocks and watches to be made for the first time. Today's electronic watches are accurate to a few seconds per month and scientific clocks regulated by the vibrations of atoms are accurate to one second in tens of thousands of years.

Simple tools and machines

Man has developed all kinds of machines and tools to help him do his work faster. Among the most useful and simple machines are levers, pulleys and gears. Levers were particularly important to primitive societies and enabled heavy weights to be moved and lifted using quite simple equipment. Without levers, huge structures, such as the pyramids of Ancient Egypt, could never have been built.

Mechanisms such as pulleys, levers and gears can make a force greater. If a person were to push on one part of a mechanism with a force of ten kilograms, by using a lever or pulley, that force could be magnified to 100 or even 1,000 kilograms. This increase in force is called "mechanical advantage".

The distance moved by the force has to be greater than the distance moved by the load. This is very clear when a heavy weight is lifted using a rope or cable passed over pulley blocks. One pulley is at-

Above: Over 2,000 years ago builders used simple machines to drive piles (strong pillars) into the ground. In this picture there is only one pulley at the top, so there is no mechanical advantage in lifting the heavy stone.

Below: A pulley reduces the effort needed to lift loads. (*Left*) the effort needed is half the weight of the load. (*Right*) the effort needed is just over 30 per cent of the load. Using gears (*Bottom*), a given effort can move a large load slowly, or a small one quickly.

Below: Tower cranes can place loads anywhere within a large circle. The operator has to remember, however, that the load he can safely handle has to be reduced as the lifting carriage travels out to the far end of the jib (arm).

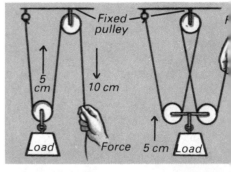

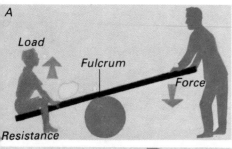

A

Load

Fulcrum

Force

Resistance

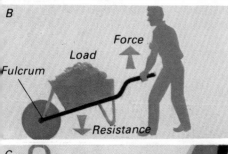

B

Force

Load

Fulcrum

Resistance

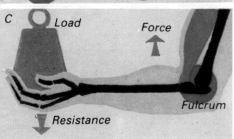

C

Load

Force

Fulcrum

Resistance

Left: The three classes of lever: (*A*), first-order; (*B*), second-order; (*C*), third-order.

Right and **below:** A lock is a way of raising or lowering boats at a point where stretches of a canal or river are at different levels. When a ship has to be raised (*A*) it enters the lock with the upper gates shut. The lower gates then close, and water is run in from the upper level through sliding sluices (*B*). When the level has reached that of the upper part of the waterway the upper gates are opened (*C*).

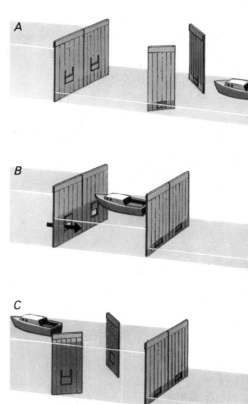

A

B

C

tached to an overhead beam while the load is suspended from a pulley lower down (as in the picture below left). The operator can lift a very heavy load, such as a car engine, but he has to pull a long length of cable or chain to move it just a few centimetres.

Some of the effort made by the operator is actually wasted during this operation. This is because the pulley, and every other mechanical device, suffers from friction. This wastes some of the force being applied, and turns it into noise and heat.

Gears

Many modern machines use gears. The most common kinds of gear-wheels have intermeshing teeth. This means that the gears run together without slipping, so little effort is lost. Friction is reduced by oiling the gears.

If two identical gears run together, they turn at the same speed. More often, a small gear runs with a large one. As the small gear turns, the large one will turn more slowly but it will overcome

much greater resistance. A system of gears enables a single person to open heavy lock gates. A small handle is wound round and round, connected to a small gear.

Levers and wedges

The lever was one of the first machines to be invented, thousands of years ago. The simplest kind of lever consists of a beam on a pivot. The pivot is called the "fulcrum". When a force is applied to one end of the beam, the effort on the other end is magnified. A see-saw is a simple kind of lever. If the fulcrum is placed near one end, a small child moving through a large distance can balance ten adults.

A tyre lever works like the see-saw. A force applied to one end of it will remove a firmly attached tyre (through a smaller distance) at the other. The see-saw and tyre lever are called "first-order" levers because the load and the effort are on opposite sides of the fulcrum. A wheelbarrow is a second-order lever, because in this case the load and effort are on the same side of

the fulcrum. When you use a wheelbarrow you have to lift the handles farther than you lift the load, but the weight of the load can be more than you could lift alone.

In the case of a third-order lever, the load moves further than the applied force. If you lift a ten-kilogram load in your hand, then the biceps muscle in your upper arm may have to pull with a force of 100 kilograms. In the picture above left you can see that the load on the elbow joint is much greater than the weight being lifted.

Ancient builders used slopes or inclines to drag heavy stones up to a height. If an incline could be wrapped up round a rod it would result in something like a screw-thread. Like levers, a screw-thread can multiply a force. A car mechanic changing a wheel may use a jack with a long screw thread to lift up a heavy car. This has an added safety advantage that the thread can be made to be irreversible. Even though it may be oiled, it cannot possibly slip back and let the car crash down on someone lying underneath.

191

Useful materials

Early man had only the natural materials he found around him. He soon found many uses for wood, and after he had discovered fire he used heat to make wood harder for making spears and tools. He also found that he could make things out of stone. Some stone objects were carved, but only after much hard work, while weaker stone, such as flint, could be split and chipped quite quickly. A special advantage of flint was that it could be given sharp edges, for cutting.

Metals

Probably the greatest single advance from stone was the discovery of metals. We think man used copper at least 6,000 years ago. He soon found that this soft metal could be turned into a harder one, bronze, by "alloying" it, or mixing it in with tin. Later, about 4,000 years ago, the first smiths were transforming iron into tools, weapons and ornaments.

The Iron Age has never really passed, because our most common metal today, steel, is nearly all iron. The strength and other qualities of metals depend a great deal upon very small amounts of other materials that may be mixed or combined in them. Pure iron is quite soft, but the addition of a trace of carbon results in steel, which is much harder and stronger. There are many kinds of steel. Some are strong when red-hot, others are stainless, and there are many special steels which can be used for anything from armour-plate to razor-blades.

Alloys

These different kinds of steel are all alloys, the name given to mixtures of metals with other metals or non-metals. Solder is an alloy specially designed to melt at a low temperature. Cupro-nickel is the "copper" used for some coins. Light alloys are those made chiefly of aluminium. Aircraft are mostly made of Duralumin and similar light alloys in which the aluminium is mixed with a little copper and

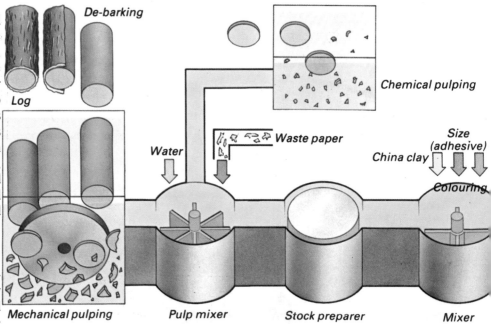

De-barking

Log

Mechanical pulping

Chemical pulping

Water

Waste paper

China clay

Size (adhesive)

Colouring

Pulp mixer

Stock preparer

Mixer

Above: Paper is today made almost entirely from wood-pulp. The soft wet mass is drawn off onto a wire gauze and dried and rolled. There are many kinds of paper, with different constituents, thicknesses or surface finishes.

Right: There is an even greater variety of pottery. Some modern plates are even made of glass, plastics or paper.

magnesium. For special purposes, more costly titanium alloys are used. Alloys, chiefly of nickel, are used in jet engines where the turbine blades have to keep their strength at almost white heat.

Electronics, as described later, has demanded a completely new set of materials, some of which are not metals at all. Transistors are often made of germanium, a member of a family called "semi-conductors". The key material in micro-electronics is now silicon, a non-metal which, next to oxygen, is the most abundant material in our earth.

Non-metals

Pottery is made of different kinds of clay, shaped by skilled hands and fired, or set hard, in a hot kiln. The finest kind is called porcelain, and is almost transparent.

The most transparent common material is glass which, like pottery and bricks, is one of a group of materials called ceramics. Glass is

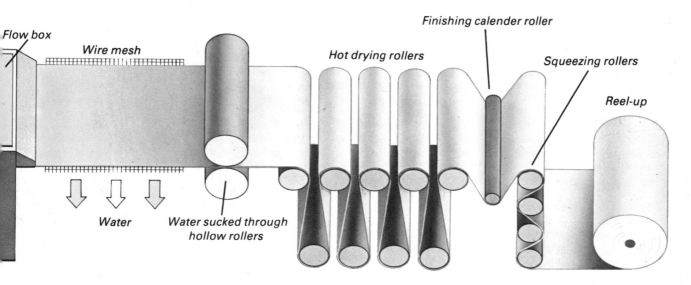

Flow box
Wire mesh
Finishing calender roller
Hot drying rollers
Squeezing rollers
Reel-up
Water
Water sucked through hollow rollers

Above: A glassblower has to work very quickly to shape red-hot glass before it cools and hardens.

Left: Running off white-hot molten iron, called pig-iron, at the bottom of the blast furnace in which it was made.

Above: Trees give us more than wood. Some maple trees yield syrup. Conifers produce turpentine. The acacia produces gum, and the sapodilla plum gives us chewing gum. Wellingtons often use natural rubber.

made by melting sand, limestone and soda in a furnace. Again, there are many kinds. Some are shaped while hot and plastic, while others, for example sheets of glass, are floated on molten tin until they set, perfectly flat.

Plastics
In the past 30 years we have seen a revolution in the form of man-made materials called plastics. Glass strengthens plastics when spun into fine glass fibres which are then moulded into useful articles with resin adhesives.

Many plastics are made in the form of fine fibres. Rayon was the first, and today we have many more including nylon, acetate and polyester fibres, all sold under various brand names. (Of course, there are natural fibres as well, including cotton, wool and silk.)

Other plastics are supplied in the form of powders, granules or solids, often already self-coloured. They are then made into objects by squeezing while hot, either in a shaped mould or by being squeezed out through a shaped hole, like toothpaste from a tube. PVC, polythene and polystyrene are well-known names, and there

are many other moulded plastics, each specially made to its own style of product.

Paper and rubber
Paper and rubber are two products vital to us today. Paper has been made for over 2,000 years, but today paper-making has become a vast, highly-mechanized industry. Rubber used to come from the sap of a tree, but modern rubber is specially made for its purpose by building up giant molecules (building-blocks) called polymers. Most modern kinds of rubber are based on oil.

Man the builder

Early man lived in caves. As the weather warmed up he began to make rough shelters from branches and reeds. These primitive dwellings gradually developed into today's houses.

Some modern houses are still simple, especially in hot countries. One way of building is to use mud. In dry places this soon sets to form a very hard shell, sometimes made stronger with straw mixed in when the mud was soft. These sun-dried materials are called adobe, and they are seen throughout the Middle East.

Quite simple houses made of bamboo and large leaves can stand up to pouring rain in the tropics. Examples of these can be found in Africa, South America and South-East Asia, many of them being made on tall poles to lift them above flood level and keep out wild animals.

European builders

Most of the ideas for new ways of building took place in Europe. Instead of making a rough shelter from wattles (long twigs), strong wood beams were used to make a frame which would last for centuries. The spaces in the framework were then filled with plaster, strengthened with straw or thinner wooden boards overlapping so that rain could not get in. The roof was usually thatched with long reeds or straws.

The strongest buildings, for example castles and cathedrals, were made of solid stone, hewn by hand into blocks that fitted together. The need to make sure that the forces all acted at right angles to the joints meant that skilled engineers and architects were needed, and since then most buildings have had to be designed by a professional.

Above: Sun-baked adobe houses are often covered with decorations, like this one in Morocco.

Below: Concrete is cheap to produce and very strong. In this building the concrete is poured between the wooden frame and the steel rods, where it sets hard. Then the frame can be taken away.

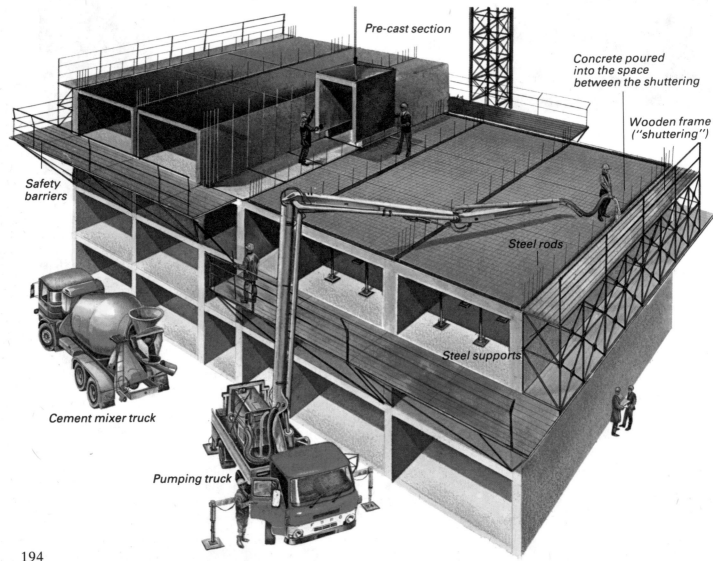

Pre-cast section

Concrete poured into the space between the shuttering

Wooden frame ("shuttering")

Safety barriers

Steel rods

Steel supports

Cement mixer truck

Pumping truck

Bricks

Stone blocks can fit together without any cement, although cement was known to the Romans 2,000 years ago and was often almost as strong as the stones it joined together. The main difficulty with stone was the time it took to cut the blocks from a quarry and form them to the exact size and shape. Bricks are a kind of artificial stone, almost the same as adobe, but in this case they are fired in a furnace called a kiln. Bricks, too, have been known for thousands of years, and are made from many kinds of natural material, usually a form of clay.

One advantage of bricks is that they are made to a standard size and shape. They can be "laid" quickly, and cemented in place to give a strong weatherproof building. In some cold climates warm houses are made of logs, with moss plugging every crack. In the

Above left: The largest structures of reinforced concrete are dams. They are curved for greater strength.

Left: A reinforced-concrete bridge under construction.

Below left: Preparing a building site with giant earthmoving machines.

Arctic, Eskimo igloos are made of blocks of hard compressed snow.

Modern buildings

Large modern buildings are made of concrete, a mixture of cement, sand, water and sometimes other material such as crushed stone. It is very strong when compressed, but when pulled apart can split. For the construction of bridges and many other structures, therefore, it has to be fitted with steel rods inside to give so-called reinforced concrete. Some tall buildings have a steel skeleton, with concrete slabs, metal or even glass filling the gaps in the framework.

Space in many cities is so expensive that buildings have to grow upwards. New York City was probably the first city to try this with its "skyscrapers", and today offices, blocks of flats and other giant structures are built with up to 100 or more floors.

A few modern buildings are mass-produced in factories, taken in large sections to the site by truck, and fixed together in two or three days.

Below: Tunnelling on a large scale is a major engineering task.

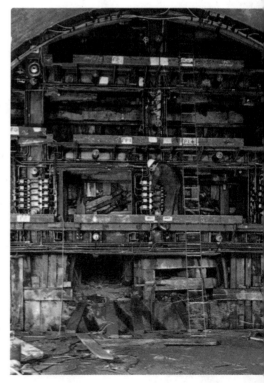

Pressure

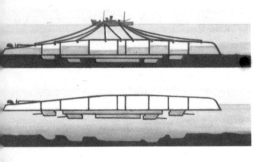

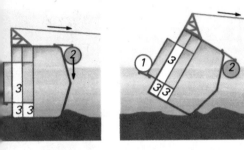

Above: Salvaging a ship is a very expensive job. In the top drawing the ship is raised by filling it with compressed air to empty it of water. The displaced water exerts an upward force thus raising the wreck to the surface, bottom up. Another method is to attach pontoons to the wreck. These are either air-filled (*1*) or water-filled (*2*). Certain compartments (*3*) are then filled with compressed air and the whole ship winched up.

On the earth, the air pressure that we regard as "normal" is, in fact, surprisingly high. Pressing down on our bodies is a column of air stretching up tens of kilometres right to the boundary with outer space. This column of air exerts a downward pressure of about one kilogram per square centimetre. Therefore the total air pressure on an average adult's head and shoulders is approaching one tonne. The reason why our bodies do not give way under the strain of supporting such a load is that, inside our bodies, there is a similar pressure and this balances the external pressure. So we are not generally aware of the surrounding air pressure. Changes in the air pressure, however, do tend to affect our bodies.

Sometimes a sudden change in air pressure may make our ears feel as if they are blocked up. This occurs because the pressure outside our eardrums has changed, but the pressure inside has not. The excess pressure on one side pushes the eardrums in slightly, making them more taut. Eventually, when the inside pressure be-

comes equal to the outside pressure, the eardrums return to normal and hearing is restored.

Changes in air pressure affect the temperatures at which liquids boil. In the process of boiling, molecules leave the liquid and escape into the atmosphere as vapour or steam. If the air pressure above the liquid is quite low, it is easier for the molecules to escape, so boiling occurs at a lower temperature. This makes it difficult to brew a good cup of tea on top of a high mountain. If the water is heated in a kettle, it never gets hot enough because it boils away before reaching its normal boiling point of 100° centigrade. The opposite effect is used in the pressure cooker. As the container is sealed, steam cannot escape, so the pressure builds up, allowing the remaining water to rise above its normal boiling point. The high temperature causes food inside the container to cook very quickly.

Sounds are transmitted through the air by means of pressure waves. These are set up by vibrating objects and travel through the air to our ears. There the pressure

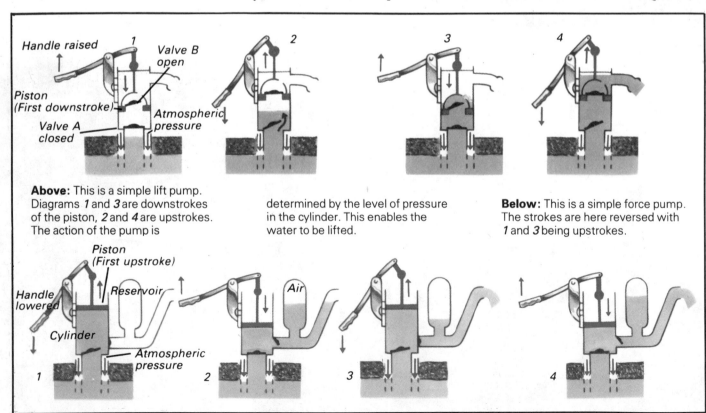

Above: This is a simple lift pump. Diagrams *1* and *3* are downstrokes of the piston, *2* and *4* are upstrokes. The action of the pump is

determined by the level of pressure in the cylinder. This enables the water to be lifted.

Below: This is a simple force pump. The strokes are here reversed with *1* and *3* being upstrokes.

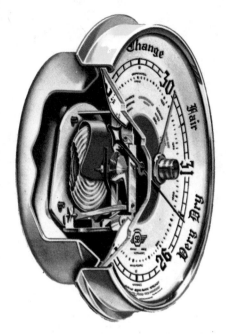

Above: A barometer is used in many homes as a guide to the day's weather. It works by registering changes in air pressure.

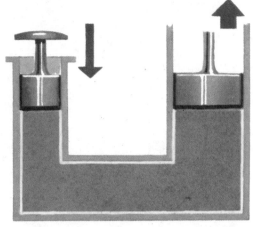

Above: This diagram shows the principle of the hydraulic jack. If the larger piston has an area ten times that of the smaller one and the small piston is pressed downward ten centimetres with a force of ten kilograms, the pressure transmitted to the large piston will raise a weight of 100 kilograms up one centimetre.

Right: Three different hydrometers:
1 General purpose model
2 Saccharometer (test for sugar)
3 Model for testing liquids heavier than water

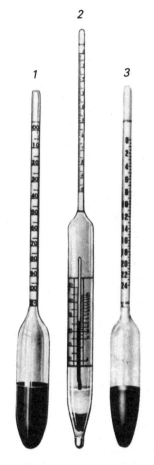

variations make our eardrums vibrate, thus giving us the sensation of sound.

In contrast to the rapid air-pressure variations of sound waves are the much slower variations associated with changes in the weather. Warm air is less dense than cool air and, therefore, exerts less pressure. Air from a high-pressure region will flow towards this low-pressure zone and the winds which will come as a result may bring rain. Barometers are instruments used to forecast the weather by measuring atmospheric pressure.

Many kinds of machines and devices depend on air pressure. The high air pressure inside an inflated tyre forces a valve shut, thus preventing the air from escaping. Compressed air is used to operate both delicate dental drills and the powerful drills used for road work.

Water pressure

Water, like air, exerts a pressure on the objects which it surrounds. As it has a higher density than air, water exerts a much greater pressure which increases steadily with depth. If a body is gradually lowered into water, the upward pressure on it increases, thus reducing its apparent weight. Eventually the pressure may become sufficient to support the entire weight of the object so that it floats. If the object is made of light material, the water pressure soon supports it and the object therefore floats in the water. Objects made of materials with a greater density sink lower before the pressure becomes sufficient to support them.

An object may be of such a great density that, even when fully submerged, the water cannot support its full weight. On lowering the object still deeper into the water, there is no further decrease in apparent weight. This is because

Right: Divers wear face masks to which compressed air is supplied from cylinders which are carried on their backs. The diver's suit reduces the body's heat losses and allows the diver to stay for longer periods in the water.

although the water pressure below still increases with depth, the top of the object is now also dependent on water pressure and this is increasing at the same rate. Once below the surface, therefore the object continues to sink. As the Greek Archimedes explained, the loss in weight is always equal to the weight of liquid displaced by the body. Denser liquids therefore give greater support. This principle is used in the hydrometer which is a float with marks on for measuring the density of liquids.

Nature's power house

Early men had only one source of power: animal muscle-power, including their own. It was muscle-power that built the Pyramids, the Great Wall of China and all the ancient cities. Slave labour rowed the first large ships, and even after someone made the discovery that the wind can help propel a ship, large numbers of slaves were kept on to row. This was to make ships go faster and to keep them on course in a flat calm, or against the wind.

The discovery of the wind-driven ship, several thousand years ago, however, set men thinking. Eventually someone invented the windmill while at about the same time the water-wheel came into use. We do not know the inventors, or when they lived, but we know water-wheels were used by the Romans. The first windmill we know of was built about A.D. 644 in Persia (now Iran).

Water power
Water is nearly 800 times more dense than the atmosphere near

Above: This hydro-electric dam was built as part of the great St Lawrence Seaway scheme in Canada.

Below: Windmills use the power of the wind to turn water wheels. These transfer water from nearby canals to the fields.

the earth's surface. This means that water can generally develop more useful power than air.

Even today, nearly all water power comes about by water falling down to the sea from a height. The oldest way of controlling this power was with a water-wheel, built on a fast-flowing river. Traditionally there were two types. In one, the undershot wheel had paddles with the lower part immersed in the water. The wheel was turned by the water flowing past. In the other, the overshot wheel had paddles more like narrow buckets. The water poured on from above, and it was this weight that pushed the wheel round.

Today almost all water power is generated as electricity. Water pours down large pipes and past a turbine. All of this is designed to change as much water energy as possible into turning a shaft. Usually the shaft drives an electric generator.

Wind power
The first windmills were made of

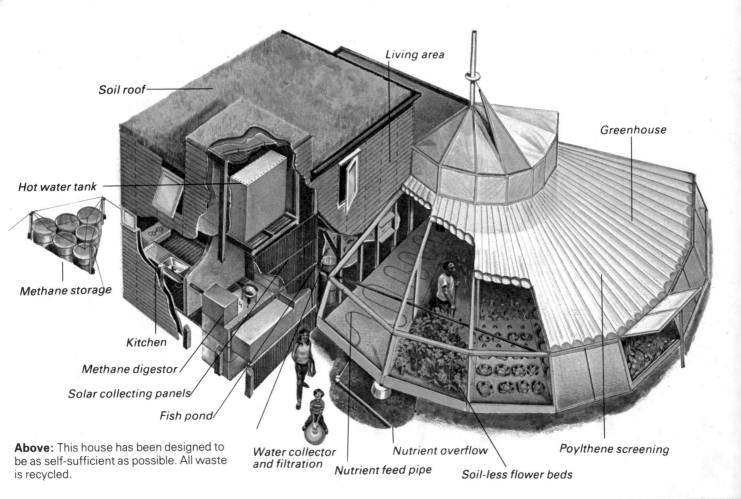

Soil roof

Living area

Greenhouse

Hot water tank

Methane storage

Kitchen

Methane digestor

Solar collecting panels

Fish pond

Water collector and filtration

Nutrient feed pipe

Nutrient overflow

Soil-less flower beds

Poylthene screening

Above: This house has been designed to be as self-sufficient as possible. All waste is recycled.

wood. They were very large, but worked extremely slowly. Millers used them to grind corn, and many were so large that they kept turning slowly even in a light breeze. They were, however, extremely inefficient.

Modern wind power generators are being built in areas of the world where the wind blows all the year round at an average speed of more than 32 kilometres per hour. The energy they will produce may be a possible supplement to nuclear and other energy. Wind power generators have the great advantage that they do not use up fuel or cause pollution. A lot of research is currently going on to find the most efficient sail design for these modern windmills.

In recent years engineers have discovered that another way of harnessing the power of the wind is to first concentrate it in the waves of the ocean. Special rows of floats off the coasts can then rock up and down as the waves pass and generate electric power.

Solar energy
Sunshine is essential to most life on earth. We can also use the Sun's energy directly. One way is to concentrate its heat, by using giant mirrors. In sunny places this is used to make furnaces, or to boil steam to generate electricity. Even where the sky is often cloudy, solar heaters are often worthwhile. Some houses have special hot-water systems using solar collectors on the roof. At present, however, it takes a long time to save the cost of installing the system.

Sunlight can also be changed straight into electricity via solar cells. These are small flat pieces of different semiconductor materials, such as silicon. When light falls on them it sets free electrons, so that if thousands of cells are wired together, a useful current can be generated. These cells are used in large solar panels on spacecraft.

Right: These solar panels lie in the French Pyrenees. It is one of many recently developed schemes to harness the power of the Sun.

Coal, oil and gas

Coal, oil and natural gas are the most important natural fuels found in the earth's crust. Gas is found in many forms. Geologists (people who study the rock formations of the earth's crust) are usually not sure where the gas came from, but oil and coal are known to be the remains of prehistoric animals, plants and trees. Over a period of millions of years the early forms of life changed as the result of great downward pressures over a long period. They became "fossilized" and coal and oil are today called fossil fuels.

Men began to use coal many hundreds of years ago. From about 1600 onwards it was found in homes and factories as a useful solid fuel that could be burned in a simple fireplace. The demand grew until in 1910 almost the entire

Derrick

Stand-by boat

Drill string

Mud tanks

Drill floor

Revolving crane

Pipe rack

Helideck

Lifeboat

Anchor line

This oil rig floats on pontoons (large buoyancy chambers), located about 15 metres below the surface of the water. The rig is kept in position by heavy anchors sunk into the seabed.

Living quarters

Pontoon

industry of the developed world, together with trains and ships, relied totally upon coal. Coal was also cooked in containers to produce another fuel, coal gas, which was piped to almost every house not only for heat but also for light. Gas-lights directed a flame through a special piece of fabric, called a mantle, which glowed a brilliant white when heated.

Coal today

Gradually electricity replaced gas as a source of light, and oil took the place of coal in transport. But today coal is as important as it ever was. It is the only fossil fuel that the earth possesses a great deal of. Some countries have enough to last for centuries at their present rate of mining. Even Britain, whose coal has been mined in great quantities for well over 100 years, has at least a further 100 years' supply left at present. More coal is continually being discovered and with improved methods of mining we may soon be able to dig out thin seams that at present are not worth mining from a financial point of view.

In any case, we know today that it is wasteful just to burn coal. It is one of our most valuable sources of raw material. Raw coal is washed and graded into sizes. Some is cooked in closed vessels. This is not to make gas, because many of us now have natural gas instead, but to break it down into raw materials. Insecticides, plastics, lipstick, paint, film, perfume and aspirins are all made from these raw materials.

Even coal used for heating is now used in better ways. Some is ground into powder to form pulverized (crushed) coal, which is sprayed through nozzles in most of the world's biggest power stations. Some is burned in fluidized-bed furnaces which are smaller than the old type, and have many advantages. Other coal will in future be converted into new products, such as solvent-refined coal and a form of natural gas. The aim is to get

both heat and vital raw materials, with less waste and pollution.

Oil

Petroleum also comes from prehistoric life, but in this case the original living things were not trees but small (almost microscopic) plants and animals which lived in the prehistoric seas. Countless numbers died, sank to the bottom, formed mud and then, for millions of years, were heated and compressed. Gradually pockets of thick, dark liquid formed, some near the surface and some at great depths under the land or oceans. In many cases gas was also present.

Oil products

In a few places the crude oil was seen at the land surface. In 1859 a well was dug in the United States which started the modern oil industry. At first the oil was just used like coal for burning, but it was soon realized that it can be refined. The thick crude oil is cooked and converted into hot vapour. It is then condensed into the main oil products, such as thick wax, vaseline, lubricating oil, diesel oil, kerosene and jet fuel, petrol (gasoline) and, lightest of all, the petroleum gases. These include propane and butane which are used for cooking in caravans and in camping.

Today almost all our transport is

Above: In underground mining, holes are drilled and packed with explosive in order to loosen the ore when the charges are detonated.

Above left: If the ore deposit lies beneath the surface, the covering or overburden has first to be removed. This bulldozer is stripping the overburden from a rock face.

totally dependent on petroleum. This is a serious problem, because even with fresh discoveries the oil wells are running out. By the year 2000 we must have made plans to change to other energy sources such as coal, gas and electricity.

Gas

Old-fashioned coal gas is now seldom made. Instead we use natural gas, found inside the earth. When refrigerated it becomes liquefied natural gas (L.N.G.), and is used as a liquid fuel by cars, trains and aircraft. It may later take the place of oil.

Butane and propane are found in most reserves of natural gas. Bottled gas is used not only by campers and other people needing a portable supply, but also by industry. Bottled gases, including a manufactured gas called acetylene, are mixed with oxygen to give a flame hot enough to melt steel.

Nuclear power

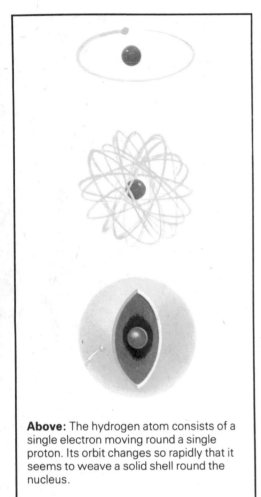

Above: The hydrogen atom consists of a single electron moving round a single proton. Its orbit changes so rapidly that it seems to weave a solid shell round the nucleus.

Nuclear energy has some advantages over older forms of energy. But problems exist concerning its use and public alarm has been expressed at accidents at nuclear power stations. The worst accident to date occurred at Chernobyl, in the U.S.S.R., in 1986. Radioactive fallout was recorded throughout Europe and even in the U.S.A.

In the first place, nuclear energy is a convenient form of energy. It is obtained by bombarding uranium atoms with neutrons, which makes the uranium split in such a way that a chain reaction starts. This process is called nuclear fission.

The first atom to be split was a special form of uranium called U235. When a flying neutron, a part of an atom, hits a U235 atom, the atom splits. Out of it come three fresh neutrons. These can hit other U235 atoms, causing fresh splits and more free neutrons.

This was first carried out during World War Two. The result was a powerful bomb which ended the war. Since then scientists and engineers have put U235 into nuclear reactors. These are not like bombs, instead the U235 is buried in large masses of graphite (carbon) which slows down the neutrons. Rods of material that absorbs neutrons, such as cadmium, are used to control the reaction.

Modern reactors

To start the reaction, the control rods are screwed out. At a certain point, as many neutrons are being generated as are being absorbed. This is called "going critical". Withdrawing the rods a little further results in the reactor sustaining a chain reaction. It gets very hot inside, and it is the heat that we want. Some reactors pump carbon dioxide gas through the hot core of the reactor. The gas then heats water in steam boilers to drive turbo-generators.

There are many other types of U235 reactor. The most common type, the sort first used in the United States, uses water under high pressure. This is heated in the reactor core to well above the normal boiling point. A common temperature inside most P.W.R.s (pressurized water reactors) is 320° centigrade. The water not only acts as the coolant but also takes the place of graphite in slowing down the neutrons.

In most of these reactors the U235 is converted into unwanted products, but most of the uranium fuel in the reactor is not U235 but the more common U238. Every time an atom of U238 is hit by one of the flying neutrons it captures the neutron and becomes a new substance, plutonium (Pu239). Plutonium did not exist before the nuclear age.

Right: The detonation of an atomic bomb releases an immense amount of energy and radiation into the atmosphere. The testing of such weapons in the Pacific Islands is a cause for concern.

Right: Particle accelerators are very large machines that accelerate sub-atomic particles to very high speeds. The particles collide with a target and they either split the atoms in the target or add on to the target's atoms.

The Future

Many nuclear physicists believe that nuclear fusion will eventually replace nuclear fission. This process involves the fusion, or combining, of the nucleii of light atoms, such as hydrogen. Fusion reactions produce intense heat and could produce cheap electricity. But recent studies suggest that fusion may create even more radioactive waste than fission. The problems of disposing of these wastes has never been satisfactorily solved. This factor, as much as any other, has weakened public confidence in nuclear energy.

Sound

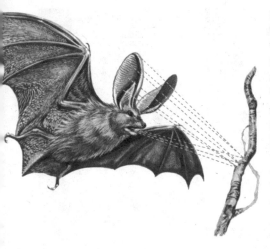

Above: Bats have poor sight and rely on a type of radar to aid their movement. They emit high frequency sounds which bounce off objects in their path and are picked up by their ears.

Few places on earth are absolutely silent because the movements of people, objects and even the wind cause vibrations that we experience as sounds. Unlike electromagnetic radiation, such as heat and light, sound cannot travel through space. There must be a medium, which can be any gas, liquid or solid, to carry the vibrations from the source of sound to our ears. When someone bangs a drum, for example, the drumskin vibrates, causing air molecules near it to vibrate too. These, in turn, make other air molecules vibrate in a similar manner. When the air vibrations reach a person's ears, they force the eardrums to vibrate too. As a result, the eardrums make movements similar to those made by the drumskin. The hearing mechanism picks up these tiny eardrum vibrations and converts them to nerve signals that our brain interprets as sound.

When sound travels through the air, the molecules are compressed together in some regions and in other places they are stretched apart. These zones move outward from the source of the sound so that each point in the sound path experiences a continual variation in pressure.

In air at normal temperatures, sound travels at about 340 metres per second, or one kilometre in about three seconds. Light, on the other hand, travels about one million times faster. This is why, at an athletics meeting, we see the

Below: Sonar can be used both to detect submarines, to chart the sea bed, and for fishing. A transducer sends out an energy impulse which is reflected back off any object. The range, depth and nature of the object are either recorded on a cathode-ray tube or as a trace on graph paper.

smoke from the starter's gun before we hear the bang. For the same reason, we see lightning before we hear the thunder, although both actually occur at the same time.

Wavelength and frequency

Any sound can be represented on a graph showing how the pressure varies along the sound path. The graph would show the alternate regions of high and low pressure and would have a wavelike appearance. For this reason, we refer to the pressure variations as sound waves. The distance between two successive waves is called the wavelength of the sound. An object vibrating quickly — that is, at high frequency — produces closely grouped waves. A high frequency, therefore, corresponds to a short wavelength and a low frequency corresponds to a long wavelength. Wavelength (λ) is measured in metres, and frequency (f) in units called hertz (Hz). One hertz is equal to one cycle (complete wave) per second. Wavelength and frequency are related by the formula $v = f\lambda$, where v is the speed of sound. Higher frequencies may be given in kilohertz, equal to 1,000 hertz.

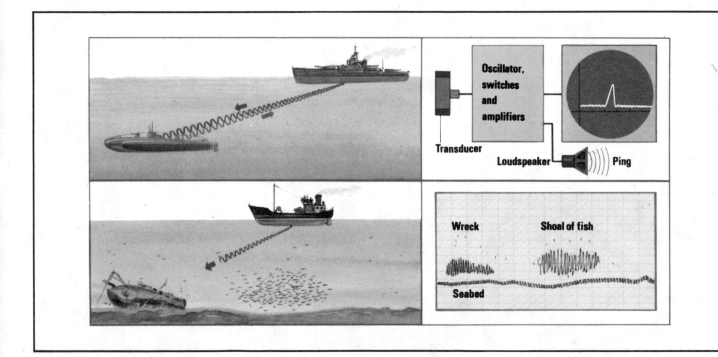

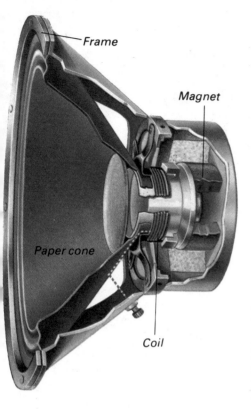

Frame

Magnet

Paper cone

Coil

Above: The most common type of loudspeaker is the moving coil. This device converts the varying electrical current in the output of an amplifier into a sound wave.

Below: Some typical microphones.
1 Small "boom", a movable platform
2 Ribbon microphone, often suspended on the "boom" arm
3 Very small microphone, often clipped to a tie
4 Multi-directional microphone picks up sounds from different sources

The perception of sound

Our reaction to vibrations in the air depends on their intensity and frequency. Below a certain intensity, the vibrations are too weak to be heard, and are said to be below the threshold of hearing. At the other end of the scale there comes a limit beyond which a person experiences pain, rather than sound. This is called the pain threshold. The physical intensity of sound is often expressed in units called decibels, while loudness is measured in phons. Unlike intensity, the loudness of a sound depends on the response of the ear as well as the physical magnitude of the vibrations. Sounds of extremely low or high frequency generally seem quieter than mid-frequency sounds of the same intensity. In fact, beyond certain limiting frequencies, we hear nothing at all.

Children generally have much better hearing than adults. A child with good ears can detect sounds ranging in frequency from about 20 hertz to 20,000 hertz but the upper limit gradually decreases with age.

When we hear a sound, we interpret its frequency in terms of pitch. The higher the frequency of a note, the higher in pitch it sounds, though even notes of the same pitch may sound quite different if they are produced by different musical instruments. This is because sounds are usually complex, consisting of a fundamental vibration and various smaller, higher frequency vibrations called harmonics. The fundamental vibration determines the pitch of the note, while the harmonics determine its character. Each instrument produces different harmonics and therefore has its own distinctive sound quality, though this may be changed according to how the surfaces in the room reflect or absorb the various frequencies of the sound. Multiple echoes give rise to the effect called reverberation. Too much can make speech unintelligible, and too little can make music sound dull. Careful design has overcome such problems in modern concert halls or auditoriums.

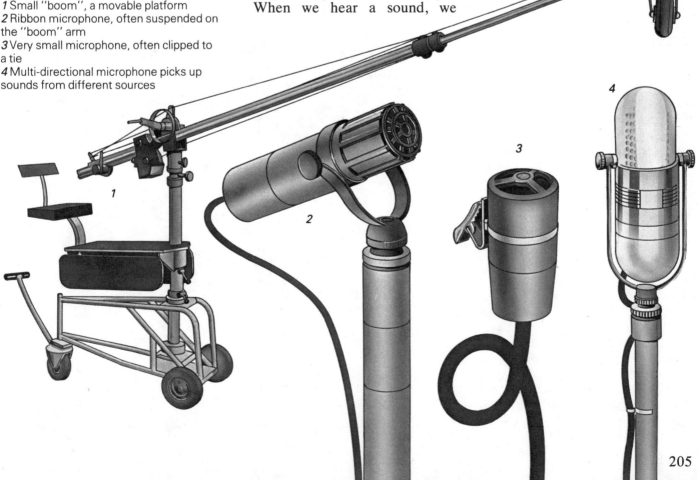

Electricity and magnetism

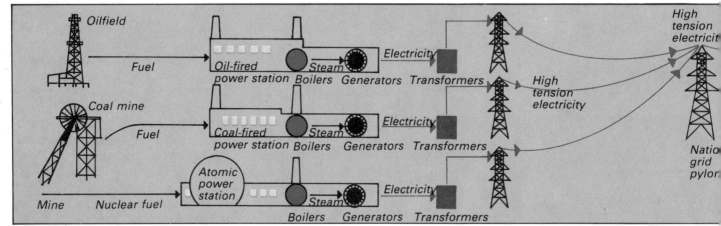

After using a nylon comb, you may find that it will attract small pieces of paper and other light objects. This happens because the comb becomes charged by friction when it is pulled through the hair. The Greeks discovered a similar effect about 600 B.C. when a piece of amber was rubbed and it attracted feathers. The Greeks, of course, knew nothing about electricity, they were simply fascinated by the mysterious power of attraction that they could give to the amber.

For more than 2,000 years, man failed to discover what caused this attraction. Then, in the late 1500s, a more scientific approach was adopted and the secret of electricity gradually emerged. In England, William Gilbert experimented by rubbing sulphur, resin and glass with a cloth. Like amber, all these substances became capable of attracting light objects. Eventually substances in this state were described as being charged with electricity. This word was derived from *elektron*, which is Greek for amber.

In the 1700s, a Frenchman called Charles du Fay discovered the important fact that there are two kinds of charge. He found that objects with different types of charge attracted each other, while substances with the same type of charge repelled or rejected each other. In that same century, Benjamin Franklin suggested that charges are always present, but cannot usually be found. We now know this is true and, to be able to

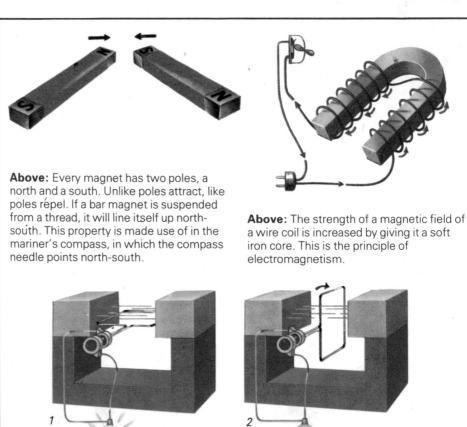

Above: Every magnet has two poles, a north and a south. Unlike poles attract, like poles repel. If a bar magnet is suspended from a thread, it will line itself up north-south. This property is made use of in the mariner's compass, in which the compass needle points north-south.

Above: The strength of a magnetic field of a wire coil is increased by giving it a soft iron core. This is the principle of electromagnetism.

Above: The generator works on the principle that every time a wire is moved through "force lines" surrounding a magnet, a voltage is set up in the wire and current will flow through it. Practical generators use coils of wire.

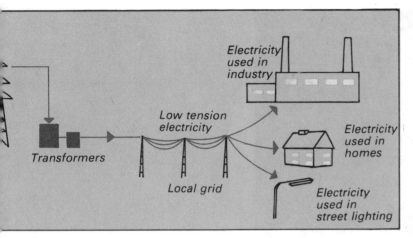

Above: The electricity generation and distribution system from mine to home.

Above: The interior of a generating house in a power station.

explain why, we have to consider the structure of atoms, the tiny building blocks from which all substances are made.

The nature of electricity

In some ways, a typical atom resembles a tiny solar system. It consists of a central core, or nucleus, with particles called electrons orbiting around it. The nucleus is made up of particles called protons and neutrons. Protons have a positive charge, while neutrons have no charge. Each electron has a negative charge equal in strength to the charge on a proton. In a normal atom, the number of electrons is equal to the number of protons, therefore their equal but opposite charges cancel out, and the atom now has no overall charge. If, however, the substance is rubbed, some electrons may be removed. As a result, the charges on some protons are no longer cancelled and the substance takes on an overall positive charge. Some substances capture extra electrons from the cloth when they are rubbed and, therefore, become negatively charged.

During the late 1700s, numerous machines were built to produce electricity by friction. Often the charges were strong enough to give large sparks or painful shocks. The sparks interested Benjamin Franklin, who realized that lightning, too, might be caused by a discharge of electricity. In 1752, Franklin performed a dangerous experiment to prove his theory. He

flew a kite in a thunderstorm and collected electricity that passed down the damp string. After this, knowledge about electricity increased rapidly. It could not be put to any practical use however, until a steady supply became available. This came in the 1790s, with Volta's invention of the electric cell.

Volta's cell

The Italian scientist Alessandro Volta was very interested in experiments carried out by another Italian called Luigi Galvani. Galvani found that a frog's legs twitched when touched with two metals in contact with each other. This observation led Galvani to believe that the frog's legs contained a supply of electricity.

Volta showed however that the two metals were of more importance in the process of producing electricity, and this led him to invent the electric cell. Volta's cell consisted of a disc of copper and another of zinc, separated by a piece of cloth soaked in salt water. Electricity produced by the cell would make the frog's legs twitch and a stack of such cells would produce sufficient electricity to give a mild shock when touched. This stack of cells, known as Volta's pile, was the first battery.

Whereas objects charged by friction would lose their electricity quickly in one sudden output,

using a battery gave a much steadier flow.

Applications

When powerful batteries became available, experimenters often found that their connecting wires became hot and a fine wire carrying a heavy current would glow brightly. These discoveries led to the invention of practical electric heaters and lamps. In 1819, a Danish scientist called Oersted discovered that an electric current also has a magnetic effect. This principle was soon used to make powerful electromagnets and it inspired the English scientist Michael Faraday to invent the electric motor in 1821 and generator in 1831.

Above: The town car of the future? This car is run on electrical batteries. It may not have a long range but it does not use up precious energy. There is also less pollution than with petrol-engines.

Electronics

Above: The battery of knobs and switches that face a sound engineer in a recording studio.

Below: The electron microscope is one of man's most valuable research tools. Its magnifying power can be increased by using a larger number of electromagnets.

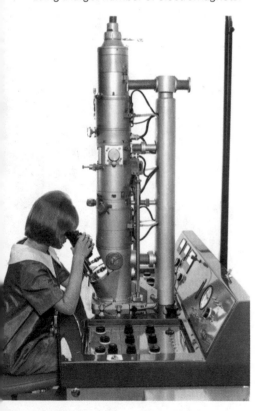

Above: A printed circuit board. It is in this field of micro-electronics that the Japanese have excelled in the past. A large-scale drawing of a circuit is made first then it is photographically reduced to its final size.

A few years ago, most people would have thought of radio, television or recording equipment when the word electronics was mentioned. Amazing changes have taken place in recent years, however, and electronic devices are playing an ever-increasing part in our everyday lives. Small, cheap calculators can now perform tasks that would once have required the use of a large computer and minute electronic regulators can ensure that our watches do not gain or lose more than a few seconds each month.

There are now many more impressive electronic gadgets available. For example, there is a tiny talking machine that teaches you to spell. It asks you to spell a word by pushing a series of lettered buttons. If you make a mistake, it may make a comment such as: "Almost right, have another try." If you spell the word correctly, the machine will congratulate you on your success and then give you a harder word to spell. This machine contains no tape or other form of recording because each word is constructed, when required, by complex electronic circuits. These produce electrical signals which match the sounds of the human voice, and the signals are reproduced on a small loudspeaker. One day, such a machine will accept spoken answers to its questions.

Another small electronic device carries out instant translations into another language. Sentences are punched into the machine on buttons and the translation is displayed immediately. If you are travelling abroad and do not speak the local language, you can use this machine to show people what you want to say.

These machines may seem amazing at the moment but there is no doubt that, in a few years time, they will be regarded as the simple beginnings of a great revolution in technology. Electronic circuits can basically be designed to do almost anything. The main problems that arise are usually concerned with size and cost. In recent years, advances in the mass production of complex, but minute electronic circuits have enabled many new devices to be produced.

Landmarks in electronics

In the late 1800s, many scientists were investigating the nature of electricity. Of particular interest were the strange glows produced by applying electricity to gases at

First, the "erasing head" magnet pulls the tiny needle-shaped iron crystals in the tape into the same direction. Then the "recording head" magnet arranges them in a different pattern for each sound.

When this new pattern passes the "playback head" the iron crystals cause variations in a magnetic field, which in turn varies an electric current. The current is amplified and fed to the speakers.

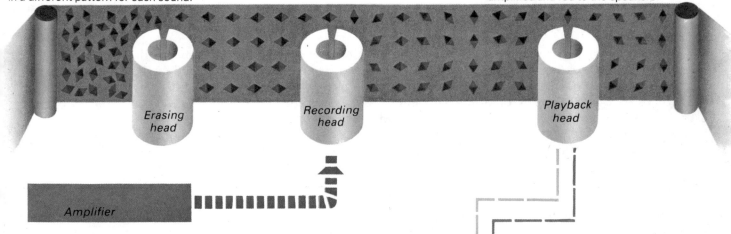

Erasing head

Recording head

Playback head

Amplifier

low pressure. Sir William Crookes devised a special tube with which to carry out these studies. The Crookes tube, as it became known, was simply a vacuum in a glass tube with a metal plate at each end. When these electrodes were connected to a battery, the low-pressure gas in the tube would glow. If the pressure of the gas was further reduced, it stopped glowing. Parts of the glass tube were now seen to glow with a greenish light. Crookes discovered that the cathode (the negative electrode) was giving out strange, invisible rays, and that these somehow made the glass glow. Crookes had thus made the first cathode-ray tube.

In 1895, Wilhelm Röntgen discovered X-rays while experimenting – with a Crookes tube. These penetrating rays were given out when the cathode rays struck a metal plate in the tube. Two years later, J. J. Thomson discovered the nature of cathode rays. His studies had shown that the rays consisted of streams of negatively charged particles of electricity, which he named electrons. Thomson's important discovery led to an understanding of atomic structure and it also enabled progress to be made in the new technology of electronics – the controlled use of electrons.

In 1904, Ambrose Fleming invented the two-electrode valve, known as the diode. This was an evacuated glass tube with an anode (positive electrode) and a heated cathode. The valve proved excellent for detecting radio signals, but it had few other uses. The real breakthrough came in 1906, with Lee de Forest's invention of the triode (three-electrode) valve. This could also strengthen signals and led to a revolution in radio and electronic design. In the late 1940s, Bardeen, Brattain and Shockly developed transistors. These were much smaller and more reliable and efficient than the valves they were designed to replace.

The introduction of transistors, therefore, led to the production of smaller and better electronic equipment. Transistors also led to the development of today's microcircuits, which are thousands of transistors and other parts assembled on a chip of silicon crystal.

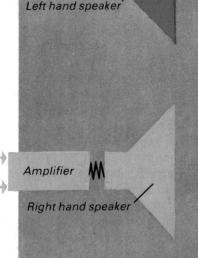

Stereo is two completely separate sound systems operating at the same time. Sound from two microphones is recorded separately on record or two-track tape. The stylus or playback head feeds each sound to a different amplifier and speaker.

Amplifier

Left hand speaker

Amplifier

Right hand speaker

Electromagnetic spectrum

One way in which movement can take place is by waves. Everyone knows the way in which wave movement occurs across a water surface. Sound waves, which are movements of air, carry sounds to our ears. When we look at an object, we are able to see it by means of light waves which travel from the object to our eyes.

Light waves are examples of a type of wave movement called electromagnetic radiation. Other familiar examples of electromagnetic radiation are radio waves. When we listen to a radio programme, radio waves travel, or radiate, outwards from a broadcasting transmitter to our receiving set. Television programmes are broadcast in a similar way.

What are electromagnetic waves?

Although we can describe ripples on a pond as movements of water, and sound waves from a gunshot as movements of air, we cannot describe forms of electromagnetic radiation as movements "of" something else. They are unique forms of energy, known as radiant energy.

But why *electromagnetic* waves? In general, these waves are created, or generated, when electrically-charged particles, such as electrons, are made to move. As the charged particles move they generate fields of electrical and magnetic energy. These two forms of energy radiate, or move outwards, from the particles as electromagnetic waves.

Radio waves move outwards in this way when they are generated by the flow of electrons within a radio transmitter. You may never have seen a radio transmitter, but certainly you will be familiar with an electric fire, which radiates heat waves, and an electric lamp, which radiates light waves. In both these cases, electromagnetic waves are generated by electrons passing through a metal wire.

Unlike water waves and sound waves, electromagnetic waves can travel through empty space. No matter what the form of electromagnetic radiation, its speed through space is the same. That speed is the speed of light, approximately 300,000 kilometres per second.

The shape of an electromagnetic wave is similar to a water wave, which vibrates up and down as the movement passes along the surface. This is known as a transverse wave. However, as an electromagnetic wave travels, it vibrates not only up and down but rates not only up and down but also in all transverse directions.

Types of electromagnetic waves

Besides light waves and radio and TV waves, electromagnetic radiation is known in many other forms. Some of these are shown in the diagram on this page. You can see that although the forms are given different names, such as X-rays, light waves and radio waves, these are really all parts of a single, continuous range, or spectrum, of electromagnetic radiation.

At one end, the electromagnetic

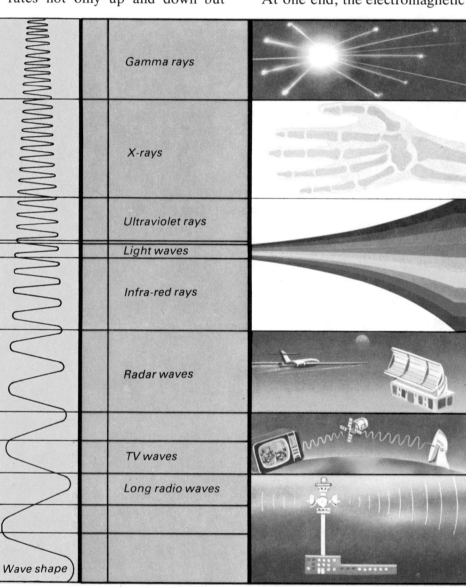

Wave shape

Gamma rays

X-rays

Ultraviolet rays

Light waves

Infra-red rays

Radar waves

TV waves

Long radio waves

Above: The electromagnetic spectrum contains wavelengths ranging from the extremely short to the extremely long. At the short end are gamma rays, found in radioactivity and also in cosmic rays that reach the earth from outer space. Much longer are the wavelengths of visible light and those of radiant heat. Longer still are the wavelengths that we use for communications, including microwaves such as those of radar and TV. Longest of all are those of long-wave radio.

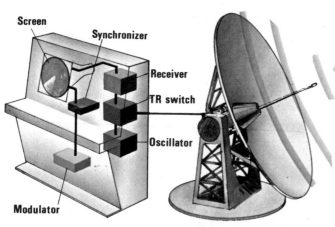

Screen
Synchronizer
Receiver
TR switch
Oscillator
Modulator

Radar equipment

Aerial

Left: Radar can detect objects at a considerable distance, such as approaching aircraft. Radar waves are broadcast outwards from an aerial, which also detects the radar waves reflected back from the object. The time taken for the radar waves to travel to and from the object indicates its distance. Both the distance and position of the object are displayed on a radar screen.

spectrum contains wavelengths that are extremely short, such as those of X-rays and gamma rays. At the other end of the spectrum are very long radio waves. These and other forms of radiation have many important uses in modern technology.

Penetrating waves

When a patient is X-rayed in hospital, the radiation passes right through the body, to produce a photographic negative, or radiograph, on the other side. X-rays, gamma rays and other forms of very-short-wave radiation all have this power to penetrate matter.

X-rays and gamma rays can even penetrate metals, and they are used in industry to look at flaws inside metal parts, particularly those which have been welded together.

Gamma rays are even more

Below: Many countries have radar installations to detect enemy missiles. Large radar aerials, which send out and receive the waves, are housed in radomes.

penetrating than X-rays. They too are used in hospitals, often to burn away cancers deep inside the body. They are one form of radioactivity, and are obtained from radioactive metals and other elements. Doctors and technologists working with these elements must handle them encased in thick lead, which absorbs the radiation. If a person comes into contact with radioactive elements, he may be seriously burned.

Ultraviolet radiation is also penetrating but to a lesser extent than X-rays or gamma rays. It is the form of radiation in sunlight which turns our skin brown.

Many substances glow, or fluoresce, when exposed to ultraviolet rays. This effect can be put to use in several ways. For example, scientists can identify minerals by the patterns with which they fluoresce.

Light itself is another form of penetrating radiation – if it were not, we would be unable to see through windows! Yet another example is radiant heat, which penetrates air which then circulates the heat round our homes. Radiant heat, which we feel but cannot see, has a slightly longer wavelength than red light. For this reason it is also known as infra-red radiation.

Longer wavelengths

Somewhat longer than infra-red waves are microwaves. These include radar, short-wave radio and TV waves. They still have some penetrating power, enough to

carry them through the air when they are broadcast. But like longer radio waves, they are easily absorbed or deflected by such dense objects as buildings. For this reason you often need an outside aerial to receive your TV signal because it is too weak to penetrate the walls of a house.

However, some shorter-wavelength microwaves are very useful because of the power they have to penetrate and heat flesh. In a microwave oven, a Sunday joint can be ready to eat in only a few minutes!

Below: Radio telescopes are giant aerials that detect radio waves coming from outer space.

Light and colour

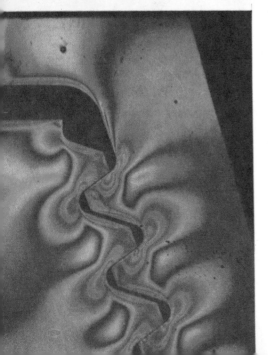

Light waves are electromagnetic waves (*see previous page*). They make up only a small part of the total electromagnetic spectrum, but they have particular importance for us.

Our eyes, and those of other animals, are especially good at detecting waves from this part of the total spectrum. This is another way of saying that we see by these waves.

The part of the total spectrum that contains waves of visible light is known as the visible spectrum. This differs slightly in range of wavelengths for different eyes. For example, a bee can see ultraviolet light, which is too short-wave for our eyes. In compensation, we can see by some light waves that are too long to be visible to a bee.

White and coloured light

White light, such as sunlight or the light from an ordinary electric bulb, really consists of a mixture of different wavelengths. When these wavelengths are separated from one another, using a transparent prism, we see the colours of the visible spectrum. In fact, a coloured light is simply light from a particular part of the visible spectrum. Shortest in wavelength is bluish light, then as the wavelength becomes longer, the light becomes in turn green, yellow and red. On sunny days, after showers, you can see the colours of the spectrum in a rainbow.

If lights of these spectral colours are mixed together in the right amounts, they will add up once more to make white light. But coloured paints or pigments will not add up in this way – a dirty brown colour would be the likelier result!

An object is the colour of the wavelengths it reflects or transmits to our eyes. For example, a red chair, seen by white light, reflects the red rays but absorbs blue, green and yellow rays. A white object reflects all wavelengths and a black object absorbs all wavelengths.

Top: A beam of white light, passing through a transparent prism, is separated out into the colours of the visible spectrum.

Centre: A laser beam sets alight a cigarette, demonstrating the power of these narrow, intense beams of light. Lasers now have many more practical uses too, such as welding and signalling.

Left: As polarized light reflects from this metal component, it reveals patterns of stress within the metal. Polarized light, as it moves along, vibrates in one direction, or plane, only. (Unpolarized light vibrates in all planes.) Special filters are used to turn ordinary light into polarized light.

Coloured lights can be mixed so that they make white light. However, when pigments of the same colours are mixed, they make a dark colour.

Movements of light

Light travels in straight lines when passing through empty space. But when it encounters matter, it is bent or scattered in various ways.

From shiny surfaces, such as that of a mirror, light is bounced back or reflected. Transparent objects, such as a pane of glass or a shallow sheet of water, allow light to pass through them. But in doing so, light is bent through an angle. This bending is called refraction.

When white light is refracted, its various wavelengths are bent through different angles. This is why we see colours when light passes through a prism.

When light passes from empty space into the earth's atmosphere, it is both refracted by the air and scattered by particles in the air. Blue rays are the most easily scattered and so the daylight sky looks blue.

When we wish to obtain a magnified view of an object, we use optical lenses such as those in a pair of spectacles, a microscope or a telescope. These lenses are specially made so that they bend light without splitting it up into its coloured wavelengths.

Quite recently, scientists have discovered that light is bent by matter even when the two do not come into direct contact. Astronomers have observed that light rays bend slightly as they pass by the huge mass of the Sun. In other words, light, like matter, is affected by gravity.

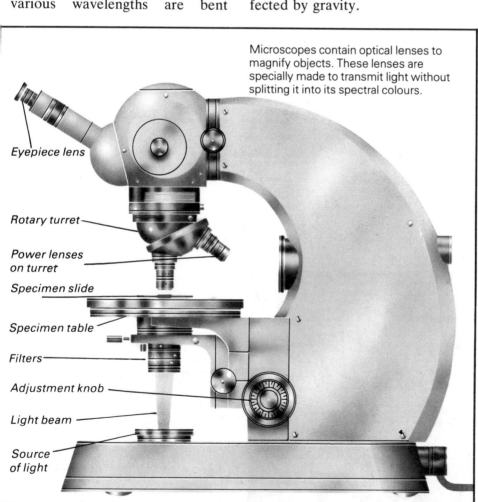

Microscopes contain optical lenses to magnify objects. These lenses are specially made to transmit light without splitting it into its spectral colours.

Eyepiece lens

Rotary turret

Power lenses on turret

Specimen slide

Specimen table

Filters

Adjustment knob

Light beam

Source of light

Throughout history, light for buildings and streets has been provided in a number of different ways. First came such methods as rushlights, candles and oil lamps (1-4). Gaslamps (5) first appeared in streets in the early 19th century. Electric lamps, or light bulbs, were invented later in that century. These included filament lamps (6 and 7) and electric arc lamps (8). Vapour discharge lamps, as used in strip lighting, appeared in the 20th century.

Heat

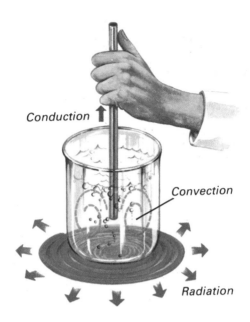

We think of heat mainly in two ways. For example, heat is what we use to cook food but heat is also what we feel when we sit by a fire. What these have in common is that in both cases, heat energy causes the temperature of a substance to rise.

All substances, including food and human flesh, are made up of molecules. The molecules are moving constantly, although in very solid substances this movement is a mere vibration.

When the temperature of a substance rises, the movement of its molecules increases. So we can say that heat energy *is* this movement of molecules. Similarly, an increase in temperature is an increase in the movement of molecules, and vice versa.

Molecules themselves consist of atoms. Substances such as some gases have molecules consisting only of a single atom. In these cases heat energy is the movement of atoms.

How heat moves

Heat moves about inside a substance, or from one substance to another, in three ways. Inside a solid substance, heat is passed along as each molecule of the substance gives its energy of vibration, or heat energy, to its neighbouring molecules. This type of heat movement is called conduction. Metals are particularly good conductors of heat.

In a heated liquid or gas, molecules also pass on their energy of movement to one another. But their molecules are more free to move about than those of solids. As a gas or liquid is heated, its molecules move about more and so become more separated from one another. This means that the gas or liquid becomes less dense, or lighter in weight, so that it rises, and heavier, unheated liquid or gas descends to take its place. This rising and falling is called a convection current, and convection is the main way in which heat moves in liquids and gases.

Thirdly, heat can travel through empty space as infra-red waves. These are electromagnetic waves *(see page 210)* which have a wavelength somewhat longer than light waves.

On earth, heat travels usually by

Below: A human hand radiates away heat in a complex pattern, as shown by this thermograph, or heat-photograph.

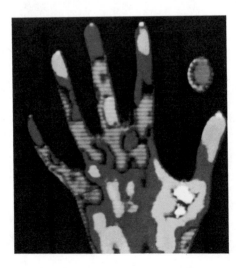

Conduction

Convection

Radiation

Above: The picture shows how heat moves in three ways. It moves by conduction through the metal rod. It moves by swirling convection currents in the heated liquid. From the heater element it moves away by radiation.

a mixture of two or more of these three ways. When we warm ourselves by a fire, heat reaches us by a mixture of air convection and radiation. When we boil water in a metal saucepan, the saucepan handle gets hot because of water convection and metal conduction.

Heat and matter

If we heat any solid substance enough, it changes its physical state, first from a solid to a liquid, then from a liquid to a gas. In a gas, molecules have so much heat energy, or energy of movement, that they fly about at great speed in all directions.

But substances can be heated to much greater temperatures still, when they change into a fourth state of matter, called a plasma. In a plasma, heat energy has not only broken up all molecules into atoms, but also has stripped off all or many of the electrons from the atoms. Inside the Sun and stars, where temperatures may be thousands of millions of degrees, all matter is in the state of a plasma.

On earth, reactions between

Right: In this heated-water central heating system, heat moves by conduction (heating coil), convection (water and air currents) and radiation (from room radiators).

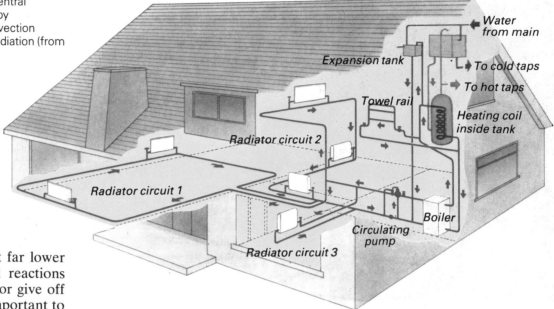

Water from main

Expansion tank

To cold taps

Towel rail

To hot taps

Heating coil inside tank

Radiator circuit 2

Radiator circuit 1

Boiler

Circulating pump

Radiator circuit 3

substances take place at far lower temperatures. Chemical reactions can either take up heat or give off heat. This is not only important to chemical industry, it is also vital to life. Just as a fuel gives off heat when it is burned, or oxidized, in air, so our food gives us energy when it is oxidized in our bodies.

At low temperatures, chemical reactions slow down and at very low temperatures they cease altogether. The chemical reactions of living bodies cease at only a few degrees below freezing. At the lowest temperature possible, or absolute zero ($-273°$ centigrade) all substances are solid and even the vibration of their molecules ceases.

Energy conversions

If you slide too rapidly down a rope, your hands burn painfully. This is an example of the conversion of mechanical energy (sliding) into heat energy (burning of hands). In general, any form of friction converts mechanical energy into heat energy.

Electrical energy can also be converted into heat energy, as in an electric fire. We have already seen how chemical energy can be converted into heat energy. In fact, heat is the type of energy "left over" after most types of reactions.

Below: Insulated by his asbestos suit, this firefighter can walk safely through flames of an oil fire.

Below: Most houses leak heat away very wastefully, mainly from windows and through the roof. Windows can be heat-insulated by double glazing. A roof can be insulated by laying down rolls of glass wool in the loft, as shown here.

Chemistry

Above: Explosives are needed for fireworks as well as warfare. The Chinese used them for both purposes 800 years ago. Modern explosives are also used for blasting, for example in quarrying rock.

Right: Scientists have discovered 92 kinds of atom, and thus 92 basic materials called elements, which can be arranged in this way. Scientists have also made artificial elements in nuclear reactors. The best known one is plutonium. Scientists have recently produced elements 104–7. These artificially made elements are not shown here.

Chemistry is the science of the different elements from which everything is made, and how they react "chemically" with each other. They can combine to form compounds, linking together in particular ways that depend on the number of outer electrons in their atomic structure. One of the most common chemical actions is oxidation (combining with oxygen), two forms of which are burning and rusting.

Chemical changes usually completely alter materials. For example, burning (oxidizing) paper results in hot gas and leaves an ash. In the chemical industry, however, many of the changes are actually physical ones, such as dissolving solids in liquids, evaporating liquids into vapour, distilling different vapours back into liquids, and then filtering them to make them into even purer substances.

Heavy chemicals

Heavy chemicals are not necessarily heavy; the term means that they are made in very large amounts. Some of the most important chemical plants or factories have an output of more than 1,000 tonnes a day, for example plants making sulphuric acid, sodium carbonate ("soda") for soap and dozens of other products, fertilizers, ammonia and plastics.

The plants that produce these vital materials can each cover several square kilometres. They work almost automatically, controlled from central computers. How were these processes first designed? Scientists experimented to get the right process on a small scale, in a laboratory. Often it was found that the efficiency was greatly improved by running part of the process at a higher temperature or pressure.

Once the method had been perfected as far as possible in the laboratory, making just a few grams of the end-product, the difficult step had to be taken to multiply this output by thousands or millions of times.

Raw material

Almost anything can be used by the chemical industry to make a useful product. Two of the most important materials are coal and oil. By oil we mean crude petroleum pumped from wells under the land or sea. This is taken to a refinery, cooked in a large vertical tube called a pipe-still, separated into constituent parts and purified.

Oil gives us countless by-products. The original oil vapour produces many liquids, such as petrols, kerosenes and lubricating

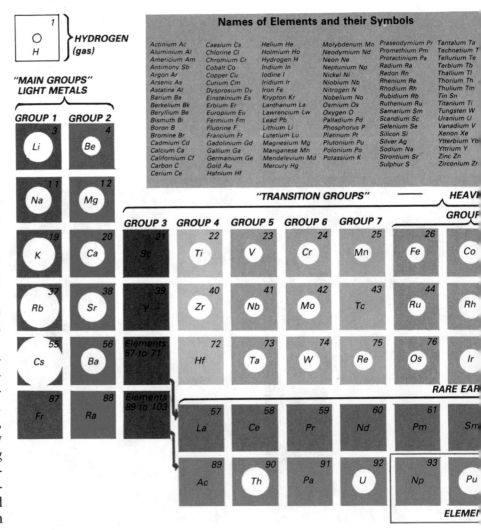

Names of Elements and their Symbols

Actinium Ac	Caesium Cs	Helium He	Molybdenum Mo	Praseodymium Pr	Tantalum Ta
Aluminium Al	Chlorine Cl	Holmium Ho	Neodymium Nd	Promethium Pm	Technetium T
Americium Am	Chromium Cr	Hydrogen H	Neon Ne	Protactinium Pa	Tellurium Te
Antimony Sb	Cobalt Co	Indium In	Neptunium Np	Radium Ra	Terbium Tb
Argon Ar	Copper Cu	Iodine I	Nickel Ni	Radon Rn	Thallium Tl
Arsenic As	Curium Cm	Iridium Ir	Niobium Nb	Rhenium Re	Thorium Th
Astatine At	Dysprosium Dy	Iron Fe	Nitrogen N	Rhodium Rh	Thulium Tm
Barium Ba	Einsteinium Es	Krypton Kr	Nobelium No	Rubidium Rb	Tin Sn
Berkelium Bk	Erbium Er	Lanthanum La	Osmium Os	Ruthenium Ru	Titanium Ti
Beryllium Be	Europium Eu	Lawrencium Lw	Oxygen O	Samarium Sm	Tungsten W
Bismuth Bi	Fermium Fm	Lead Pb	Palladium Pd	Scandium Sc	Uranium U
Boron B	Fluorine F	Lithium Li	Phosphorus P	Selenium Se	Vanadium V
Bromine Br	Francium Fr	Lutetium Lu	Platinum Pt	Silicon Si	Xenon Xe
Cadmium Cd	Gadolinium Gd	Magnesium Mg	Plutonium Pu	Silver Ag	Ytterbium Yb
Calcium Ca	Gallium Ga	Manganese Mn	Polonium Po	Sodium Na	Yttrium Y
Californium Cf	Germanium Ge	Mendelevium Md	Potassium K	Strontium Sr	Zinc Zn
Carbon C	Gold Au	Mercury Hg		Sulphur S	Zirconium Zr
Cerium Ce	Hafnium Hf				

Right: Rusting is actually exactly the same chemical process as burning – the original element is oxidized, or combined with oxygen. Slowly, this shipwreck will become encrusted with more and more rust.

oil, and even waxes, vaseline and tarry bitumen. These products are then taken to other factories to be made into detergents, synthetic rubbers, fibres and plastics.

Coal rivals oil for the number and quality of substances made from it. In fact, it can be processed physically and chemically to make new solid, liquid and gaseous fuel, as well as paint, inks, perfumes, plastics, insecticides, cosmetics and even tablets.

Food and drugs

Increasingly we buy specially processed foods, These processes are part of the chemical industry. Instead of eating potatoes we eat crisps, and instead of corn we buy packets of mass-produced crunchy shapes which people seem to enjoy. Salt, sugar and many other foods are all mass-produced in vast automated chemical plants.

Almost all the drugs that people need to keep them fit are mass-produced in the same way. By far the most common of the drugs is the tablet aspirin, many millions of which have to be made every day. This is a substance derived from coal tar, a liquid obtained from coal. Different processes then work on the aspirin to make it dissolve faster in water or taste better or act quicker in the body.

The helpful drugs are made by the pharmaceutical industry, a special branch of the chemical industry that has to set the highest standards of perfection and cleanliness. A number of modern drugs are based on moulds, many of them being antibiotics for killing viruses and other disease-causing germs. Every day a scientist somewhere discovers a new drug that will help mankind. The pharmaceutical industry then has to work out how to mass-produce it.

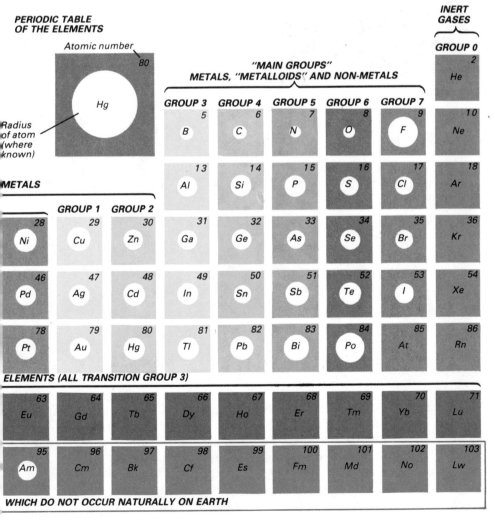

PERIODIC TABLE OF THE ELEMENTS

Advances in medicine

Modern medicine and surgery began only about 150 years ago, when doctors started to use a chemical called an anaesthetic which put patients to sleep so that they felt no pain during a surgical operation. The first anaesthetics to be used were chloroform and ether. Before their widespread use, many patients had died from the shock that followed operations.

Later in the 19th century, the discovery of germ-killing antiseptics, such as carbolic acid, made surgery far safer still by eliminating infections.

Modern drugs

From ancient times until the end of the 19th century, drugs to fight disease were nearly always natural substances extracted from plants, but it was not often known how they worked.

By contrast, the first synthetic (man-made) drugs were invented to have a specific action. Salvarsan, a drug patented in 1910, was developed to kill the bacteria that cause syphilis. It became known as the magic bullet because it was so effective at doing this.

In the 1930s a whole range of powerful new drugs, the sulfa drugs, helped to stamp out many bacterial infections. However, these early "wonder drugs" had the drawback that they were often poisonous to the patient if given in large amounts. At the start of the World War Two, another, far less poisonous type of wonder drug appeared — the antibiotic.

Antibiotics are drugs actually made by microbes (bacteria) themselves, which act most specifically against other microbes. Penicillin was the first one to be discovered.

Vaccines were a different type of drug with a specific action that had been in existence for well over a century. The first vaccine was invented by Edward Jenner in 1796, for the cure of smallpox. Jenner did not know how his vaccine worked, nor that smallpox was a virus disease. Even in 1885, when Louis Pasteur developed a

Top left: Louis Pasteur (1822-95) first proved that infections are caused by bacteria and other disease microbes. He also developed the first rabies vaccine.

Above: Robert Koch (1843-1910) identified many kinds of disease bacteria and made the first vaccine against the cattle disease anthrax.

Left: Marie Curie (1867-1934) discovered radium, the first substance used in radiotherapy for the treatment of cancer.

Below: Alexander Fleming (1881-1955) identified the mould that makes penicillin, the first of the antibiotic drugs.

vaccine against the dreaded virus disease rabies, no virus had ever been seen.

Nowadays, with the aid of the electron microscope, viruses can be seen, and many more vaccines are available for treating infections by viruses and bacteria. A vaccine, or a related type of drug called an antiserum, causes antibodies (bodies within the blood) to attack and kill infectious microbes.

Another new class of drugs, the immunosuppressive drugs, does the very opposite by preventing the formation of antibodies. These drugs are used after "transplant" operations. Without the drugs, new hearts or kidneys are rejected due to a build-up of antibodies.

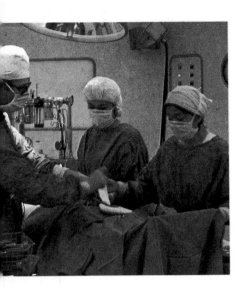

Left: Major surgical operations today are precisely controlled, safe and painless. Standards of hygiene are extremely high. Every surgical instrument is sterilized before use.

Right: In developing countries immunization with vaccines is the major weapon against infectious disease.

Below: A radiologist examines X-ray photographs, or radiographs, of a patient's chest region.

Bottom: Acupuncture is a form of treatment invented by the ancient Chinese. The picture shows a modern version called electro-acupuncture. This type of stimulation is now believed to cause the body to produce natural pain-killing substances.

Medical machinery

Many complex and powerful machines are now available to doctors for the diagnosis, cure and prevention of diseases. X-ray machines have long been used to reveal abnormalities hidden deep in the body. A more recent type of body scanner uses not X-rays, but ultrasonic waves – sound waves pitched too high to hear.

Yet another type of scanner detects abnormalities in the body by the heat these give out. Other large machines will show if anything is wrong in the heart or brain by detecting the tiny electrical impulses within these organs.

For burning away cancers and other tumours (growths), intense beams of radiation are used.

The development of new drugs and medical machinery has led to an increased understanding of how complicated a machine the body is. Great advances have been made in prosthetic surgery – the replacement of defective parts of the body with strong, synthetic materials and devices.

It is now quite common for surgeons to replace diseased joints with plastic and metal ones, or to fit artificial limbs which are electronically controlled. Other electronic devices, such as heart pacemakers, are safely fitted inside the body.

The self-healing body

Physicians have always recognized

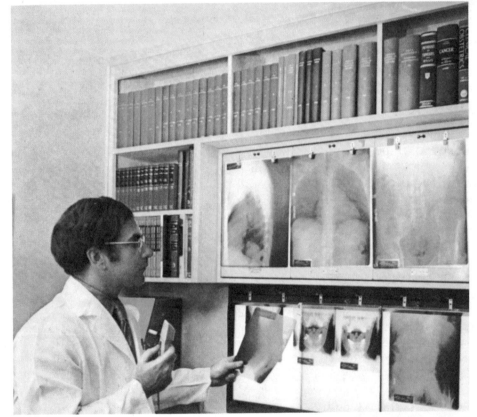

the power of the body to heal itself. With the help of modern biochemical knowledge, they are becoming even more aware of it.

Early among these biochemical discoveries were the hormones, chemical messengers of the body, and the enzymes and vitamins, which enable most of the body's chemical reactions to take place. More recent discoveries are the endorphins and encephalins, which are made by the brain and control the feeling of pain.

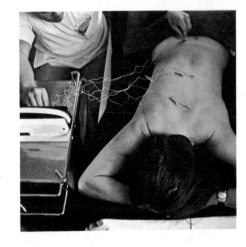

Early land transport

Man first transported loads too heavy to carry by simply sliding them over the ground. To make the task easier, the loads were sometimes moved on sledges, but an even better method was to use a platform with rollers underneath. These were made from straight tree trunks. As the platform was hauled forward, men took away the rollers at the back, carried them forward and placed them in front of the platform. Providing a rolling action made movement easier by reducing frictional losses between the load and the ground. Another improvement, and one of man's greatest inventions, came over 8,000 years ago. Instead of rollers, thin round slices of logs were pivoted to a platform to provide the required rolling action. The wheel had arrived!

Although more convenient than massive rollers, solid wheels made early carts quite heavy. So holes were sometimes cut in the wheels. This greatly reduced their weight with only a slight loss in strength. Later, even better wheels were made by fixing wooden rims to a central hub with straight wooden spokes.

Early carriages

The horse-drawn chariots used by the Romans had two wheels mounted on an axle that supported the body of the vehicle. These fast carriages were designed to carry a person rather than his belongings. Horse-drawn carriages, similar in basic design, were still being used in the 1800s, although many improvements had been incorporated by this time. Strong springs between the carriage body and the wheel axle acted as shock absorbers, so the ride was much more comfortable, especially over bumpy ground. Four-wheeled carriages gave even greater stability. They had a pivoted front axle to enable them to turn corners easily. Many carriages had a canopy to protect passengers in bad weather, while others were fully enclosed and fitted with doors. By this time,

Moving statue on rollers

Before the invention of wheels heavy objects were pulled along the ground by teams of men or animals. Rollers placed under the objects made the task easier. This was how the wheel was developed.

Early solid and spoked wheels

Early wheels were discs made of solid wood. Later, spokes made them lighter. The Roman chariot had two wheels fixed to the end of an axle. Because the chariot body rested directly on the axle, journeys over rough ground were bumpy.
The driver stood up to avoid being bruised or getting thrown out of the chariot.

Roman chariot

By about 200 years ago carriages were being built in two parts. The wheels were still on axles, but were fitted to a separate part called a chassis. The body was suspended from the chassis by leather straps which helped to cushion the bumps.

steam-driven carriages had appeared on the roads. But it was the petrol engine that eventually enabled the horseless carriage to dominate road traffic.

The horseless carriage

The age of steam started in 1698, when Thomas Savery patented a simple steam engine for pumping water. Other inventors improved on this design, and James Watt patented a much more efficient steam engine in 1769. It could be used to drive many kinds of machines, and to power vehicles. That same year, a Frenchman called Nicolas Cugnot built a steam-driven carriage for hauling

heavy field guns. This was the world's first self-powered vehicle on the roads. Unfortunately, it ran out of steam every 30 metres and had to stop until sufficient pressure had built up again. Its maximum speed was only four kilometres per hour! Later, much better steam-powered vehicles were developed and, by the 1830s, some were providing regular passenger services.

The main disadvantage of the steam engine was its size. It needed a large boiler so that it did not keep running out of water. Another problem was that it could not be started instantly. It took time to bring the water to boiling point in

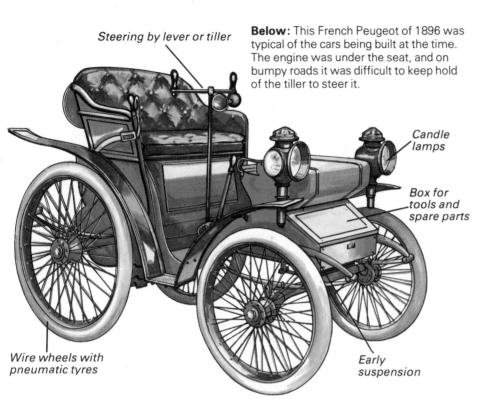

Steering by lever or tiller

Below: This French Peugeot of 1896 was typical of the cars being built at the time. The engine was under the seat, and on bumpy roads it was difficult to keep hold of the tiller to steer it.

Candle lamps

Box for tools and spare parts

Wire wheels with pneumatic tyres

Early suspension

Above: Henry Ford with his wife in his first motor car. He built this simple petrol-driven vehicle in 1896, and later, he mass-produced his famous *Model T*.

order to make steam. So, many inventors worked to produce a smaller, more convenient engine with quicker starting.

Explosive engines

Since the late 1600s, attempts had been made to power an engine by a series of controlled explosions. In 1680, Christiaan Huygens tried to use gunpowder as fuel in an engine. The experiments of Huygens were not successful and little progress was made in this field

until the 1800s.

Realizing the need for an improved engine for the horseless carriage, several inventors developed engines powered by explosive gases. In 1862, J. Etienne Lenoir built the first motor car driven by an internal combustion engine. It used large quantities of expensive coal gas for fuel. Lenoir's car was extremely noisy and slow.

Edouard Delamare-Deboutteville produced the world's first

successful petrol-driven car in 1883. But the general public took little notice of this development. Then, two years later, a German called Karl Benz built a small petrol-driven tricycle. In 1888, he made a more powerful model and drove it around the streets of Munich. This aroused great interest, and Benz was swamped with orders for his vehicle. As a result of the interest in his invention, Benz set up the world's first motor car factory that same year. But, in

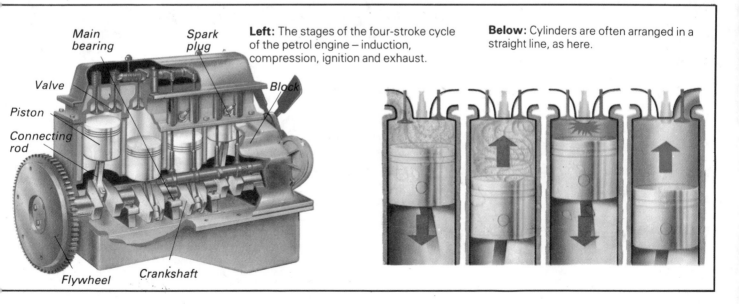

Main bearing

Spark plug

Valve

Piston

Connecting rod

Block

Flywheel

Crankshaft

Left: The stages of the four-stroke cycle of the petrol engine – induction, compression, ignition and exhaust.

Below: Cylinders are often arranged in a straight line, as here.

The motor car era

the United States it was Henry Ford who realized the need for a cheap, reliable car. Using mass-production techniques, he built his famous *Model T* by the million and became one of the world's richest men. In the early years of this century, Henry Ford's *Model T* – or "Tin Lizzie" as it was commonly called – revolutionized motoring in the United States. Being relatively cheap, it soon became popular. As orders for it rose, Ford was able to increase the speed of production and decrease the cost of the car. As a result, the price of the same basic car dropped by nearly 70 per cent between 1908 and 1927.

European developments

Like America, Europe had a need for cheap, reliable cars. At first, this demand was partly satisfied by importing the *Model T*. Then, after the end of World War One (1914-18), several European manufacturers boosted their output by adopting mass-production techniques. In England, Austin produced their highly successful *Austin Seven*. Like Ford's "Tin Lizzie" in the United States, the *Austin Seven* made motoring possible for millions of people previously unable

to afford it. The rapid spread of mass-production techniques on both sides of the Atlantic put great economic pressures on the smaller car manufacturers. Many small firms were ruined because demand for their high-quality vehicles decreased, and they could not afford to set up mass-production lines in order to compete with the big companies. But other small firms survived by merging together to form large organizations.

Assembly-line production

In a typical modern car factory, the preparation and assembly of parts is split into numerous stages. Each stage is carried out by a group of skilled workers in a separate part of the factory. The cars and components are transported from one section of the factory to the next on moving tracks and overhead conveyer belts. Many of the components, such as tyres and head-lamps, are produced by separate specialist companies. From orders received from car salesrooms, the manufacturer works out what materials and components he requires. He then compares this information with a list of what he already has in stock. The manufac-

turer can then work out what he needs to reorder from suppliers to replenish his stocks. Efficient stock control is extremely important as the whole factory may come to a halt if one essential component is unavailable. Although it may be possible to carry out some stages of production, cars cannot be sold until complete, and storage space for unsold cars soon runs out.

The manufacturing process starts in the bodywork department, where a giant press stamps out each car body from sheet steel in a single, powerful blow. Separately produced bodywork components, such as the doors and boot cover, are then fitted. After cleaning, the bodywork is primed and then sprayed with several coats of quick-drying paint. Next the instrument panels are fitted. In another part of the factory, each body receives an engine, steering equipment and other parts. The engines are bolted on to the body, and the car's electrical gear is installed and wired up. After fitting the wheels, seats and other remaining items, the cars are inspected for faults and tested for roadworthiness. Any observed faults are corrected, and the cars

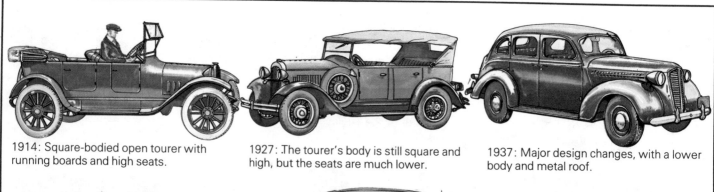

1914: Square-bodied open tourer with running boards and high seats.

1927: The tourer's body is still square and high, but the seats are much lower.

1937: Major design changes, with a lower body and metal roof.

1950: More streamlined shape. The wings and headlamps merge with the body, and the running boards are very narrow.

1960: The wings have disappeared altogether, the windscreen is curved, and boot and bonnet are the same size.

1974: The modern car, with highly streamlined shape to reduce wind resistance at top speeds.

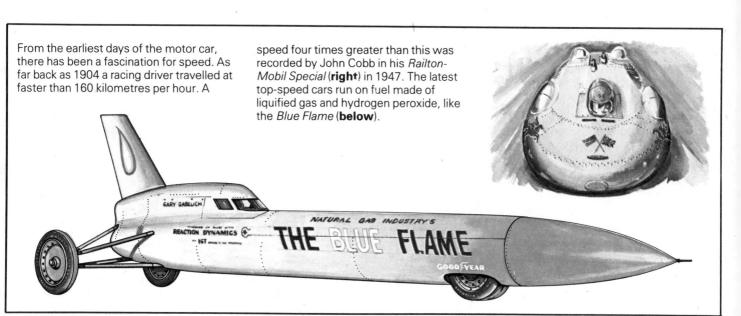

From the earliest days of the motor car, there has been a fascination for speed. As far back as 1904 a racing driver travelled at faster than 160 kilometres per hour. A speed four times greater than this was recorded by John Cobb in his *Railton-Mobil Special* (**right**) in 1947. The latest top-speed cars run on fuel made of liquified gas and hydrogen peroxide, like the *Blue Flame* (**below**).

are washed before being taken by truck to the salesrooms.

Pollution and the car

Today's rapidly expanding road traffic has increased the pollution of the atmosphere by waste gases from engine exhausts. Pollution can be greatly reduced by fitting devices designed to absorb some of the poisonous exhaust gases, but this significantly increases manufacturing costs. However, world petroleum supplies are running low, so scientists have the opportunity of choosing a less polluting fuel for cars of the future. Hydrogen is an interesting possibility. It is easy but expensive to obtain from water, and could only be used in conventional cars with certain modifications. Apart from some oxides of nitrogen only harmless steam would be produced in the exhaust.

Below: Porsche *917-10K CanAm*. This turbo-charged Porsche was a very successful racing car during the 1972 Canadian-American series of race meetings. The engine alone cost £24,000 to develop.

Below: A bird's eye view of the *Countach*, a fast, modern sports car of unusual appearance. It is made by the Italian firm of Lamborghini. The *Countach*, which costs more than £10,000, can reach speeds of over 300 kilometres per hour.

The birth of the railway

Railways were in use centuries before powerful steam locomotives thundered their way across the countryside. In the 1500s, horse-drawn wagons were used in England for transportation in mines and ports, and sometimes loads were shifted on trucks that ran freely down gently sloping rails. But with the development of efficient steam engines in the late 1700s, many inventors started to design steam-powered vehicles.

The first to build a steam-powered railway locomotive was Richard Trevithick. In 1802, he tested his vehicle on a small, circular track in London. After some modification, Trevithick's locomotive was put to work in 1804. At the Penydaren ironworks, South Wales, the engine successfully hauled a ten-tonne load and 70 men a distance of about 15 kilometres. However, the new machine did not prove popular for long. It never went much faster than walking pace, and the brittle cast-iron rails often broke under the heavy loads. As a result, interest in the locomotive faded, and horse-drawn wagons remained in use for some time. Trevithick tried to perfect his engine, but he was forced to give up when he ran out of money.

Most people thought that the idea would never work. It seemed obvious to them that the metal wheels would slip on the metal rails if the engine tried to haul heavy loads at speed. However, William Hedley thought otherwise. In 1812 he built two steam locomotives and these went into service the following year at the Wylam colliery in the North of England.

A young man called George Stephenson had followed the progress of the railways with great interest. Like his father, Stephenson started work as a miner. He had received little education, and could neither read nor write when he started work. Still, he was destined to become a highly skilled railway engineer known as the "father of British railways". In

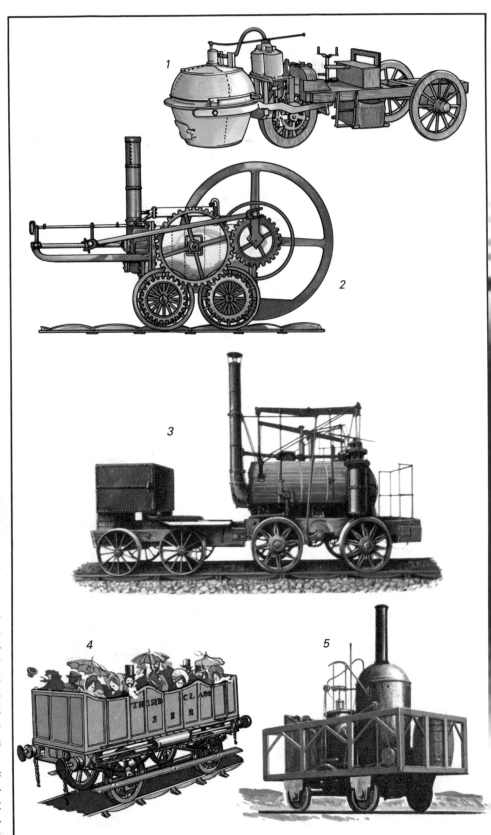

Cugnot's steam tractor (*1*) was the first self-powered vehicle in the world.

Trevithick's locomotive (*2*) of 1803 could travel at about 8 kilometres per hour.

The *Puffing Billy* (*3*) was built in 1812. It was used to haul coal in a colliery.

A third class coach of 1835 (*4*).

In 1830 a race took place between the tiny locomotive *Tom Thumb* (*5*) and a horse. The horse won!

1814, at the age of 33, Stephenson completed his first locomotive. And, within a few years, he had become recognized as an expert in this field. As a result, he was able to persuade the builders of the Stockton and Darlington Railway to use steam trains. In 1825, Stephenson drove his *Locomotion No. 1* to haul 600 passengers along the line and open the first ever passenger railway service.

The first passenger railway to rely entirely on steam power was the Liverpool and Manchester. In 1829, at Rainhill near Liverpool, the railway company held a contest to find the best locomotive for their line. Before a crowd of 10 to 15,000 George Stephenson's *Rocket*, fitted with a French boiler, won the contest and a prize of £500. On 15th September 1830, the line was officially opened. This proved to be an important stage in the history of the railways. For the Liverpool and Manchester line proved such a success that new lines began to spread across the country at an incredible rate.

The great expansion
In the early 1830s, numerous small railways were built in Britain.

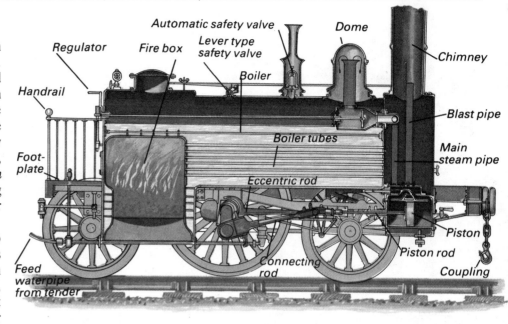

Below: An American locomotive of 1867 that ran on the Central Pacific line. In 1869, this was joined with the Union Pacific line to form America's first transcontinental railroad.

Many were later incorporated in major trunk routes. George Stephenson's son Robert played an important part in this expansion and became an expert in building tracks and bridges and in general railway planning. Another notable British railway engineer was Isambard Kingdom Brunel. After assisting his father, Sir Marc Kingdom Brunel, in tunnel construction, he joined the Great Western Railway Company. Working as chief engineer, Isambard Kingdom Brunel built numerous lines, tunnels and bridges. By 1844, British railway routes totalled 3,600 kilometres and, by 1850, this figure had almost trebled.

Europe and America
Experienced British engineers

Above: A typical express engine of 1848. Coal burning in the fire box heats water to produce steam. The pressure of the steam forces the pistons back and forth in cylinders and turns the wheels.

were often called in to help develop the railways in other countries. As a result, some features of British railways were adopted in the foreign systems. In Germany, for example, the gauge of the rails (distance between them) was made to take locomotives imported from Britain. Robert Stephenson built the locomotive that opened Germany's first public railway in 1835. Stephenson also built the first line of Belgium's railway network, which opened in that same year. At this time, the French Government were trying to encourage companies to build railways. After a slow start, rapid progress was made in the late 19th century. In Europe, railways mainly provided a fast and convenient means of travel. But in America railways were responsible also for the spread of civilization.

In the early 1800s, few people lived in the American West. But railways developed rapidly in the 1830s and gradually crept inland. Then, in 1869, the Union Pacific line from the east was joined with the Central Pacific line from the west. This paved the way for settlers and eventually led to the development of great new cities.

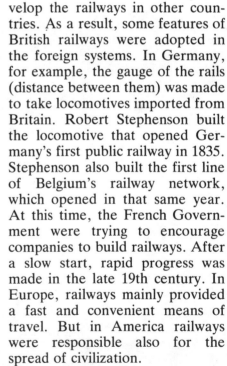

Twentieth-century railways

Pre-1914 Orient Express

Riviera Express

N° 598

Trans-Siberian Express

Top: Before World War One, the *Orient Express* made three journeys a week from Paris to Constantinople (now Istanbul). The trip via Munich, Vienna, Budapest and Belgrade took about 65 hours.

Centre: The *Riviera Express* ran from Berlin to Italian and French resorts on the Mediterranean coast.
Bottom: The *Trans-Siberian Express* on its ten-day, 8,000-kilometre journey.

By the early 1900s, powerful expresses were making regular journeys across countries throughout the world. Trips that once would have taken weeks to complete by road now lasted only a few days. In Canada, for example, it used to take five months to travel the 4,800 kilometres from Montreal in the east to the west-coast town of Vancouver. But the train journey on the Canadian Pacific line took a mere five days. Besides reducing travelling time drastically, the railway companies had also made efforts to increase the comfort of their passengers. Buffet and dining cars, toilets and sleeper cars had been introduced on a number of trains and these facilities gradually became established as part of normal service on longer rail journeys.

Special trains

In 1914, the outbreak of World War One gave the European railways an important new role to play. At first, ordinary trains carried troops, ammunition and supplies to the front lines and returned with wounded men.

Then, as the war progressed, specially designed trains were brought into service for military use. To cope with the ever increasing numbers of casualties, hospital trains were introduced. These carried drugs, medical equipment, doctors and nurses so that wounded soldiers could be given vital treatment. Early hospital cars were made by converting the luggage cars of ordinary trains. These mobile medical posts led to the introduction of purpose-built hospital trains complete with operating theatres. Another product of the war was the armoured train, with light guns for defensive purposes, or heavy artillery for long-range offensive bombardment.

Because the railways were so important to the war effort, tracks and trains were often attacked by enemy aircraft. As a result, Europe's railways had suffered extensive damage by the time the war ended in 1918. However, this gave the railway companies a chance to improve their systems during rebuilding.

Alternatives to steam

For over 100 years, steam power had dominated the railways. But other means of hauling trains had not been ignored. As early as 1839, the Baltimore and Ohio Railroad Company ran an experimental electric engine from Washington to Bladensburg. Another experimental electric type was tested on the Edinburgh and Glasgow Railway in 1842. But this locomotive was destroyed by steam-engine crews who feared they might lose their jobs if it was introduced into regular service. However, the American company persevered and, in 1894, carried out the first electrification of a mainline railway. This was a section through Baltimore.

In the spring of 1895, the first electric passenger trains were introduced. In Britain, the North Eastern Railway was the first to operate regular electric passenger trains on existing standard track, this service starting in March 1904. But development in Britain was slow, and mainline electric services did not start until the 1930s.

Diesel locomotives were introduced much later than electric types, but their subsequent development was more rapid. In 1912, the first experimental diesel locomotive ran on the Prussian-Hessian State Railway. This trial proved unsuccessful but, nine years later, the first regular diesel service started in Tunisia.

After another period of destruction in World War Two (1939-45), railways underwent further modernization. More lines were ·electrified, and steam locomotives slowly disappeared from the scene. Latest developments include gas-turbine locomotives, and the tracked air-cushion vehicle (TACV), which is a hovercraft train running on cushions of air along a specially-designed smooth track.

Above: Not all engineering problems are successfully solved. The A.T.P. (Advanced Passenger Train) developed by British Rail had a tilting mechanism on the coaches which enabled the train to take corners at high speed. After trials, the A.P.T. went into service in 1984, but was withdrawn later that year. The engineers stated that they could not get the tilting mechanism right.

Right: A stretch of dead-straight railway track 525 kilometres long runs across the Great Nullabor Plain in Australia.

Below: Trans-Europe Expresses link important cities throughout Western Europe.

Sailing ships

Early travellers often found they needed to cross water in order to continue their journey. Sometimes they could wade or swim across. In Mesopotamia (present-day Iraq), bags made from animal skins were inflated and used as floats, rather like water wings. This made the crossing much less hazardous. But it was more convenient and less tiring to float across the water on a log or bundle of reeds, and this soon led to the development of real boats.

The dug-out canoe was made by hollowing out a log. This greatly reduced the log's weight so that loads could be carried. Rafts made from several logs or bundles of reeds lashed together proved to be extremely stable in the water and useful for transporting goods. Another early boat, called the coracle, consisted of a light wicker frame covered with animal skins treated to make them waterproof.

Early rowing boats

The first simple craft were propelled by paddling with the hands, but this soon gave way to the use of wooden paddles, which proved much more effective. Another technique was to punt the boat, using a long pole to push against the bottom of a river or lake. The main disadvantage of punting was that the long pole required was heavy and difficult to manipulate in deep water.

The most successful means of hand propulsion was the oar, invented by the Egyptians around 3000 B.C. Soon long ships called galleys, rowed by teams of slaves, were speeding across the seas. By this time, the use of sails was well established and many boats and ships were equipped with both oars and sails.

Phoenician ships

Besides being used for trading and transport, ships often carried troops to invade foreign lands or to attack other vessels. When naval battles occurred, the great control provided by skilful oarsmen won

Dug-out canoe (6000 B.C.)

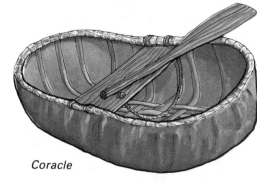

Coracle

The first boats

One of the earliest kinds of boats we know about is a craft hollowed out from a single tree trunk. Similar dugout canoes are still used today in some of the Pacific islands. Skin-covered vessels like the coracle have probably developed from primitive craft which used a bundle of reeds wrapped in an animal skin to form a float. A third kind of early boat was the raft. Polynesian peoples of 1,500 years ago may have built balsa wood rafts, and the Egyptians built rafts from reeds.

Balsa wood raft

Later developments

During the Dark Ages, the Angles, Jutes and Saxons built long open boats in which they crossed the North Sea. The Vikings' longships developed from these, and many people believe the Vikings went as far as America in them. Viking merchant ships relied on sails rather than oars. The sails were reinforced with bands of material to prevent the cloth tearing in high winds.

Long boat

Viking merchant ship (7th to 10th century)

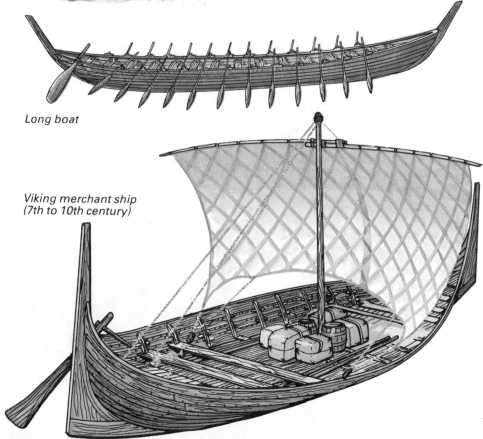

many victories against ships under sail. Around 1000 B.C., the Phoenicians dominated the Mediterranean with numerous merchant vessels protected by effective fighting ships. The Phoenician pentekonter, with a single square sail and a team of 50 oarsmen, was itself a dangerous naval weapon. For the front of the ship's 15-metre hull tapered to form a vicious, pointed ram. When rowed directly at an enemy vessel, the ram would penetrate it below the water line with disastrous results.

After the decline of the Phoenicians around 800 B.C., the Greeks and then the Romans continued the development of shipbuilding in the Mediterranean region. The slim naval vessels still relied on oars for manoeuvrability. But the broader merchant ships generally used two large, square sails, each on a separate mast. Over the centuries, these gradually developed into the three-mast carracks, used by Columbus and other explorers in the 1400s, and the four-mast ships of the 1500s to increase the area of the sails and thus their speed. This great period of exploration was inspired by Europe's need to expand her trade. It was made possible by the improved reliability of ships and advances in navigational skills.

Right: The *Victory* was Admiral Nelson's flagship at the Battle of Trafalgar, 1805. The ship was built between 1759-1765.

Below: The *Cutty Sark* was one of the fast clipper ships built to transport China tea.

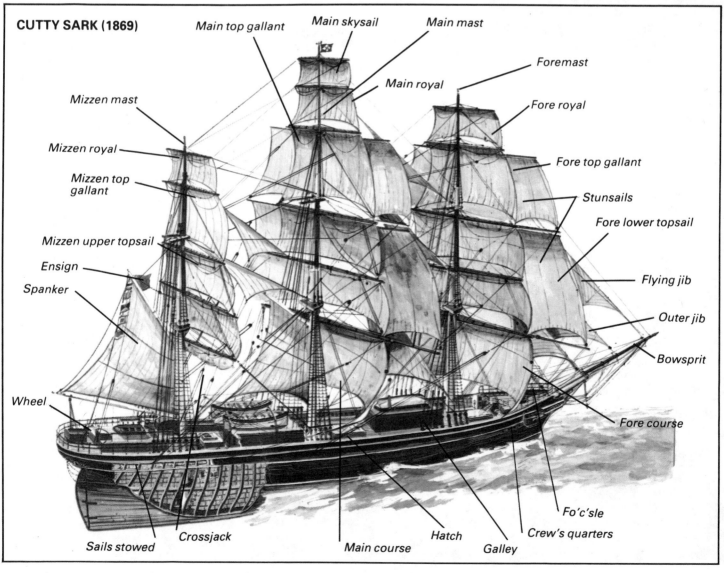

CUTTY SARK (1869)

Main top gallant · Main skysail · Main mast · Foremast · Main royal · Fore royal · Mizzen mast · Fore top gallant · Mizzen royal · Stunsails · Mizzen top gallant · Fore lower topsail · Mizzen upper topsail · Flying jib · Ensign · Spanker · Outer jib · Bowsprit · Wheel · Fore course · Sails stowed · Crossjack · Main course · Hatch · Galley · Crew's quarters · Fo'c'sle

Steam ships and the modern age

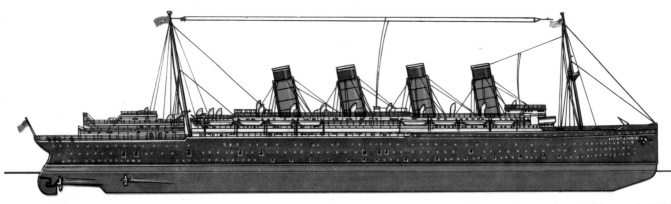

Atlantic liners
The history of Atlantic liners began in 1838 when the Great Western started a packet delivery service. The first regular Cunard crossing followed in 1840. Cunard introduced steam turbines in 1907 when the *Mauretania* **(top)** and the *Lusitania* were launched.

The speed record for the Atlantic crossing was held by the *Mauretania* until 1929, when the German ship *Bremen* **(above)** set a new record. Today, modern passenger liners are designed more as floating holiday resorts. The SS *France* **(below)** is an example of a luxury liner.

Throughout the 1600s and 1700s, wooden-hulled sailing ships continued to advance in size and design. This trend persisted into the next century. But a new age of shipping was dawning following two important events that took place in England in the late 18th century. In the early 1770s, James Watt developed an efficient steam engine. And, in 1771, an unusual vessel was launched on a Yorkshire river. Although only a small pleasure craft carrying 15 passengers, its appearance marked an important innovation in boat design – the use of an iron hull. These two developments were eventually combined in the iron steamships of the 1800s.

Paddle boats
Ideas for propelling boats by rotating paddles were centuries old and inspired by an ancient invention – the water wheel. If moving water could turn a paddle wheel then, it was reasoned, a turning paddle wheel should be able to propel a boat. A design produced in Roman times showed a vessel with three pairs of oxen turning vertical shafts. Gear wheels coupled the shafts to a series of paddle wheels along the sides of the craft. In 1472, Valturio illustrated several small man-powered paddle boats in his military manual *De Re Militari*. And one of Leonardo da Vinci's sketches of that period showed a treadle-operated paddle boat. Ideas were plentiful, but the oar proved more effective than the paddle wheel for human operators, and the powerful animals needed to turn the wheel took up much

valuable space and greatly increased the vessel's weight.

The age of steam

Steam engines were being introduced into factories around 1780, and the first practical steamboat appeared in 1783. This 42-metre paddleboat was built in France by the Marquis de Jouffroy. As early as 1790, America introduced the world's first commercial steamboat service. This operated on the Delaware River between Trenton and Philadelphia. But the boats could not compete successfully with the much faster stagecoaches linking the same towns, so the service was discontinued after a few months.

Regular commercial steamboats did not reappear until Robert Fulton started the *Clermont* paddle steamer service between Albany and New York in 1807

By this time, the screw propeller had been used in submarines. And, in 1804, Colonel John Stevens demonstrated the first successful steamboat to use propellers instead of paddle wheels. *Little Juliana* reached a top speed of about 13 kilometres per hour during trials in New Jersey. Another important design change appeared in 1822, with the launching of the British built *Aaron Manby,* the first iron-hulled steamer.

All the early steamers carried sails, as their engines were rather unreliable and often broke down. In the 1820s, more and more steamers took to the seas and oceans, but the first Atlantic crossing made entirely under steam did not take place until 1833. This first voyage, from Nova Scotia to the Isle of Wight, was made by a Canadian ship called the *Royal William* and took 18 days. Five years later, Isambard Kingdom Brunel's *Great Western* started the first regular steamship service across the Atlantic.

Brunel also designed the *Great Britain.* Launched in 1843, this was the first liner driven by screw propeller. In 1845, she became the first iron-hulled steamship to operate on the transatlantic route.

Below the surface

In 1615, a Dutchman, Cornelius Drebbel, built the first submarine. Propelled by 12 oars, it had a wooden frame covered with leather. In the United States, David Bushnell built a submarine in the 1770s driven by a hand-turned propeller. The first all-electric submarine was built by two Englishmen, Campbell and Ash, but its range was extremely short. Then in 1895, J. P. Holland built a submarine for the United States

Above: Nuclear submarines only need refuelling every year or so, and can stay submerged for months at a time.

Above: Hovercraft travel on cushions of air and are powered by jet engines of the type used in large airliners. Huge

hovercraft ferries cross the English Channel carrying up to 30 cars and 250 passengers.

Right: Tankers are the largest kinds of ships in the world. Many are used to carry vast quantities of oil from the Persian Gulf round Africa to European oil refineries. Fully laden, the bulk of a tanker lies below the waterline.

government. The vessel was named the *Plunger* and was propelled by steam on the surface and by electricity when submerged. An improved design, built in 1900, formed the basis for later submarines.

Today's nuclear submarines have a built-in atomic power station to generate electricity for their motors. The fuel is used so slowly that several trips around the world can be made before refuelling.

Pioneers of the air

Throughout history, man has wanted to fly. Many brave adventurers have been killed trying to flap their way through the air with wings in bird-like fashion. But man's first successful flight was made without using wings.

In November 1782, a Frenchman called Joseph Montgolfier suddenly got the inspiration that led to man's first ascent into the atmosphere. Staring into a fire, he noticed the hot smoke rising. Perhaps, he thought, a bag filled with hot air would rise too. So he made a small silk bag and filled it with hot air from the fire. On being released, this small hot-air balloon promptly rose to the ceiling. Joseph told his brother Etienne what had happened so they started experimenting with much larger balloons.

In November 1783, the Montgolfier brothers prepared a balloon for the first manned flight. A fire

Below: The German airship *Graf Zeppelin* flew around the world in 1929, taking just over 21 days for the trip. In 1930 the British *R 101* crashed killing 47 people.

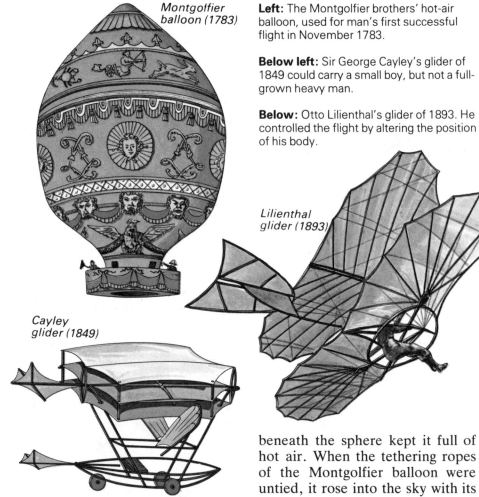

Montgolfier balloon (1783)

Cayley glider (1849)

Lilienthal glider (1893)

Left: The Montgolfier brothers' hot-air balloon, used for man's first successful flight in November 1783.

Below left: Sir George Cayley's glider of 1849 could carry a small boy, but not a full-grown heavy man.

Below: Otto Lilienthal's glider of 1893. He controlled the flight by altering the position of his body.

beneath the sphere kept it full of hot air. When the tethering ropes of the Montgolfier balloon were untied, it rose into the sky with its pilot Pilâtre de Rozier and his passenger the Marquis d'Arlandes. Twenty-five minutes later, the balloon landed safely.

Giants in the sky

A different kind of balloon was constructed by another Frenchman, J.A.C. Charles, in the same year (1783). His balloon was lifted into the air not by hot air but by hydrogen.

But, although man could now fly with reasonable safety, he had no control over direction. That depended entirely on the wind. Attempts were made to use oars, flapping wings, sails and other devices to control the balloons, but the wind remained in command. Then, in 1852, Henri Giffard suspended a steam engine from a long hydrogen balloon. The engine turned a propeller and there was a rudder for steering. Although unsuccessful, Giffard's airship encouraged others to perfect this new

form of transport. In the 1890s the German Count von Zeppelin built petrol driven airships with rigid frameworks. Zeppelin had great success, and, in 1910, his *Deutschland* provided the world's first scheduled passenger air service.

Heavier-than-air machines

In 1853, one year after Giffard's first airship, came a much more important development.

After years of research, an Englishman called Sir George Cayley was ready to test a man-carrying glider he had built. With difficulty, he persuaded his coachman to take the controls. This unwilling man flew the glider across a valley and became the first pilot of a heavier-than-air flying machine. Later that century, the German Otto Lilienthal made over 2,000 successful controlled glider flights. But he was killed in August 1896, when his machine crashed.

In 1903, the American brothers Wilbur and Orville Wright fitted a

Above right: A French *Deperdussin* racer of 1913. In that year, Maurice Prévost flew a *Deperdussin* at a record speed of 204 kilometres per hour.

Right: Towards the end of World War One fighter planes like this one were in service.

Below right: The *Supermarine S.6B* seaplane was the fastest plane in the Schneider Trophy race of 1931.

glider with a propeller and petrol engine. With Orville at the controls, the machine took off. Only 12 seconds later, it touched down again, no more than 30 metres from where it started. It never rose much more than three metres from the ground. But these facts disguise the great importance of this first aeroplane flight. For it had demonstrated to the world that the aeroplane was capable of controlled, powered flight. Swift progress followed and, by 1913, speeds of over 200 kilometres per hour had been achieved. Man had conquered the air.

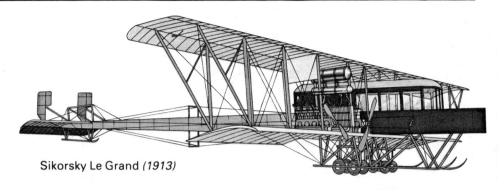

Sikorsky Le Grand *(1913)*

Above: The world's first four-engined aeroplane, built by the Russian Igor Sikorsky in 1913. This giant aircraft had a wingspan of 28 metres. The following year, Sikorsky built an even larger version, the *Ilya Mourometz*.

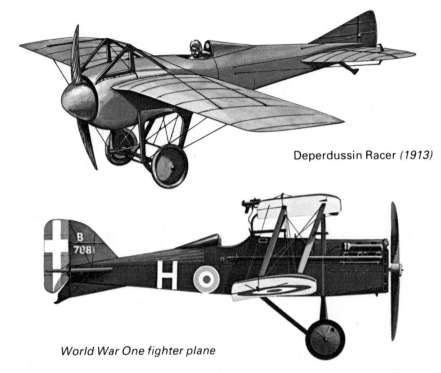

Deperdussin Racer *(1913)*

World War One fighter plane

Modern aircraft

The early 20th century saw many landmarks in the history of aviation. On 25th July 1909, a French pilot Louis Blériot became the first person to fly across the English Channel in an aeroplane. The crossing from Baraques to Dover took just 37 minutes. Ten years later, the first transatlantic flights were made. On 16th May 1919, Lieutenant-Commander Albert Read of the United States Navy took off from Newfoundland in Canada in a Curtiss *NC-4* flying boat with a crew of five. Eleven days later, they arrived in Lisbon, Portugal. Several stops were made on the way, but the first non-stop Atlantic crossing was less than three weeks away.

On 14th June 1919, Captain John Alcock and his navigator Lieutenant Arthur Brown left Newfoundland in a Vickers *Vimy* biplane. In 16 hours and 12 minutes, they reached the Irish town of Galway and won a £10,000 prize for the aircraft company.

These historic flights demonstrated the rapid progress in aircraft technology. And, while advances were made with conventional aeroplanes during the 1920s and 1930s, the helicopter and gas turbines were also being developed.

Helicopters

When an aeroplane moves forward, its specially shaped wings experience increased air pressure below and decreased pressure above. This pressure difference over the whole wing is called lift, which at least equals the weight of the aircraft and enables it to fly. In a helicopter, the rotating blades are, in effect, moving wings. The lift the blades receive allows the machine to rise without having to move forward like an aeroplane. And the helicopter can descend vertically too. As a result, it can take off and land in confined spaces where aeroplanes cannot (except for the vertical take-off *Harrier* jet).

As early as the 1300s, children played with simple toy helicopters – spinning devices that would rise into the air. But the development of a man-carrying helicopter had to wait until a suitable engine became available. In 1905, E. R. Mumford designed the first helicopter capable of lifting a man. Powered by an internal combustion engine, it rose into the air. But its movement was restricted by a short tethering rope. The first free flight by helicopter was achieved by the Frenchman Paul Cornu in 1907.

Above: The pilot and co-pilot in the cockpit of a modern airliner, showing the array of dials and controls.

The flight lasted only 20 seconds, and the machine rose no more than two metres. But it was an important event in aviation history.

At first, designers were happy if their machines could take off, hover and land. Only when this had been mastered did they tackle

Above: Supersonic airliners, like *Concorde,* are best suited for long flights, especially over unpopulated areas, when they can fly at their top speeds.

Right: The *Phantom* combat aeroplane first flew in 1958. It can fly at two and a half times the speed of sound and can climb to 20,000 metres in less than three minutes.

the problem of forward flight. Sustained forward flight by helicopter was not achieved until 1924, and practical helicopters came only in the mid-1930s.

The Jet Age

Rockets and jet engines both work on the principle that for every action there is an equal and opposite reaction. When applied to a rocket or jet engine, this means that the force with which the engine expels gases from the back gives rise to an equal and opposite force on the engine. This causes the engine to move forward. For most types of aeroplane, jet engines have proved to be a more satisfactory means of propulsion than rockets. Jets use oxygen from the air to burn their fuel, while rockets carry their own supply.

Designs for jet aircraft first appeared around 1910. In the late 1920s, Britain's Frank Whittle designed a jet engine and patented it in 1930. He later formed a company to develop his engine, but the Germans were ahead of him and produced the first jet aeroplane in 1939. Designed by Dr Hans von Ohain, the Heinkel *He 178* made its first flight in August that year. Meanwhile, Whittle persevered with his own design and, in May 1941, the Gloster-Whittle *E. 28/39* took off for the first time. Whittle's engine proved superior to the German type and inspired the world-wide development of jet planes.

Above: Before every flight teams of maintenance engineers check the aircraft. Flying is a very safe form of transport.

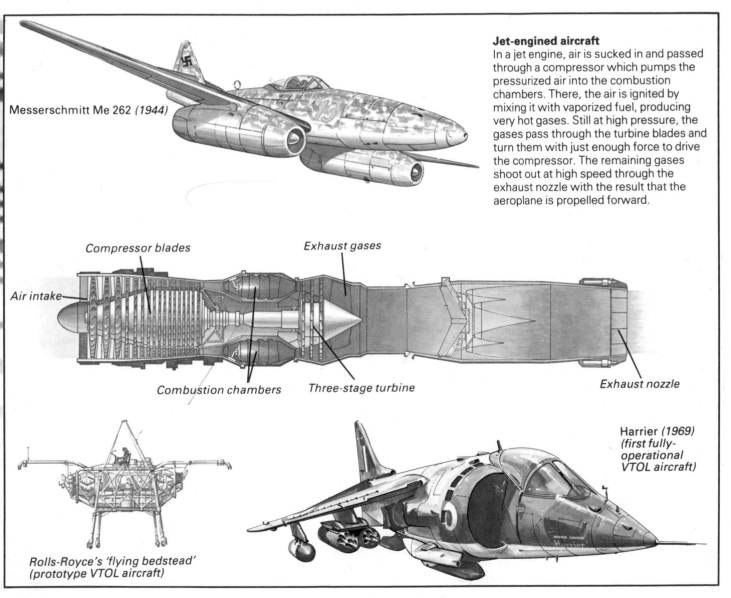

Messerschmitt Me 262 *(1944)*

Jet-engined aircraft

In a jet engine, air is sucked in and passed through a compressor which pumps the pressurized air into the combustion chambers. There, the air is ignited by mixing it with vaporized fuel, producing very hot gases. Still at high pressure, the gases pass through the turbine blades and turn them with just enough force to drive the compressor. The remaining gases shoot out at high speed through the exhaust nozzle with the result that the aeroplane is propelled forward.

Compressor blades

Exhaust gases

Air intake

Combustion chambers

Three-stage turbine

Exhaust nozzle

Harrier *(1969)* *(first fully-operational VTOL aircraft)*

Rolls-Royce's 'flying bedstead' (prototype VTOL aircraft)

235

The space age

Above: Apollo 11, with a three-man crew, made the first manned landing on the Moon in July 1969. The lunar landing vehicle, *Eagle*, was photographed returning from the Moon to dock with the command module 100 kilometres above the Moon's surface. The earth looms over the Moon's horizon.

Above: An astronaut climbs out of the command module to carry out a simple maintenance job. Any work done outside a spacecraft is usually termed E.V.A. (extra-vehicular activity).

Below: Unmanned spacecraft have successfully touched down on Mars and Venus. A lot of information about these planets has been relayed back to earth. The Mariner spacecraft, one of which is

The fascination of space and the idea of space travel has inspired writers since ancient times. In the second century, the Greek writer Lucian described how a ship sailing from Gibraltar was propelled to the Moon by a freak waterspout. He warned readers that the story was pure fiction, for people at that time were apt to believe almost anything about the unknown.

In more recent times, Jules Verne wrote of a voyage to the Moon in a spaceship. The book, published in 1865, was called *From the Earth to the Moon.* Verne was aware that the spaceship would have to reach a speed of about eleven kilometres per second in order to escape from the earth's gravitational field. In the book, this high "escape velocity" was achieved by firing the spaceship from a huge cannon.

For technical reasons, such a system as Verne suggested would not be satisfactory. But, soon after the turn of the century, a Russian teacher called Konstantin Tsiolkovsky had worked out the principles of a practical method for sending a vehicle into space. His proposed system of using a multi-stage rocket formed the foundation

for astronautics – the science of space travel.

Rocket propulsion

According to Isaac Newton's third law of motion, for every action there is an equal and opposite reaction. If, for example, a person jumps from the back of a small boat with a certain force (action), an equal force (reaction) will tend to move the boat forward through the water. In the same way, jets and rockets move forward by forcing out gases from the back.

Both types of engine produce these gases which thrust them forward by burning fuel with oxygen. But, whereas the jet obtains its oxygen from the air, the rocket is entirely self-contained. With its own oxygen supply, it can operate in outer space.

Rockets were invented around the year 1000, probably by the Chinese, who used them as missiles in battle. A design for a rocket-propelled bird appeared in the 1400s, and rockets were proposed as a means of powering balloons in the late 1700s. Around 1900, Konstantin Tsiolkovsky proposed the use of liquid, rather than solid fuel for increased power and con-

shown being launched in the photograph, were a series of space probes sent to explore the solar system. In 1974 Mariner 10 sent back television pictures of Venus, and then went on to Mercury.

trol. The Germans' spectacular *V-2* rocket-bomb of World War Two was powered by alcohol and liquid oxygen. From this were developed today's powerful space rockets and space exploration began.

Exploring space

Rocket-powered aircraft carried their pilots briefly to the fringes of space in the early 1950s. But the space age really began in October 1957, with the launching of the first artificial satellite, the Russian *Sputnik 1.* It measured only 58 centimetres across, and carried scientific instruments and a radio transmitter. It was put into orbit by a powerful Russian rocket.

The following month, the Russians' *Sputnik 2,* carrying a dog called Laika, was put into earth orbit.

In 1958, America launched her first satellite, *Explorer 1.* Although even smaller than the first Russian satellite, its instruments sent back important information about the radiation belts around the earth.

The first manned orbital flight was made in 1961 by the Russian cosmonaut Yuri Gagarin. Travelling in the five-tonne spacecraft *Vostok 1,* he made one orbit of the earth. America's first man in orbit was John Glenn who, in 1962, went around the earth three times in his *Friendship 7* capsule. After this, progress was rapid and, in 1969, American Neil Armstrong became the first man to walk on the Moon.

Space stations

There have been several manned flights to the Moon since, but recently, both Russia and America have been more interested in developing manned space stations.

The construction of space stations orbiting just outside the Earth's atmosphere has involved the perfection of complicated "docking" manoeuvres. The first major manned space station was Skylab, launched in 1973. Crews lived on board it for up to 84 days. Scientists are studying the effects of long periods of weightlessness on astronauts. As part of this research, Yuri Romanenko spent a record 326 days in the Soviet Mir space station in 1987.

An artist's picture of a future space station. Before the end of this century huge space stations like this one may be in orbit round the earth. Astronauts and scientists will live and work in them, for possibly years at a time. On board, solar energy may be turned into electricity, and industries may start production in space.

Telecommunications

The word telecommunications simply means communications at a distance. The first example was telegraphy (writing at a distance) which appeared in the last years of the 18th century.

The first telegraphs
In the earliest telegraphs, electrical signals from the newly-invented electrical battery were sent along metal wires a kilometre or more in length. Commercial telegraphs of the mid-19th century, however, were powered more efficiently by the electric generator, which had been invented by Michael Faraday in 1831.

Morse code
In the first telegraph systems, electrical signals were received in various ways, but most successfully as a sort of code using the ringing of an electric bell.

In the 1840s an American, Samuel Morse, improved on this idea by inventing the Morse code, in which letters and numbers were represented by various combinations of dots and dashes. Morse

Below: The telegraph sender invented by Samuel Morse in 1837. Messages in Morse code were sent by moving a "comb" under a contact lever. This instrument was soon afterwards replaced by the more familiar Morse code key.

Below right: A modern telegraphic instrument, the Telex machine.

How a telephone works

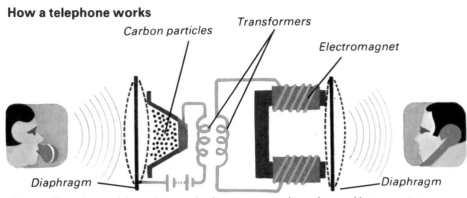

Above: Sound waves from the speaker's voice cause a diaphragm to vibrate, so also vibrating the carbon particles. This produces a pattern of electrical impulses in the telephone circuit. The message also invented an instrument for sending this code along his own 65-kilometre telegraph line between Washington and Boston.

The Morse telegraph soon became very widely used. Morse-code messages were usually received as the buzzing sounds of an electromagnet activated by the electrical impulses.

Teleprinters
The hand-key method of sending Morse code is still employed today, for example in the sending of personal messages between ship and land. However, as a method of transmitting large amounts of information, it is far too slow.

Machines for telegraphing information much more rapidly were invented as long ago as the 1860s. Teleprinters, as they came to be pattern is exchanged between two transformers and passes to the listener's earpiece. Here, it rapidly switches an electromagnet on and off, so vibrating a diaphragm, which reproduces the voice.

called, are typewriter-like machines that both send out and receive messages in a modified form of Morse code.

Earlier forms of receivers included the ticker-tape machines by which brokers and gamblers on stock exchanges received news about changes in share prices. A much more recent type of telegraph system, Telex, conveys typed messages via a telephone exchange network.

The telephone
The first telephone to work at all satisfactorily appeared in 1876, as the invention of an American engineer, Alexander Graham Bell. Its mouthpiece contained a thin disc, or diaphragm, which vibrated to the sound waves of speech.

This in turn caused movements

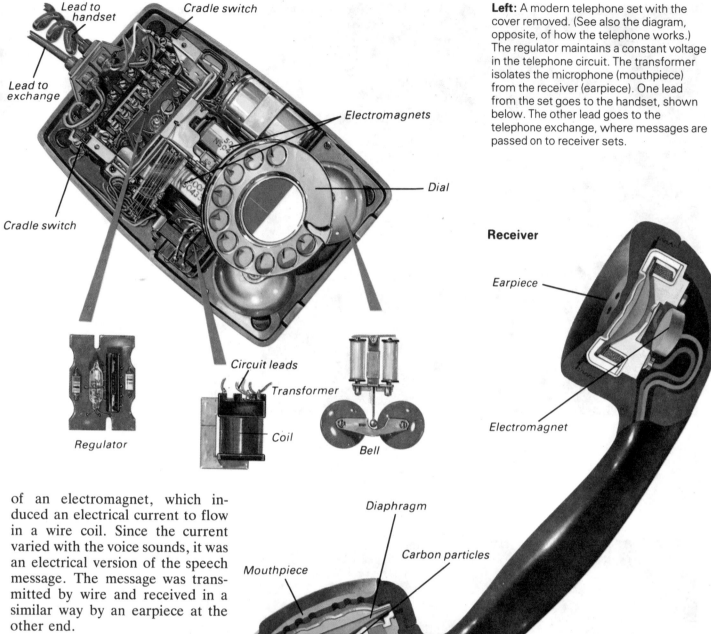

Lead to handset

Cradle switch

Lead to exchange

Electromagnets

Cradle switch

Dial

Left: A modern telephone set with the cover removed. (See also the diagram, opposite, of how the telephone works.) The regulator maintains a constant voltage in the telephone circuit. The transformer isolates the microphone (mouthpiece) from the receiver (earpiece). One lead from the set goes to the handset, shown below. The other lead goes to the telephone exchange, where messages are passed on to receiver sets.

Circuit leads

Transformer

Coil

Bell

Regulator

Receiver

Earpiece

Electromagnet

Diaphragm

Carbon particles

Mouthpiece

Above: A telephone handset. When it is resting on the main unit, shown above, the handset presses down the cradle switch, so isolating the outgoing line.

of an electromagnet, which induced an electrical current to flow in a wire coil. Since the current varied with the voice sounds, it was an electrical version of the speech message. The message was transmitted by wire and received in a similar way by an earpiece at the other end.

Bell's telephone had a limited range because the electromagnet induced only a very weak current. Shortly afterwards, Thomas Edison solved this problem by replacing the electromagnet in the mouthpiece with a carbon-particle resistance unit, as shown in the diagram. This produced a much stronger electrical signal.

Later developments in telephony and telegraphy included wireless transmission, the sending of messages by radio. But even the wire-and-cable part of a modern telephone network can extend over many millions of kilometres and includes complex electronic switch-

ing exchanges for the automatic relaying of a huge flow of messages.

Telemetry
The space age has brought its own great advances in telecommunications, most familiar of which are the television programmes and weather bulletins relayed and

broadcast by satellite.

Satellites and space probes are controlled, and their radio messages received, by methods of telemetry, a word which means measurement at a distance. The information transmitted, received and interpreted by these telemetry systems is so complex that it demands the use of computers.

Radio and television

Above: A complex team of people work together to make a television programme. In the studio, the floor manager (on the right of the picture) gives the actors a cue when to start. Several cameras are used to film the action.

Below: In the darkened control room, the director and his assistants oversee what happens in the studio. A number of "monitor" screens show the pictures taken by each camera. The director selects the "shot" he wants.

Cathode ray tube

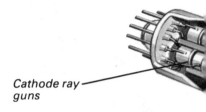

Cathode ray guns

Right: The cathode ray tube is a device for receiving electrical energy and changing it into an electron beam. The beam in a television tube only lights up one tiny dot on the screen at a time. We manage to see a complete picture on the screen because the beam sweeps over the entire surface of the screen very rapidly.

Radio waves were first produced thousands of millions of years ago, soon after the formation of the universe. Many stars give off radiation in the form of radio waves as well as light, but because radio waves are invisible, their existence remained a secret until quite recently.

In the 1860s, James Clerk Maxwell stated that it should be possible to make a changing electric current generate invisible radiation. Some 20 years later, Heinrich Hertz made this statement come true. In 1887, he used a high voltage to produce sparks between two metal rods. When a spark passed between the rods, another spark jumped across the gap in a nearby metal ring. Radio waves from the rods had travelled to the ring where they had produced electricity and this had caused the sparking. Hertz and other inventors soon found ways to increase the range of their radio equipment. The most outstanding person in this field was Guglielmo Marconi. In 1901, he successfully transmitted a signal across the Atlantic Ocean. Early transmitters sent signals in the dots and dashes of the Morse code. Then, in the early 1900s, the triode valve was invented. This made possible the transmission of sound and vision by radio.

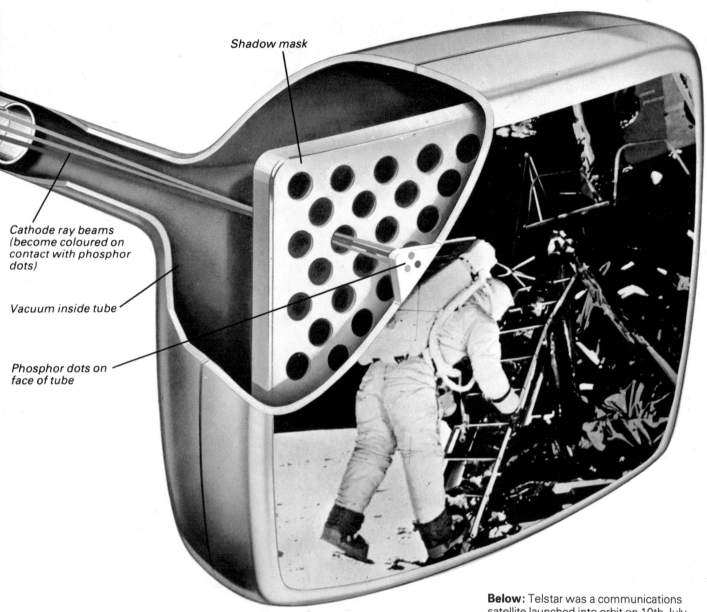

Shadow mask

Cathode ray beams
(become coloured on
contact with phosphor
dots)

Vacuum inside tube

Phosphor dots on
face of tube

Radio and T.V. broadcasting

In a radio transmitter, a device called an oscillator produces an electric current that varies rapidly in a wave-like manner. The rate at which the waves of current are produced is constant, and their strength is constant too. When such a current flows into an aerial, radio waves are sent out.

The radio signal described above is called a carrier, for it can be used to "carry" sound or vision signals. In sound broadcasting, signals from a microphone, record player or tape machine are used to vary the carrier. In amplitude modulation (A.M.), they modulate (vary) the amplitude (strength) of the carrier. In frequency modulation (F.M.), they modulate the frequency (rate of production) of the waves. In television broadcasting, separate sound and vision carriers are modulated by signals coming from the studios.

Vision signals are produced by a technique called scanning. In the 1920s, John Logie Baird used a rotating disc with holes in it to scan across an image formed by a lens. Light passing through the holes was changed into electricity using a photo-electric cell. In the modern television camera, a special cathode-ray tube forms the vision signal. In the receiver, this signal is used to build up the picture, line by line, in a cathode-ray tube with a fluorescent screen.

Below: Telstar was a communications satellite launched into orbit on 10th July 1962. The day after the launch, Telstar transmitted the first live television pictures across the Atlantic Ocean. Satellites like Telstar can also handle thousands of international telephone calls at any time.

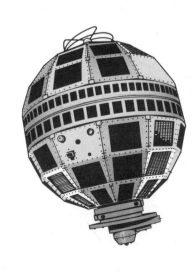

Photography and the cinema

The origins of photography date back to the 1500s, when artists first used the camera obscura as a drawing aid. A lens at the front of the camera formed an image on a screen. The artist would simply trace this image in order to produce a quick, realistic sketch. Photography – "drawing by light" – started when the light itself was made to produce permanent pictures by allowing the images to fall on flat plates coated with light-sensitive chemicals.

Many artists and inventors experimented with photography in the 1820s but most of the pictures produced soon faded away. However, Nicéphore Niépce managed to make permanent pictures, and a view taken in 1826 from his attic window still survives to this day. Louis Daguerre perfected a better system in the late 1830s. His photographic plates were more sensitive, and so needed a much shorter exposure to light. The images produced were of remarkably high quality. By this time, Fox Talbot had invented a different system. He produced negative images on light-sensitive paper and could then use the negatives to make any number of normal, or positive prints. The earliest surviving print made from a paper negative shows Lacock Abbey, Fox Talbot's home in Wiltshire, England. This picture was taken in 1835. Daguerre's system gave better results than Fox Talbot's, as far as quality was concerned. Fox Talbot's process was more convenient, however, and led others to invent new negative-positive processes of higher quality.

Photography became a popular hobby following the introduction of the Kodak camera by George Eastman in 1888. This was the first camera to use roll film. Millions of photographs are now taken and processed each day. Many kinds of film are available, both black-and-white and colour, to suit different types of photography. High-quality enlargements can be made, even from the tiny negatives produced

cameras have a confusing number of knobs, levers and dials. The most important of these control the shutter speed, aperture (lens opening) and focus. The first two limit the intensity and the amount of light falling on the film, so that it can be correctly exposed. The focus control enables the photographer to ensure that the image is sharp. Many modern cameras automatically adjust themselves for correct exposure. Some have a built-in flashgun for use in dim light. Others even have an automatic device for focusing.

Developing and fixing processes make the images on a film visible and permanent. They may be formed as positives for projection, or as negatives for making prints.

Motion pictures

Motion pictures do not really move at all. We really see a series of still pictures, each one slightly different from the last. These are taken in rapid succession by a movie camera and projected onto a screen at the same quick rate. We see that the images appear to merge, forming a life-like moving picture. This effect was demonstrated in many interesting gadgets made long before the invention of the cine-camera.

Below: This photograph of a busy street at night was taken by leaving the shutter open for a fairly long time. The lights of moving cars appear as red and white streaks on the film because of the time exposure.

Above: Filming a "shoot-out" scene for a Western. Film sets rarely look "real", but through the "eye" of the camera most sets are convincing enough. In the drawing above, the saloon has only three walls and no ceiling. All around are lights, cameras and microphones.

The image we see on a cinema screen is made up of separate shots projected onto the screen in rapid succession. To make the image appear continuous to the eye, 24 separate shots, or frames, are projected onto the screen every second.

by many popular cameras. Cameras themselves have evolved from simple, box-like structures to electronic wonders.

Basic photography

In a camera, the shutter allows light to enter when the photographer wants to take a picture. A lens forms this light into an image and a light-sensitive film makes a permanent record of the image. Simple cameras have few other features but some complex

Writing and printing

Man has always needed to make permanent records of important events as information passed down from one generation to another by word of mouth was liable to lose its meaning or become forgotten altogether at some stage. One way to record an event was to show it in a painting or drawing. A sequence of events could be described in a series of drawings and these were often simplified so that they could be drawn or carved more quickly. In this way, symbols were gradually invented to represent objects and actions.

The first people to adopt this system were probably the Sumerians, who lived in the eastern Mediterranean region called Mesopotamia. The symbols were either pressed into soft clay or carved in stone. In order to be able to describe a wide range of subjects, the Sumerians devised more than 2,000 symbols. This made their writing so complicated that few people could understand it all. The Egyptians devised a better system called hieroglyphics, a word meaning sacred carving. The Egyptian alphabet consisted of a few dozen symbols and these could be used to spell thousands of words. Further advances were made by the Phoenicians, and their alphabet was later improved by the Greeks. After being changed many times by the Etruscans and Romans, this alphabet closely resembled the one used in this book, in fact we still refer to it as the Roman alphabet. Some alphabets used today, for example the Chinese, still consist of large numbers of symbols like the ancient pictographs.

Words in print

Early books were written by hand and, because this took so long, they were made in very small quantities. Often, only one copy of a book was produced. Throughout the years, many books were lost or deliberately destroyed, and an enormous amount of information was lost to mankind for ever. The development of printing has ensured that disasters of this kind can never occur again.

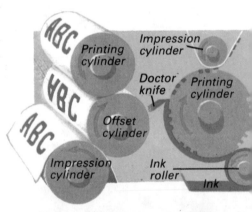

Above: A later development of Sumerian writing was called cuneiform. The script looked more like pictures than letters.

Above right: The diagram on the left shows an offset lithograph printing press, and on the right a photographic press. With offset lithography, the printing plate does not come into direct contact with the paper (i.e. offset), but with photogravure it does.

Right: A four-colour lithograph machine. Most colour-illustrated books are printed on a machine like this.

invented the Linotype process. This enabled a keyboard operator to put together or cast complete lines of type at high speed. In the Monotype process, invented in the 1880s by Tolbert Lanston, each character is cast separately. This simplifies the task of making corrections at a later stage. Today, photographic techniques are replacing molten-metal typecasting systems. The whole production process is now being made even faster by the use of complex computer-controlled equipment.

The postal service

The year 1840 was the turning point in the organization of postal services, when Rowland Hill introduced Britain's penny post. For the first time, letters could be sent to any destination in the country at this low rate. Similar systems were adopted throughout the world, and over 1,000 million letters are now posted daily. At sorting offices, machines separate parcels from letters. Coded dots typed onto the envelopes enable other machines to sort them at high speed.

Above: An author may write two or three draft texts for his book.

The earliest printed book known to exist is a Chinese work on Buddhism bearing the date A.D. 868. Illustrations were carved into a wooden block, which was then covered with ink and pressed onto the paper. In the same way, all the words for a page were printed from a single carved block. Smaller printing blocks, bearing separate characters, had appeared in the East by the 1400s. These blocks were assembled into lines as required. After printing, they were taken apart and then rearranged in order to print something else.

The first European to use movable type to print a book was probably Johannes Gütenberg of Mainz, Germany. *The Gütenberg Bible,* written in Latin and published in 1456, does not have Gütenberg's name on it, but he is thought to have put together the type from which it was printed. Gütenberg may have printed books before this date, but there is no reliable information available.

For centuries, printing was a slow process carried out on hand-operated printing presses. Then, in the early 1800s, a German printer by the name of Friedrich König invented an automatic press powered by a steam engine. With the aid of his mechanic, Friedrich Bauer, König built two of these machines for British newspaper companies. On the morning of the 29th November 1814, *The Times,* produced for the first time on one of König's machines, announced the new revolution in printing. Using fewer people printing could now be carried out at up to four times the speed previously possible. Since that time, many other important inventions have been made in this field. In 1863, William Bullock invented the rotary press, still used by newspapers today.

In 1876, Ottmar Mergenthaler

Above: A typesetter sets the author's typescript on to punched tape. The tape is then photographically changed into plastic film.

Index

Index

Index

Index

Acknowledgements

The publishers have made every effort to trace the ownership of all copyrighted material in this publication and to secure permission from the holders. Photographs have been credited by page number and position: (T) top, (C) centre, (B) bottom, and combinations, for example (TR) top right.

The publishers would like to thank the following:

Aberdeen Refinery: 190BL
AGA UK: 215BL
Air Products Ltd: 36CL
Asbestos Information: 215BL
Heather Angel: 73TR CR, 75B, 80TL
Associated Press: 202, front cover R
Paul Brierley: 212TL
British Museum: 124TR, 127BL, 143TR, 174TL
British Tourist Authority: 170T
British Transport Films: 227T
Bundesarchiv, Koblenz: 170B
CGTA: 193CL
CIT: 227BL
Camera Press: 125B
Tim Canadine: 125TR
J. Carter Photos: 24TL
J. Allan Cash: 160-161T, 182, 183
Martin Chillmaid: 32BR, 245CB
Peter Clayton: 120B
Coloursport: 181T
Commission des Communautés Européens: 40T
Courtauld Institute: 137T
Daily Telegraph Colour Library: 212CL
Tony Duffy: 180BR, front cover BL
EMI Ltd: 208TL
Mark Edwards: 142TR
Robert Estall: 25BR
Mary Evans Picture Library: 141B, 145BR, 218CT
Geological Survey: 31BL
Glaxco Ltd: 219TL, back cover TL
Sally and Richard Greenhill: 171B
Lionel Grigson: 40B
Sonia Halliday: 32BL, 33BL, 130BR
Robert Harding Associates: 33BR
Brian Hawkes: 180BL
Michael Holford: 179T
Inbel: 168BL
Institute of Geological Sciences: 29TR
Interfoto: 145BL
Italian Institute: 133T
Joyce Jason: 171T
Keystone: 219CR
Tom Lonsdale: 162TL
Macdonald Educational/Shaun Skelly: 240B
Macmillan, London: 177TR
Geoffrey Magney: 180T
Mansell Collection: 169T, 184TL, 218TR CL

Marshall Cavendish Ltd: 219BR
Denis Moore: 167TR, 172TL, 181B
Dr. Pat Morris: 114T, 115T, front cover BC
Musée des Arts Décoratifs, Paris: 176L
Museum of London: 169CR
NASA: 17BR TR, 155TR
National Army Museum: 116-7T
National Parks Service of America: 28L
National Portrait Gallery: 117R
National Tourist Organization of Greece: 122R, 174-5T
NHPA/Brian Hawkes: 23TL, 77T
P&O Lines: 148T, 149TR
Pegussa: 208TR
Photri: 236-7
Pictor: 108T
Picturepoint: 41B, 175TR, 194T, 219TR
Popperfoto: 173CR
The Post Office: 238BR, 245T
Prado Museum, Madrid: 136T
Queen Mary's Hospital Medical School: 218B
Radio Times Hulton Picture Library: 124CB, 132T, 142BR, 144TL, 168-9B
Rex Features: 199BR
G.R. Roberts: 198TR
Ann Ronan Picture Library: 184TR
Scala: 132B, 144TR-145TL
SEF: 177BL
Shell Photo Services: 36TL
Francis Skinner: 143BR
Society for Cultural Relations with U.S.S.R.: 139B
Spectrum: 175B
Syndication International: 154B
Tate Gallery, London: 148B
Total, France: 30T
Transworld Feature Service: 154TR
Sarah Tyzack: 31CB
USIS: 33T, 155B
Victoria and Albert Museum: 127T, 142TL
Roger Viollet: 138T
John Watney: 187TR, front cover TC
Western Americana: 146B
Bryan Woodriff: 176T
Yale University Art Gallery: 140B, 146T
Yorkshire Television: 240T
ZEFA: 10BL, 10-11, 48T, 52TB, 54B, 116-117B, 160BL, 161TR B, 173TL, 216TL, 217TR

Title page: Concorde
Endpapers: Radio telescope

Contributors and Consultants
John E. Allen
Linda Bennett
Arthur Butterfield
Peter Clayton
Dougal Dixon
Bill Gunston
Robin May
Ron Taylor
Stephanie Thompson
Keith Wicks